# Music
## *of the*
## Baroque

# Music of the Baroque

*An Anthology of Scores*

DAVID SCHULENBERG

New York • Oxford
OXFORD UNIVERSITY PRESS
2001

Oxford University Press

Oxford   New York
Athens   Auckland   Bangkok   Bogotá   Buenos Aires   Calcutta
Cape Town   Chennai   Dar es Salaam   Delhi   Florence   Hong Kong   Istanbul
Karachi   Kuala Lumpur   Madrid   Melbourne   Mexico City   Mumbai
Nairobi   Paris   São Paulo   Shanghai   Singapore   Taipei   Tokyo   Toronto   Warsaw

*and associated companies in*
Berlin   Ibadan

Copyright © 2001 by Oxford University Press, Inc.

Published by Oxford University Press, Inc.
198 Madison Avenue, New York, New York 10016
http://www.oup-usa.org

Oxford is a registered trademark of Oxford University Press

ISBN 0-19-512233-X

Printing (last digit): 9 8 7 6 5 4 3 2 1

Printed in the United States of America
on acid-free paper

# Contents

# PREFACE

This is an anthology of scores to accompany *Music of the Baroque*, a study of European music from the late sixteenth through the mid-eighteenth centuries. The present volume can also be used independently as a collection of study scores. A complete discussion of each work, including its historical and cultural context, biographical material on its composer, and analysis, is in the accompanying volume. The present volume gives not only the score but the verbal text of each vocal work (with translation, where necessary), commentaries on the edition used and on any performance issues raised by the work, and information about the work's sources. The accompanying volume includes plot summaries and other supplementary material, much of it in the form of tables and boxes readily distinguished from the main text for easy reference.

The music selected for presentation comprises complete works and musically self-contained excerpts. The few exceptions, such as the ornament tables extracted from several French Baroque sources (Selection 29), are self-explanatory. Where excerpts rather than complete works are given, as with operas, an effort has been made to present a coherent portion of each work, such as a series of successive scenes. In several cases, additional, briefer extracts appear in the text volume in the form of musical examples.

This anthology includes a number of "noncanonical" selections, including works by women composers, alongside familiar standards. Also present are a few pre- and post-Baroque selections to illustrate the opening and closing chapters of the text volume, which provide transitions to music from other historical periods. The commentaries point out specific features of each score, such as any significant editorial emendations or notable aspects of notation. They also mention important issues of performance practice raised by each work. Translations are as literal and preserve as much of the original syntax as possible.

A word about the editions used is appropriate. A number of works are presented in new editions. But no apology is needed for the fact that, like most anthologies of this type, the present volume also depends on editions reprinted from other sources, an expedient dictated by the need to present a broad variety of compositions in an affordable format. This feature can be turned to an advantage in a study collection, for a musician or music historian must be familiar not only with various types of recent editions—which differ significantly from one another in physical appearance and editorial policy—but also with facsimile reprints from older editions and from original sources. The commentaries accompanying the scores will assist readers in understanding the diverse types of edition that are increasingly available and, indeed, indispensible for anyone studying, performing, or listening to European music of the past.

All of the editions reproduced here employ modern notation, and only a few use unfamiliar "old" clefs for certain parts. A few facsimiles from original printed sources employ clef and note shapes somewhat different from those in current use, but experience has shown that students have little difficulty in adjusting to this. Moreover, the experience of having done so empowers them to make practical use of a much wider variety of sources than would otherwise be the case.

Where works appear here in new editions, the musical and verbal texts have been established wherever possible through comparison with primary sources. Although it is impractical for a volume of this nature to include a formal text-critical apparatus, an effort has been made to identify all editorial additions or emendations in the commentaries or in the scores themselves.

It is a pleasure to close by acknowledging the generous response of a number of publishers and editors to requests to reproduce their editions in the present volume. Specific acknowledgments are included in the individual commentaries.

# Music
## *of the*
# Baroque

# 1. Giovanni Pierluigi da Palestrina (1525/6–1594),
## *Dum complerentur* (motet)

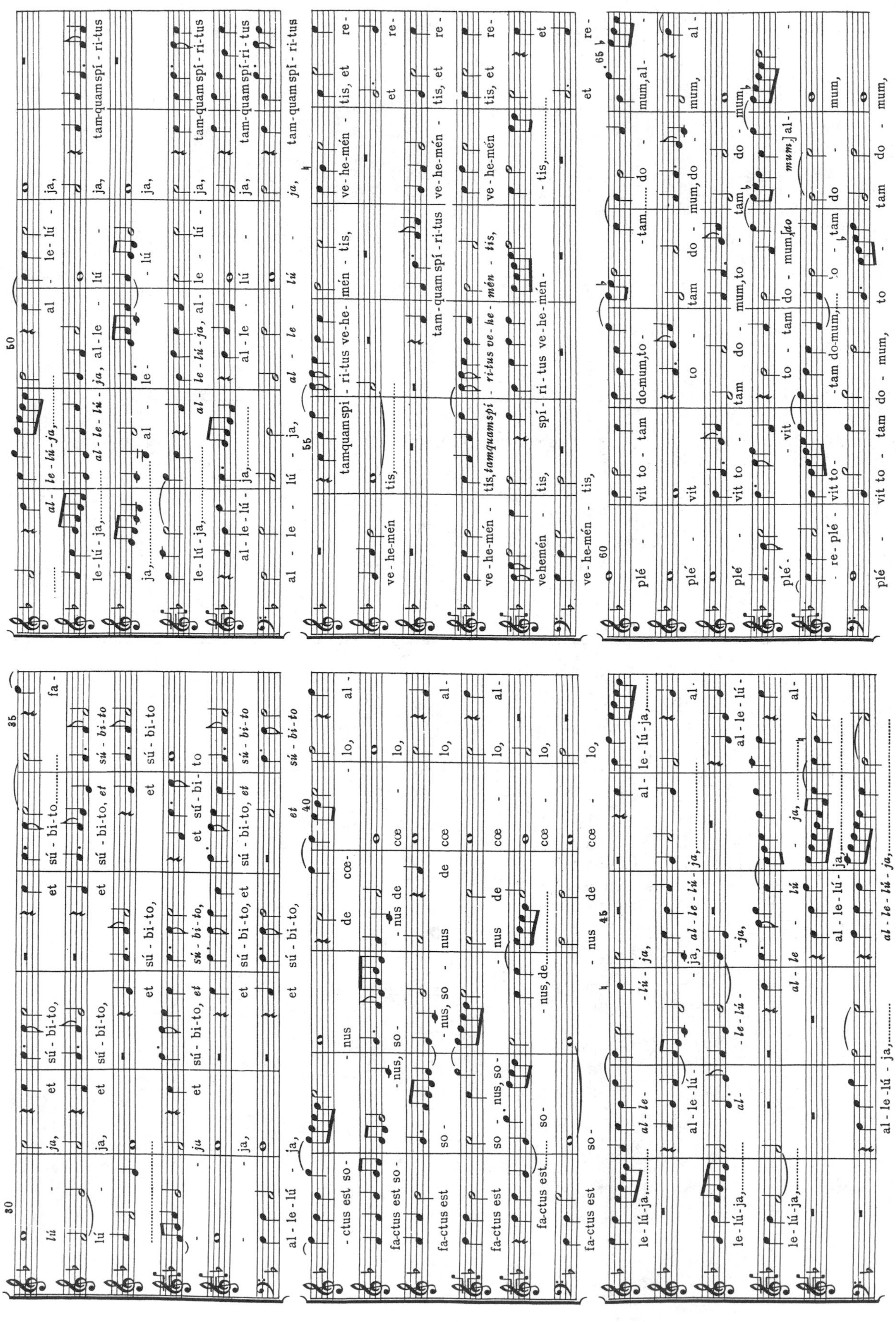

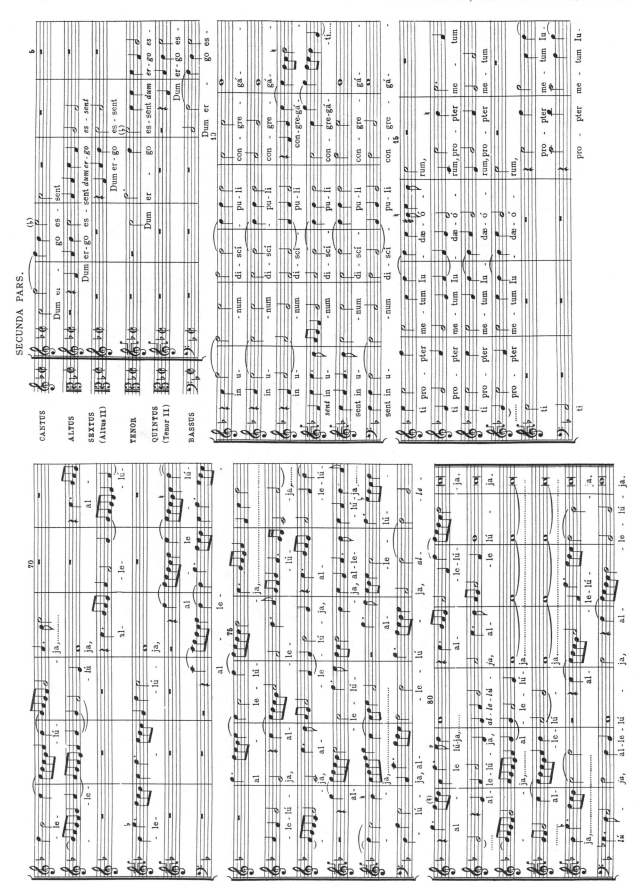

# TEXT AND TRANSLATION

## Prima pars

**Part 1**

1 Dum complerentur dies Pentecostes,
2 erant omnes pariter dicentes alleluja,

3 et subito factus est sonus de coelo,
    alleluja
4 tamquam spiritus vehementis,
    et replevit totam domum, alleluja.

When the feast of Pentecost was come,
all [the disciples] were together, saying
    hallelujah,
and suddenly a sound was made from heaven
    —hallelujah!—
as from a rushing wind, filling
the entire house—hallelujah!

## Secunda pars

**Part 2**

5 Dum ergo essent in unum discipuli
    congregati,
6 propter metum Iudaeorum,
7 sonus repente de coelo venit super eos,

8 tamquam spiritus . . . .

—Acts 2:1–2, with additions

Thus, when the disciples were gathered
    together as one
because of fear of the Jews,
a sound from heaven suddenly came over
    them,
as from a wind . . . .

# EDITION

Like most modern scores of sixteenth-century music, this edition has been prepared from the individual vocal parts in which the work originally circulated. The layout in score is the work of a modern editor, as are the addition of barlines and other aspects of the notation necessary for presenting it in score.

At the beginning of the score, the six parts are labeled with the names given them in Palestrina's original printed edition. Also shown are the original clefs, which differ from those used in the modern edition except in the top part. The editor has also suggested modern equivalents (given in parentheses) for the original labels *sextus* and *quintus*.

In the text, the editor has added accent marks to indicate syllables that would receive a stress when spoken aloud. Some repeated words and phrases of the text are printed in italics (*like this*). These represent editorial additions; in the original printed edition, not all repetitions of words were written out.

Accidentals placed above the notes, such as the natural in the quintus part in measure 11, are editorial suggestions. Commonly referred to today as *musica ficta*, these editorial accidentals correspond in most cases to alterations that singers probably would have made in performance in Palestrina's day.

## PERFORMANCE ISSUES

The question of what types of voices should be used, or how many should sing each part, cannot be settled by examining the score. For example, the editor has suggested that the sextus part be sung by a second alto, but modern performers must decide whether this means a boy or girl alto, an adult female alto or contralto, or an adult male falsetto singer. In Palestrina's performances at the Sistine Chapel in Rome, adult men probably sang all six parts. Instrumental participation, although banned in the Sistine Chapel, might have taken place in performances elsewhere.

Closely related to the issue of voices and instruments is that of original pitch. The modern concept of a fixed, absolute pitch (a' = 440 Hz) did not exist in Palestrina's day; thus, regardless of the notated pitches, in practice the actual pitch level of any work might have been higher or lower than what we would assume. There is some evidence that purely vocal music such as this motet was usually sung at Rome at a significantly lower pitch than the notation would indicate to us.

The score provides no indications of dynamics, tempo, or other aspects of musical in-terpretation now deemed essential to performance. As noted above, the accent marks in the text are editorial. Palestrina's music tends to set these accented syllables on higher or longer notes, or with melismas; thus, these syllables would not require an additional stress accent as well. Other issues that performers might consider include the pronun-ciation of the Latin text and the addition (if any) of improvised ornamentation and em-bellishment, a common practice in Palestrina's time although not necessarily employed in all works. Modern performers resolve these issues based on their understanding of historical performance practice and their analysis of the score. In addition, many deci-sions, now as in Palestrina's day, must depend on the circumstances of an individual performance: whether the latter takes place in a large church, a small private chapel, or a concert hall—the latter being a uniquely modern venue for a sacred motet of the Renaissance.

## SOURCES

The score has been reproduced from *Le opere complete di Giovanni Pierluigi da Palestrina*, ed. Raffaeli Casimiri, vol. 5 (Rome: Fratelli Scalera, 1939), 149–58. The work was orig-inally published in Palestrina's *Liber primus . . . motettorum* (Rome: Dorico, 1569); this edition is based on the reprint of 1600 (Venice: Scotto).

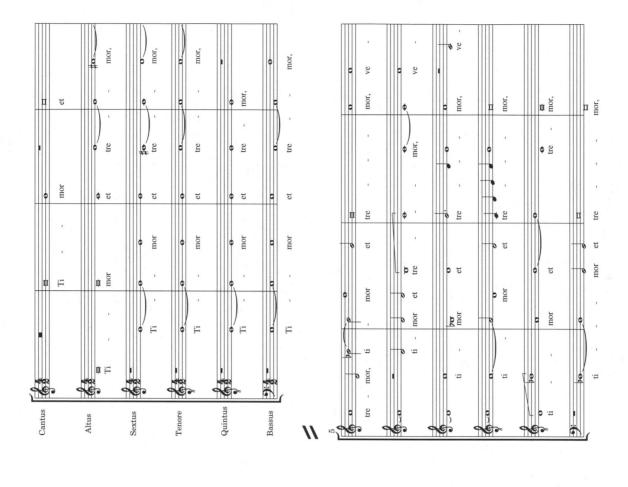

**2.** Orlando di Lassus (1530/2–1594),
*Timor et tremor* (motet)

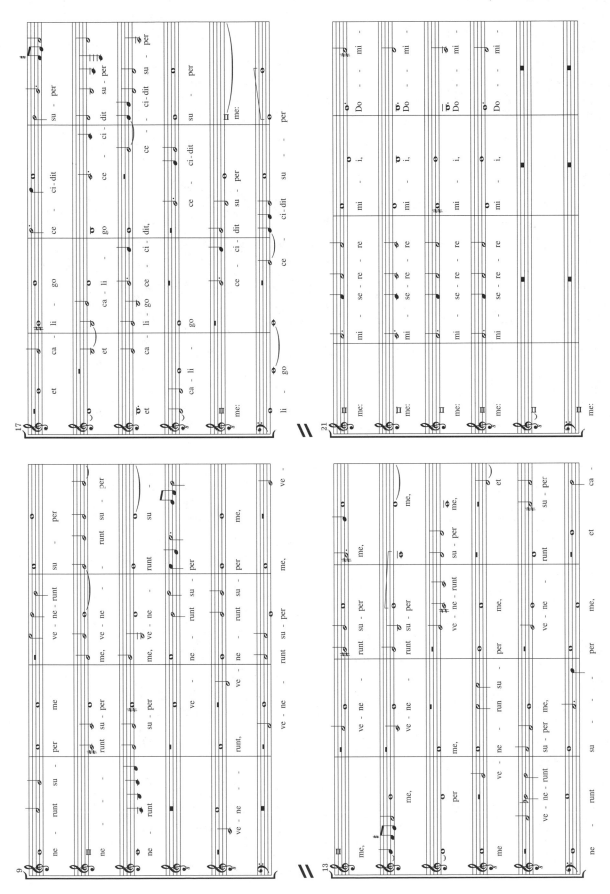

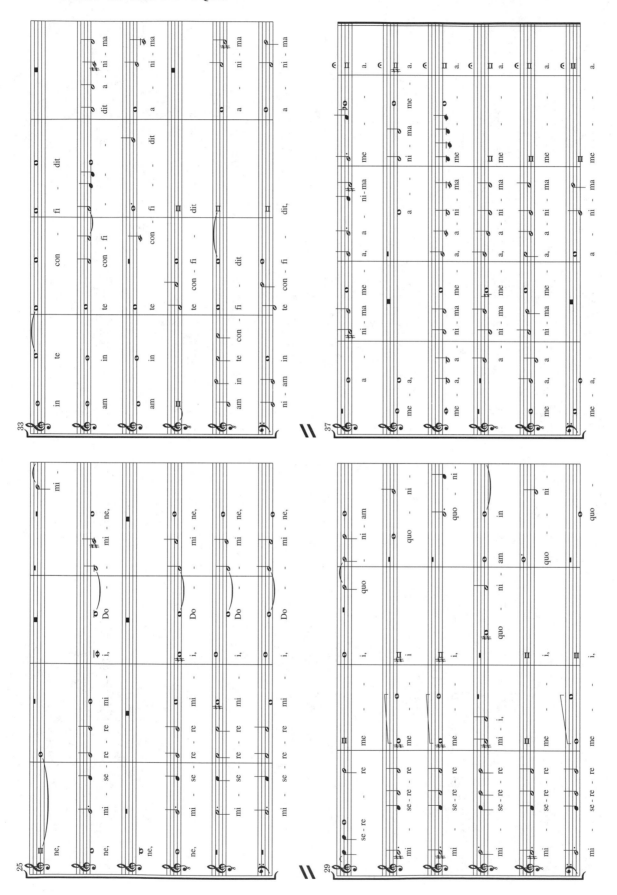

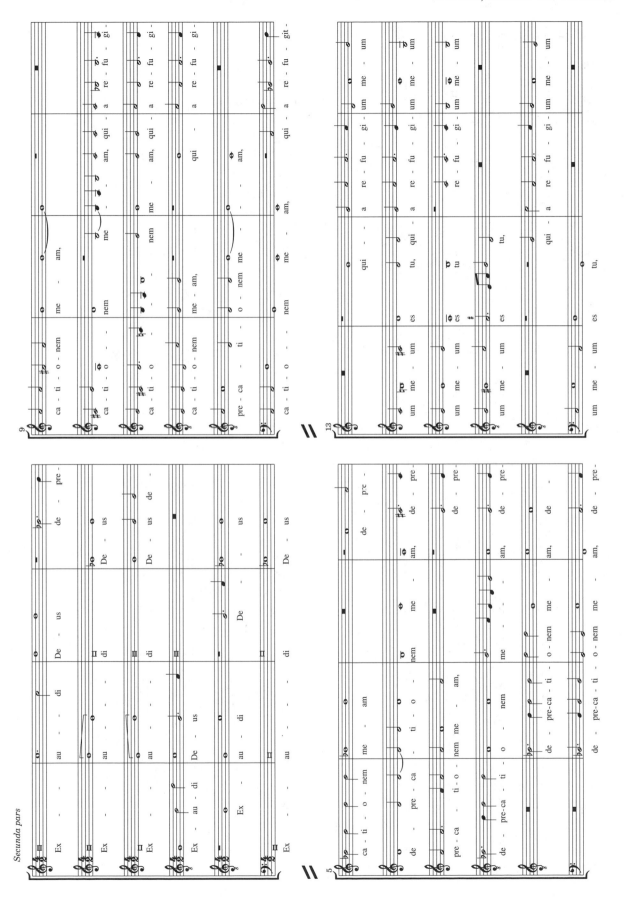

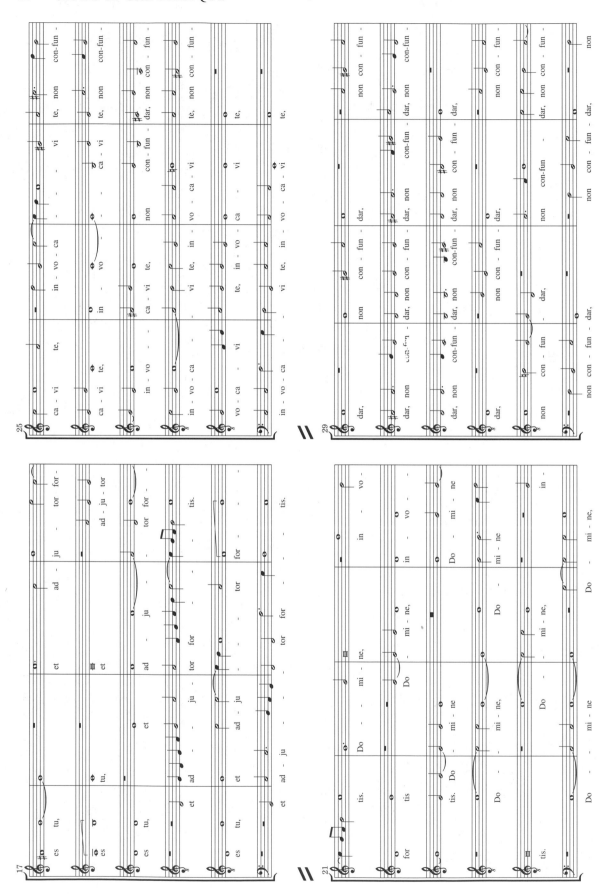

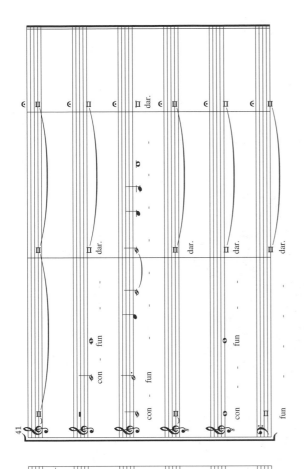

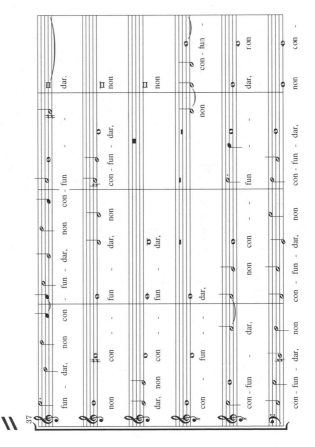

# TEXT AND TRANSLATION

*Prima pars*

*Part 1*

1 Timor et tremor venerunt super me

Fear and trembling have come over me,

2 et caligo cecidit super me.

and darkness has fallen on me.

3 Miserere mei, Domine,

Have mercy on me, Lord,

4 quoniam in te confidit anima mea.

for in you trusts my soul.

*Seconda pars*

*Part 2*

5 Exaudi Deus deprecationem meam,

Hear, God, my prayer,

6 quia refugium meum es tu et adjutor
  fortis.

for you are my refuge and my strong helper.

7 Domine, invocavi te,

Lord, I have called on you;

8 non confundar.

do not confound [me].

# EDITION

Our edition is again a modern transcription of an early printed edition in the form of individual vocal parts. The score resembles that of the Palestrina work (Selection 1), reflecting the general similarities in style and notation between the two motets. Nevertheless, modern editors do not always present similar compositions in similar ways, and the present score differs in some ways from that of the Palestrina work.

For example, this score lacks editorial indications for accentuation in the Latin text. More significantly, it gives the notes in their original rhythmic values; in the Palestrina score, each note is shown in half the value of the original print. The Lassus score thus contains a preponderance of whole notes and half notes, whereas the Palestrina score comprises mainly halves and quarters. The Lassus score even contains some instances of the *breve*, a square note shape in common use during the Renaissance but rarely seen today; it is equivalent to two whole notes (as in the first note of the altus part). These large note values might suggest a slow tempo to a modern performer, but in fact this motet was probably performed at roughly the same tempo as the Palestrina motet; that is, a whole note here has approximately the same duration as a half note in the Palestrina score.

A few of the longer notes in this score are joined together by brackets, as in part 1, measure 5 (quintus). Each bracket indicates the presence in the original of a *ligature*: a special symbol used as shorthand for two or more separate notes, usually of relatively long duration. A holdover from medieval notation (in which they were used far more frequently), ligatures were falling out of use during the sixteenth century. They may sometimes have functioned somewhat as slurs do in later music; in sixteenth-century music, the notes of a ligature are almost always sung to a single syllable.

## PERFORMANCE ISSUES

This work raises much the same questions of performance as does Selection 1. The composer is perhaps more likely to have envisaged instrumental participation in this work, but purely vocal performance remains equally possible. The large rhythmic values of the present score do not imply an unusually slow tempo, despite the seriousness of the text. The present notation implies placing the beat on the whole note, and any needed changes in tempo are written into the music: the initial motion predominantly in whole notes leads to lively movement in smaller values by the end of Part 2.

## SOURCES

Our score is based on the edition in Orlando di Lasso, *Magnum opus musicum . . . Theil X*, ed. Franz Xaver Haberl, *Sämtlicher Werke* 19:6–9. Haberl's source was the *Magnum opus musicum* (Munich, 1604), a posthumous compilation of Lassus's works. An edition based on the first printing of this work in *Thesauri musici tomus tertius* (Nuremberg: Montanus and Neuber, 1564) is anticipated.[1]

---

[1] To appear in vol. 3 of *Orlando di Lasso: The Complete Motets*, Recent Researches in the Music of the Renaissance (Madison, Wis.: A-R Editions).

**3.** Don Carlo Gesualdo, Prince of Venosa (ca. 1560–1613),
*Beltà, poi che t'assenti* (madrigal)

## TEXT AND TRANSLATION

| | | |
|---|---|---|
| 1 | Beltà, poi che t'assenti, | Beauty, since you have consented, |
| 2 | Come ne porti il cor, porta i tormenti. | As you carry off my heart take also my torments. |
| 3 | Che tormentato cor può ben sentire | For a tormented heart can well feel |
| 4 | La doglia del morire, | The pain of dying, |
| 5 | E un'alma senza core | But a soul without a heart |
| 6 | Non può sentir dolore. | Cannot feel sadness. |

## EDITION

Unlike Selections 1 and 2, Gesualdo's madrigals appeared not only in printed partbooks but in score, a rare form of publication for this type of music.[2] Gesualdo's score includes barlines, but in keeping with the practice of the time these were placed irregularly, creating measures of varying length. The present score follows Gesualdo's barring; thus, for example, measures 20–22 are only half as long as those at the beginning. In modern terms the time signature at the opening should be $\frac{4}{2}$, changing to $\frac{2}{2}$ at measure 20. The original meter sign ("C-slash") has nevertheless been left at the beginning of the score; the value of the notes remains constant throughout the composition.

Otherwise the modern edition raises few issues not already encountered. One small point involves the Italian text, in which certain vowels are joined by curved lines that indicate the presence of *elisions* (as on the words *porti il cor* in m. 4). In an elision, adjacent vowels are combined into a single sound, forming one syllable where there might otherwise be two or even three. Elision is an important device in Italian poetry, since elided syllables are counted as one for the purposes of prosody (poetic meter).

## PERFORMANCE ISSUES

This score remains, in principle, purely vocal. The secular text would, at the time of composition, have permitted the use of female as well as male adult singers. The difficulty of singing the chromatic progressions in tune suggests that Gesualdo had professional singers in mind, possibly accompanied by lute, harp, or harpsichord, as was the case with performances by the "Three Ladies" of Ferrara, for whom works such as this might have been intended. Such performers would undoubtedly have added improvised ornamentation, although this particular score leaves little room for elaborate embellishment.

Like Selection 2, this score contains a built-in accelerando, opening with relatively large note values but concluding with predominantly smaller ones. It is therefore likely that Gesualdo, like his predecessors, envisaged a fairly steady beat throughout the madrigal. Performers might have taken a somewhat more flexible approach in this type of music, however, employing ritards at the ends of phrases (as in m. 4) and pushing forward when the rhythm flows more swiftly in quarter notes. Nevertheless, this music was still performed from independent part books, without a conductor; this would have made extreme or sudden changes of tempo difficult to coordinate without extensive rehearsal.

The chromatic progressions raise the issue of tuning and temperament. Modern singers, accustomed to accompaniment on the equal-tempered piano, often overlook the

---

[2]Parts: *Madrigali a cinque voci, libro sesto* (Naples: Carlino, 1611); score: *Partitura delli sei libri de' Madrigali a cinque voci*, ed. Simone Molinaro (Genoa: Pavoni, 1613).

possibility of alternative tuning systems or *temperaments*. But Gesualdo and his contemporaries knew many different tuning systems, some of which would have deepened the expressive effects of his chromatic progressions. For example, in certain temperaments the chromatic half step sung by the soprano at the outset (g′–g♯′) is smaller than the diatonic half step that follows (g♯′–a′). The lute, which might have participated in performances of this work, is in principle an equal-tempered instrument, like the modern piano. Other temperaments would have been used on the harp or the harpsichord, and Gesualdo and his Ferrarese patrons must have known of special keyboard instruments with extra keys (to distinguish, e.g., G♯ from A♭) that would have been useful in training and accompanying singers in this type of music.

# 4. Claudio Monteverdi (1567–1643),
## *Luci serene* (madrigal)

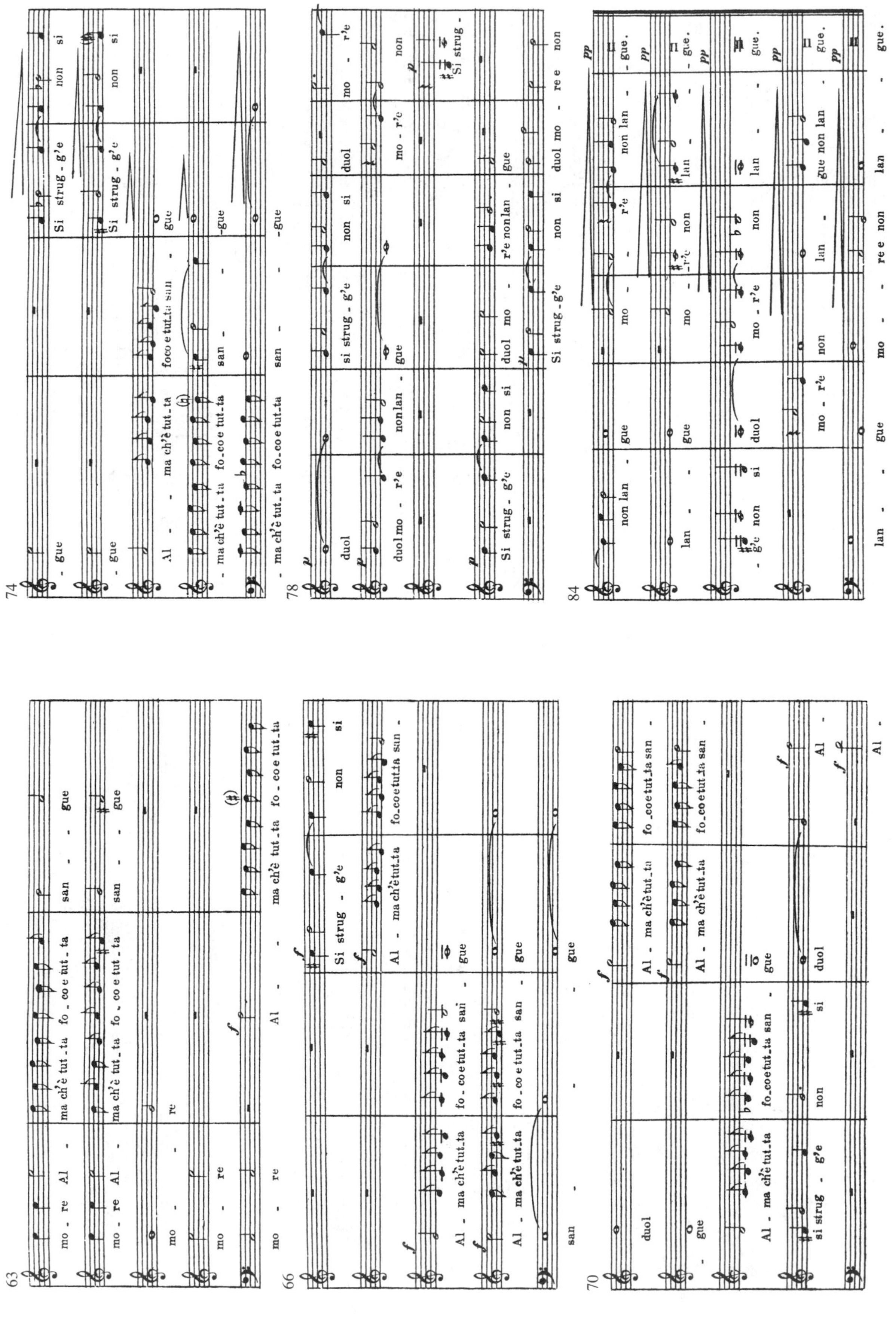

## TEXT AND TRANSLATION

1 Luci serene e chiare,
2 Voi m'incendete, voi, ma prov'il core
3 Nell'incendio diletto, non dolore.

4 Dolci parole e care,
5 Voi mi ferite, voi, ma prov'il petto
6 Non dolor ne la piaga, ma diletto.

7 O miracol d'amore:
8 Alma ch'è tutta foco e tutta sangue
9 Si strugg'e non si duol, muor e
   non langue.

—Ridolfo Arlotti

Eyes serene and clear,
You inflame me, you, but my heart feels
In burning delight, not pain.

Sweet words and dear,
You pierce me, you, but my breast feels
Not pain in the wound, but delight.

Oh, [such a] miracle of love:
That a spirit that is all fire and all blood
Is consumed but does not suffer, dies but
   does not languish.

## EDITION

Our score is based on the individual vocal parts of Monteverdi's Fourth Book of Madrigals. An edition from the earlier twentieth century, it includes editorial dynamic markings such as **mf** (*mezzoforte*) in measure 1 and the crescendo symbols in measures 13–16. Also editorial are the tempo marking (*andante*), all parenthesized accidentals, and the occasional slurs (as in mm. 7 and 9), although the latter serve only to mark melismas. The clefs used for the original printed parts are shown in parentheses at the opening.

Two wrong notes in the edition must be corrected: in measure 5, note 1 of the basso should be A, not G; in measures 36–87, the tied note in the canto should be a', not f'.

## PERFORMANCE ISSUES

Like the preceding work, this madrigal may have been conceived with instrumental participation in mind. Indeed, two of the many seventeenth-century reprints of this work included an instrumental accompaniment in the form of a basso continuo part, that is, a bass line for a keyboard or other instrument on which the player improvised chords, guided by numbers and other symbols written above the notes.[3] Although often described today as optional, such parts may have reflected the usual practice of the time.

The editorial dynamic markings in our edition are arbitrary additions, but Monteverdi probably expected singers to employ dynamic contrasts in response to the changing emotional character of the text. The editor's *andante* marking is somewhat misleading; the tempo throughout should probably be such that the eighth notes beginning in measure 42 are lively enough to represent the image of "fire" present in the text at that point. As in Selection 3, changes of pacing are written into the music, although some freedom of tempo was no doubt taken for granted.

## SOURCES

This edition is reproduced from *Tutte le opere di Claudio Monteverdi*, ed. Gian Francesco Malipiero, vol. 4 (Asola, 1927). The source for the latter was Monteverdi's *Quattro libro de madrigali* (Venice, 1603).

[3]The basso continuo part appeared in an edition published in 1615 in Antwerp (in modern Belgium); it is included in *Claudio Monteverdi: Madrigali a 5 voci: Libro quinto*, ed. Elena Ferrari Borassi, *Opera omina*, vol. 5 (Cremona: Fondazione Claudio Monteverdi, 1974), 128–33.

## 5. Giulio Caccini (1551–1618), *Sfogava con le stelle* (continuo madrigal)

Sfo-ga-va con le stel - le       Un in-fer-mo d'a-mo - re,       Sot-to not-tur - no

cie - lo il suo do-lo — re,       E di-cea fis - so in lo - ro:       O,

o, im-ma-gi-ni bel - le dell' i - dol mio ch'a-do - ro, Si       co-me a me mo-stra -

- te,       Men-tre co-sì splen-de - te La sua ra — ra bel-ta-te Co - sì mo-stra-te a

le - i, Men-tre co-tan-to ar-de-te I vi - vi ar-do - - - - - - ri

mie - i.    La fa-re-ste col vo-stro au-reo sem-bian-te Pie-to-sa si,    pie-to - sa si,    co-

11 #10 14          ♭                                                    ♮

- me me fa - - - te a-man - te,    La fa-re-ste col vo-stro au - reo sem-bian-te Pie-to-sa

6          6     11 #10 14

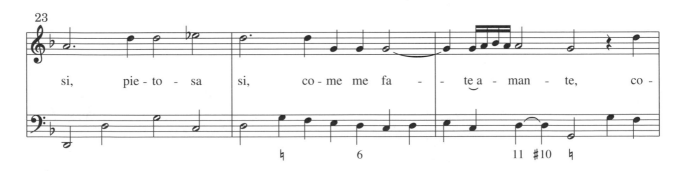

si,    pie-to - sa    si,    co - me me fa - - - te a - man - te,    co-

♮          6                11 #10  ♮

- me me fa - - - - - - - te a - man - te.

6  6          ♮                              #10 11          11 #10 14

## TEXT AND TRANSLATION

| | |
|---|---|
| 1 Sfogava con le stelle | To the stars, under the nighttime sky, |
| 2 Un infermo d'amore, | A lovesick man |
| 3 Sotto notturno ciel il suo dolore, | Poured out his sadness |
| 4 E dicea fisso in loro: | And said, his eyes fixed upon them: |
| 5 O, immagini belle | "O lovely images |
| 6 Del idol mio ch'adoro, | Of my idol whom I adore, |
| 7 Sì come a me mostrate, | Just as you show me, |
| 8 Mentre così splendete | By shining so splendidly, |
| 9 La sua rara beltate | Her rare beauty, |
| 10 Così mostraste a lei, | Show her |
| 11 Mentre cotanto ardete | That, as strongly as you burn |
| 12 I vivi ardori miei. | Are my own hot flames. |
| 13 La fareste col vostro aureo sembiante | Make her, through your golden semblance, |
| 14 Pietosa sì, come me fate amante. | As merciful as you make me ardent." |

—Ottavio Rinuccini

## EDITION

This edition is a verbatim transcription of the original printed score for voice and basso continuo, which is notated as a figured bass.

## PERFORMANCE ISSUES

Caccini left no indication of the type of voice or instrument(s) intended, despite his inclusion of a lengthy preface on the intended manner of singing. Caccini's figured bass differs from later examples in its use of compound figures; for example, measure 25 uses the numerals 11–10 where later composers would have written 4–3. The tied bass notes in the same measure indicate the precise rhythm of the upper voice of the continuo realization as it moves from 11 (g′) to 10 (f♯′); this type of notation also was abandoned within a few years of this work.

Other editions provide written-out realizations of the figured bass. However, it is practically impossible to notate a stylish realization of this figured bass for the lute, probably the preferred instrument at the time.[4]

## SOURCES AND ACKNOWLEDGMENTS

This edition is based on the original edition of Caccini's *Le nuove musiche* (Florence, 1601), available in facsimile (New York: Broude, 1973).

---

[4]For a keyboard version, see the edition by H. Wiley Hitchcock (Madison, Wis.: A-R, 1970).

# 6. Claudio Monteverdi (1567–1643), *Orfeo*, Act 2 (opera: selections)

a. Sinfonia and two arias: "Ecco pur ch'a voi ritorno" and "Mira ch'a se n'alletta"

pur ch'à voi ri - tor - no___ Ca - re sel - ve e piag - ge a - ma - te, Da quel

Sol fat - te be - a - te Per cui sol mie nott' han gior - no. Ec - co

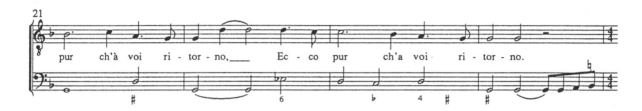

pur ch'à voi ri - tor - no,___ Ec - co pur ch'a voi ri - tor - no.

**Ritornello**

*Questo Ritornello fu suonato di dentro da un Clavicembano, duoi Chitaroni, & duoi Violini piccioli alla Francese.*

*Pastore (C4)*

Mi -

b. "Mira, deh mira Orfeo" through chorus, "Ahi, caso acerbo"

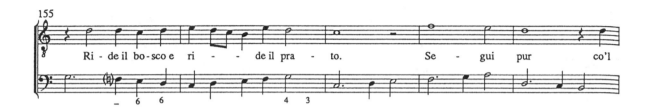

*Un Clavic[embalo], chitar[one] & viola da bracio.*

171 **Pastore (C4)** ... **Messagiera (C1)**

Qual suon do-len-te il lie-to di per-tur-ba?    Las - sa,    dun - que deb-b'i - o

174

Men-tre Or - feo    con sue no - te il Ciel con-so - la    Con le pa-ro - le mie pas-sar-

177    **Pastore (C3)**

- - - gli il co - re?    Que - sta è Sil - via gen - ti - le    Dol-cis-si-

180

-ma com-pa - gna Del-la bell' Eu-ri-di - ce:    ò quan-to è in vi-sta Do-lo-ro -

183

- sa:    hor    che fia?    deh som-mi De - i Non tor-ce-te da noi be-ni-gno il

**186**  *Messagiera (C1)*

guar - do.   Pas - tor   la - scia - te il can - to,   Ch'o - gni no - stra al - le - grez - za   in

**189**  *Orfeo (C4)*

do - glia è vol   -   ta.   D'on - de vie - ni?   o - ve vai?   Nin - fa che por - ti?

**193**  *Messagiera (C1)*

A   te   ne ven-go Or-feo___   Mes-sa-gie-ra in - fe - li - ce   Di ca-so più in-fe-li   -   ce e più fu-ne-

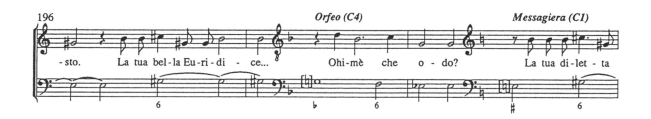

**196**                                                      *Orfeo (C4)*                          *Messagiera (C1)*

- sto.   La tua bel-la Eu-ri-di - ce...   Ohi-mè che o - do?   La tua di -let-ta

**199**                                  *Orfeo (C4)*              *Messagiera (C1)*

spo - sa   è mor - ta.   Ohi - mè.   In   un fio - ri - to pra - to   Con

l'al - tre sue com - pa - - gne  Gi - va co - glien - do fio - ri  Per

far - ne u - na ghir - lan - da à le sue chio - me,  Quand' an - gue in - si - di - o - so  Ch'e-

- ra fra l'er - be a - sco - so,  Le pun - se un piè  con ve - le - no - so den - te.

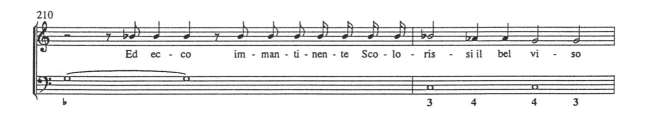

Ed ec - co  im - man - ti - nen - te  Sco - lo - ris - si il bel vi - so

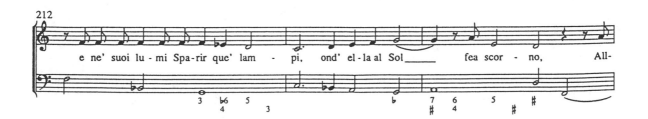

e ne' suoi lu - mi  Spa - rir que' lam - pi,  ond' el - la al Sol____  fea scor - no,  All-

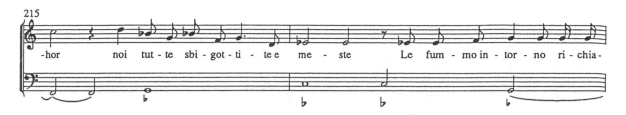

-hor noi tut-te sbi-got-ti-te e me-ste Le fum-mo in-tor-no ri-chia-

-mar ten-tan-do Gli spir-ti in lei smar-ri-ti Con l'on-da fre-sca e co' pos-sen-ti car-mi; Ma__

__ nul-la val-se, ahi las-sa, Ch'el-la i lan-gui-di lu-mi al-quan-to a-pren-

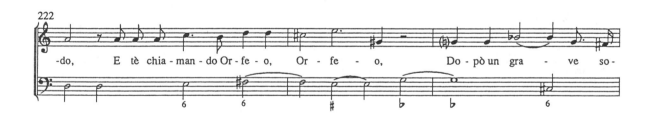

-do, E tè chia-man-do Or-fe-o, Or-fe-o, Do-pò un gra-ve so-

-spi-ro Spi-rò frà que-ste brac-cia, ed io ri-ma-si Pie-na il cor di pie-

228

ta - de e di spa-ven - to. Ahi,___ ca - so a-cer-bo, ahi fat' em - pio e cru - de - le, Ahi,

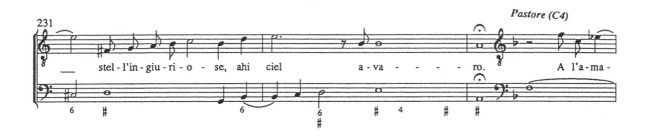

231

___ stel - l'in - giu - ri - o - se, ahi ciel a - va - - - - ro. A l'a - ma

234

- - ra no - vel - la Ras - sem - bra l'in - fe - li - ce un mu - to sas - so, Che per trop - po do - lor non

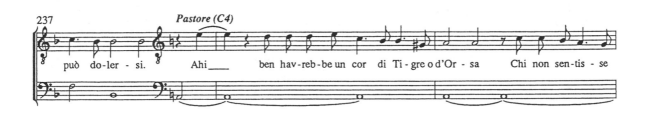

237

può do - ler - si. Ahi___ ben hav - reb - be un cor di Ti - gre o d'Or - sa Chi non sen - tis - se

240

del tuo mal pie - ta - te, Pri - vo d'o - gni tuo ben mi - se - ro a - man - - - te.

Orfeo
Tu_____ se' mor - ta se' mor - ta mia vi -

*Un organo di legno e un chitarone*

-ta, ed io re-spi - ro? Tu se' da me par-ti - ta,

se' da me par-ti - ta Per mai più, mai più non tor-na - re, ed io ri-man-

--go? Nò, nò,_____ che se i ver-si al-cu - na co - sa pon - no

N'an-drò si-cu - ro a più pro-fon-di a-bis - si, E in - te-ne - ri-to il

cor      del Rè de l'Om - bre      Me - co trar - ròt - ti    a   ri - ve - der   le

stel -    le:      O  se  ciò  ne - ghe - ràm - mi em - pio  de - sti - no

Ri - mar - rò  te - co    in com - pa - gnia   di  mor - te,    A  dio  ter - ra,

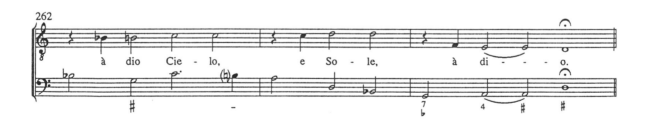

à   dio  Cie - lo,      e  So - le,    à  di - - o.

## TEXT AND TRANSLATION

### Orfeo

Ecco pur, ch'à voi ritorno,
Care selve e piagge amate,
Da quel sol fatte beate
Per cui sol mie nott'han giorno.
*Questo ritornello fu suonato di*
*Dentro da un clavicembano, duoi*
*chitaroni, & duoi violini piccioli*
*alla francese.*

### Pastore

Mira ch'à se n'alletta
L'ombra Orfeo de que'faggi,
Hor che'nfocati raggi
Febo da ciel saetta.

Sù qual'herbosa sponda
Posianci, e in varii modi
Ciascun sua voce snodi
Al mormorio de l'onde.

. . .

Mira, deh mira, Orfeo, che d'ogni
    intorno
Ride il bosco e ride il prato,
Seguì pur co'l plettr'aurato
D'addolcir l'aria in si beato giorno.

### Messaggiera

*(un organo di legno & un chit{arone})*

### Orpheus

Here I am, returning to you,
Dear woods and beloved country
Who are blessed by the same sun
By whom my nights are made days.
*The following ritornello was played*
*backstage by a harpsichord, two*
*large lutes, and two small violins*
*in the French style.*

### Shepherd

See how Orpheus is enticed
By the shade of these beech trees,
As Phoebus [the sun god] shoots
Burning rays from heaven.

On this grassy shore
Let us rest, and in varying ways
Let each blend his voice
With the murmuring of the waves.

See, ah see, Orpheus, that all around you

The forest and the meadow laugh;
Go on with your golden plectrum,[5]
Sweetening the air on this lovely day.

### Messenger

*(accompanied by a wood-pipe organ and a large*
*lute)*

---

[5]A plectrum is a pick used to pluck an instrument such as a lute.

Ahi caso acerbo, ahi fat'empio e
   crudele
Ahi stelle ingiuriose, ahi ciel avaro.

**Pastore**

*(un clavic{embalo} & viola da bracio)*
Qual suon dolent'il lieto dì perturba?

**Messaggiera**

Lassa, dunque debb'io
Mentre Orfeo con sue note il ciel
   consola
Con le parole mie passargli il core?

**Pastore**

Questa è Silvia gentile,
Dolcissima compagna
De la bell'Euridice: ò quanto è in vista
Dolorosa: hor che fia? deh, sommi Dei
Non torcete da noi benigno il guardo.

**Messaggiera**

Pastor, lasciate il canto,
Ch'ogni nostr'allegrezza in doglia è volta.

**Orfeo**

Donde vieni? ove vai? Ninfa, che porti?

**Messaggiera**

A te ne vengo, Orfeo,
Messaggiera infelice
Di caso più infelice e più funesto.

La tua bella Euridice . . .

**Orfeo**

  Ohimè, che odo?

**Messaggiera**

La tua diletta sposa è morta.

**Orfeo**

  Ohimè.

**Messaggiera**

In un fiorito prato,
Con l'altre sue compagne,
Giva cogliendo fiori
Per farne una ghirlanda à le sue
   chiome,
Quand'angue insidioso
Ch'era fra l'erbe asconso
Le punse un piè con velenoso dente,
Ed ecco immantinente

---

Ah, bitter fortune; ah, cruel, pitiless fate;

Ah, unjust stars; ah, envious heaven.

**Shepherd**

*(accompanied by harpsichord and a {bass} violin)*
What sad sound disturbs this happy day?

**Messenger**

Alas, must I,
While Orpheus charms heaven with his
   notes,
Pierce his heart with my words?

**Shepherd**

This is noble Sylvia,
Sweetest companion
Of the beautiful Euridice; oh, how her face is
Saddened—what has happened? Ah, great gods,
Do not turn from us your benevolent gaze!

**Messenger**

Shepherd, cease your song,
For all our happiness to sadness has turned.

**Orpheus**

From where do you come? where are you
   going? Nymph, what [news] do you bring?

**Messenger**

I come to you, Orpheus,
An unfortunate bearer
Of tidings [even] more unfortunate and
   unhappy.
Your beautiful Euridice . . .

**Orpheus**

  Oh no, what do I hear?

**Messenger**

Your beloved bride is dead.

**Orpheus**

  Ah, no!

**Messenger**

In a flowery meadow,
With her companions,
She was wandering, gathering flowers
To make a garland for her hair,

When a treacherous snake
That was hidden in the grass
Struck her foot with poison fangs,
And at once

| | |
|---|---|
| Scolorissi il bel viso e ne'suoi lumi | Her lovely face grew pale, and in her eyes |
| Sparir que'lampi, ond'ella al sol fea scorno. | Grew faint the light by which the sun was outshone. |
| Allhor noi tutte sbiggottite e meste | Meanwhile we, all terrified and sad, |
| Le fummo intorno richiamar tentando | Were about her, trying to bring |
| Gli spriti in lei smarriti | Her lost senses back to her |
| Con l'onda fresca e co'possenti carmi; | With cold water and powerful incantations; |
| Ma nulla valse, ahi lassa, | But nothing worked, alas, |
| Ch'ella i languidi lumi alquanto aprendo | And at length, opening her fading eyes |
| E tè chiamando, Orfeo, | She called for you, Orpheus, |
| Dopò un grave sospiro | Then, with a deep sigh, |
| Spirò fra queste braccia, ed io rimasi | Perished in these arms, and I am left |
| Piena il cor di pietade e di spavento. | With my heart full of pity and fear. |

**Pastore**

**Shepherd**

| | |
|---|---|
| Ahi caso acerbo, ahi fat'empio e crudele | Ah, bitter fortune; ah, cruel, pitiless fate; |
| Ahi stelle ingiuriose, ahi ciel avaro. | Ah, unjust stars; ah, envious heaven. |

**Pastore [secondo]**

**[Second] Shepherd**

| | |
|---|---|
| A l'amara novella | At this bitter news |
| Rassembra l'infelice un muto sasso, | The unhappy one [Orpheus] seems like a mute gravestone, |
| Che per troppo dolor non può dolersi. | Afflicted with so much grief that he cannot grieve. |

**Pastore**

**Shepherd**

| | |
|---|---|
| Ahi, ben havrebbe un cor di tigre o d'orsa | Ah, one would have to have the heart of a tiger or a bear |
| Chi non sentisse del tuo mal pietate, | Not to feel pity for your misfortune, |
| Privo d'ogni tuo ben, misero amante. | Deprived of your beloved, wretched lover! |

**Orfeo**

**Orpheus**

| | |
|---|---|
| (*un organo di legno e un chitarone*) | (*accompanied by a wood-pipe organ and a large lute*) |
| Tu se' morta, mia vita, ed io respiro? | You are dead, my life, and I breathe? |
| Tu se' da me partita | You have left me, |
| Per mai più non tornare, ed io rimango? | Never to return, and I remain? |
| Nò, che se i versi alcuna cosa ponno | No, if my verses have any power, |
| N'andrò sicuro à più profondi abissi, | Surely I will go to the deepest abysses |
| E, intenerito il cor del rè de l'ombre, | And, softening the heart of the king of shades [the dead], |
| Meco trarròtti à riveder le stelle | Will lead you with me again to see the stars. |
| O se ciò negherammi empio destino | But if pitiless fate denies me this, |
| Rimarrò teco in compagnia di morte. | I will remain with you in the company of death. |
| A dio terra, à dio cielo, e sole, à dio. | Farewell, earth; farewell, heaven; and, to the sun, farewell. |

**Coro**

**Chorus**

| | |
|---|---|
| Ahi caso acerbo, ahi fat'empio e crudele, | Ah, bitter fortune; ah, cruel, pitiless fate; |
| Ahi stelle ingiuriose, ahi ciel avaro. | Ah, unjust stars; ah, envious heaven. |
| Non si fidi, huom mortale, | Trust not, mortal man, |
| Di ben caduco e frale | In good fortune, fleeting and frail, |

| | |
|---|---|
| Che tosto fugge, e spesso | Which quickly disappears; often |
| A gran salita il precipizio è presso. | A great cliff lies near a peak. |

—Alessandro Striggio

## EDITION

Our edition is based closely on the published score of 1609. The italicized phrases in Italian are the original indications of instrumentation and other performance details; these are translated above.

The parenthesized abbreviations at the beginning of the score and at the entries of voices are editorial indications of the original clefs; thus "C4" at Orfeo's entrance (m. 12) means that his part was originally written with a C clef on the fourth line, that is, a tenor clef. The figures in the basso continuo part are editorial except for a few given in larger type (e.g., 3–4–4–3 in m. 171). Realizations (not always in historically appropriate style) can be found in several older editions.

## PERFORMANCE ISSUES

Despite the presence of headings that describe aspects of the work's first performances, Monteverdi's score raises many difficult questions. For example, it is not clear exactly to what instruments some of the terms refer. Moreover, some instrumental parts are left unlabeled (as in the sinfonia that opens Act 2), and the score fails to specify whether the vocal parts of the choruses were sung by soloists or by a larger group, or whether they were doubled by instruments. The singers presumably included women as well as men, but precisely what types of voices were used is not always certain; for example, the music of the second shepherd is written in alto clef, suggesting either a high tenor voice or falsetto.

Beyond these basic issues of scoring there are the usual questions about pitch, tempo, dynamics, improvised ornamentation, and the like. To these we can add many other questions arising from the fact that this was a stage work. For example, how large was the theater and how did its size influence the style and volume of the singing and playing? What sort of lighting and costumes were employed, and did these influence the musical performance in any way? Where did the players sit and how were the vocal and instrumental ensembles directed and coordinated? (The score indicates that some of the instrumental music was heard from behind the scene.) What types of stage movement, including dance, did the soloists and chorus use: was it stylized or realistic? Did soloists reinforce their vocal projection through vigorous physical gestures, or were the latter restrained? Questions such as these have been carefully considered by performers as well as scholars; some modern performances have attempted to recreate elements of early practice, shedding new light on aspects of the work, but many proposed solutions must remain speculative.

## SOURCES AND ACKNOWLEDGMENTS

The score given here is reproduced with kind permission from the edition by Clifford Bartlett © King's Music 1993.[6]

---

[6]*Monteverdi: L'Orfeo: Favola in Musica, 1607* (King's Music, Redcroft, Banks End, Wyton, Huntingdon, Cambridgeshire PE17 2AA, United Kingdom, 1993).

# 7. Claudio Monteverdi (1567–1643),
*Il combattimento di Tancredi e Clorinda*
(*balletto* or "dramatic madrigal")

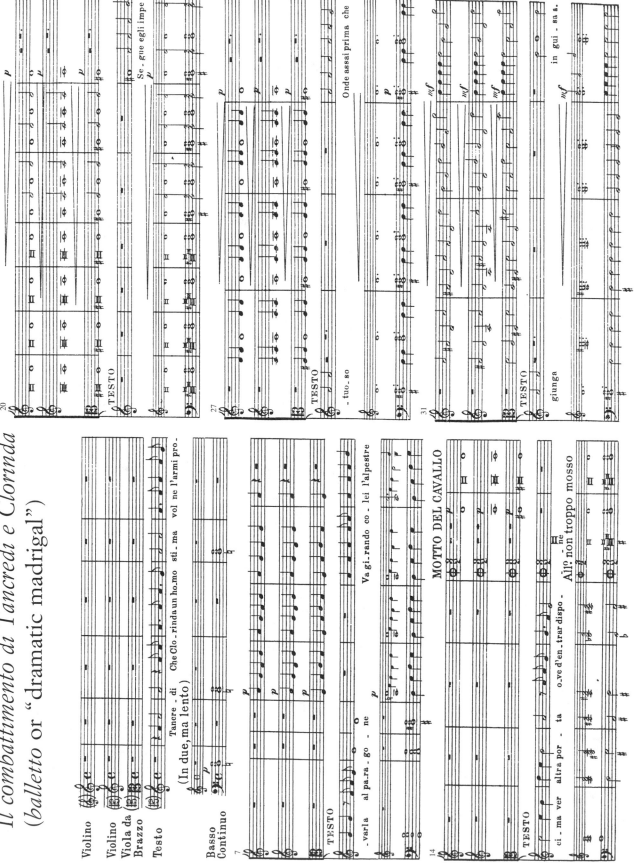

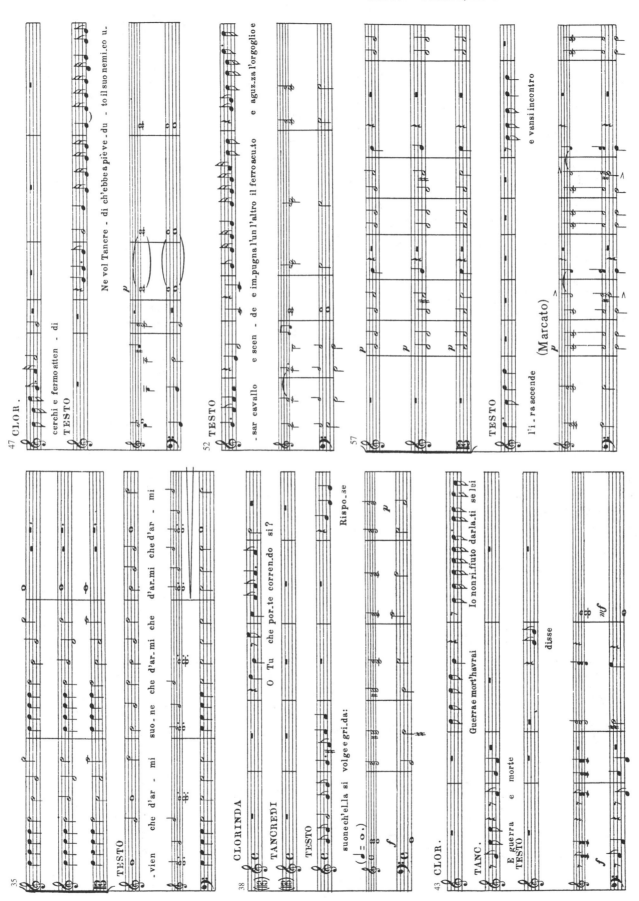

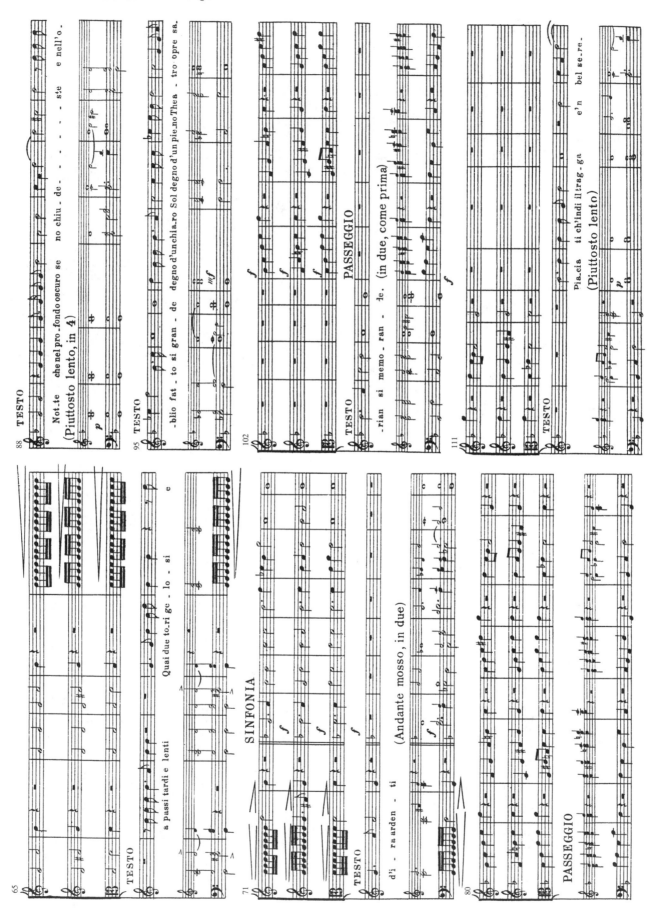

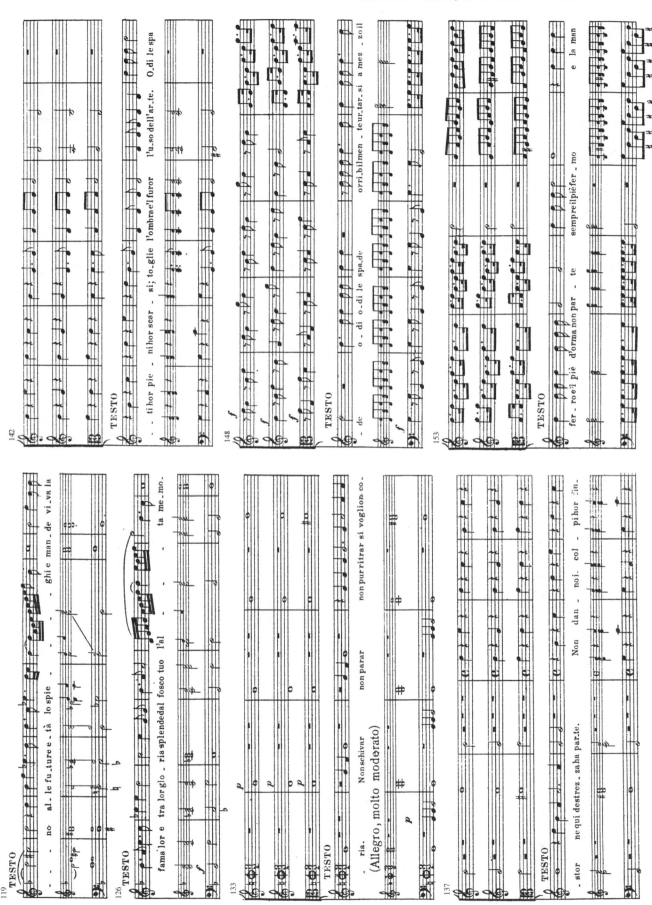

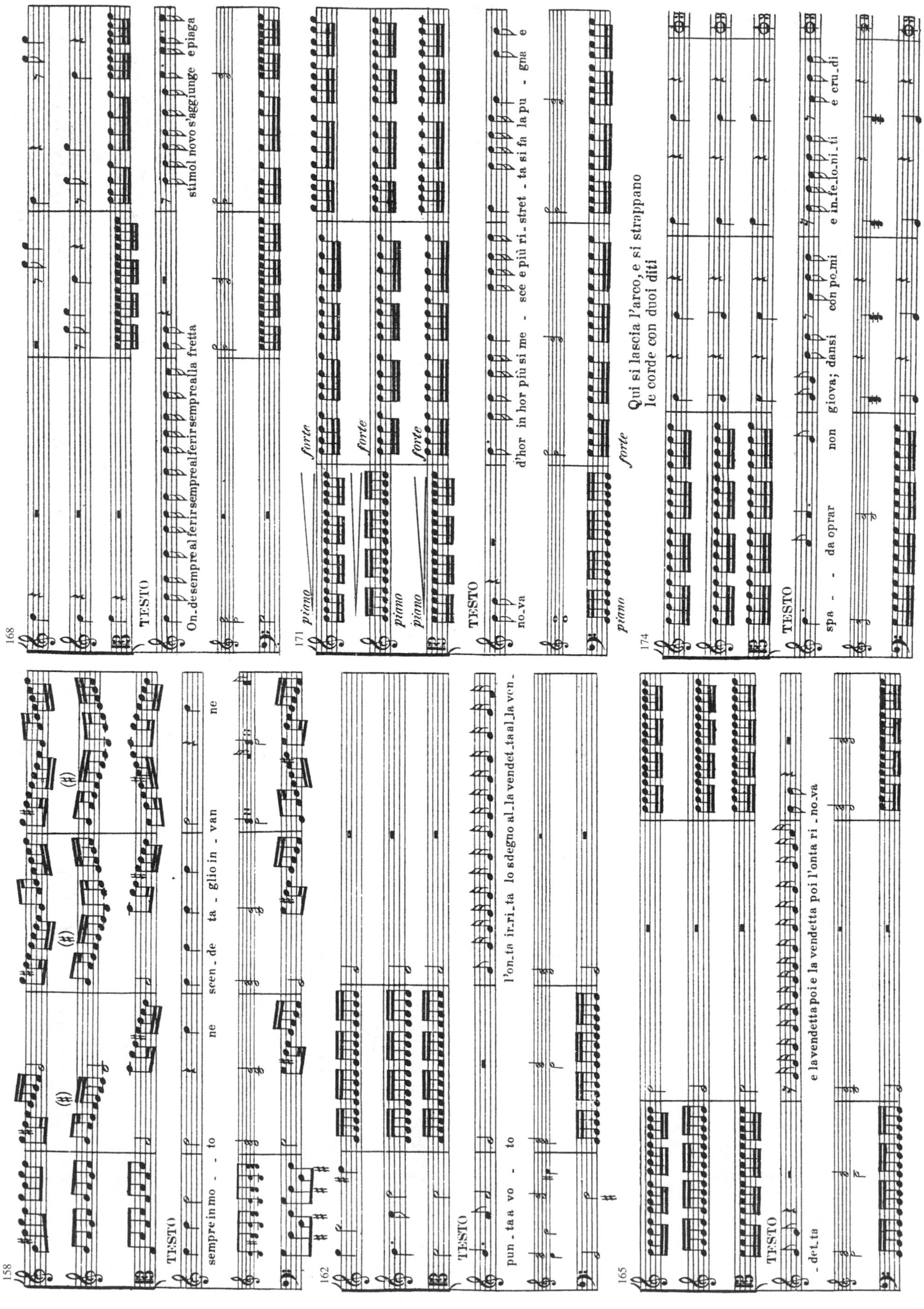
158
TESTO
sempre in mo - to ne scen - de ta - glio in - van ne
162
TESTO
pun - ta a vo - to l'on - ta ir - ri - ta lo sdegno al - la vendet - ta al - la ven -
165
TESTO
- det - ta e la vendetta poi e la vendetta poi l'onta ri - no - va
168
TESTO
On - de sempre al ferir sempre al ferir sempre alla fretta stimol novo s'aggiunge e piaga
171
piano
forte
TESTO
no - va d'hor in hor più si me - sce e più ri - stret - ta si fa la pu - gna e
Qui si lascia l'arco, e si strappano le corde con duoi diti
174
TESTO
spa - - da oprar non giova; dansi con po - mi e in - fe - lo - ni - ti e cru - di

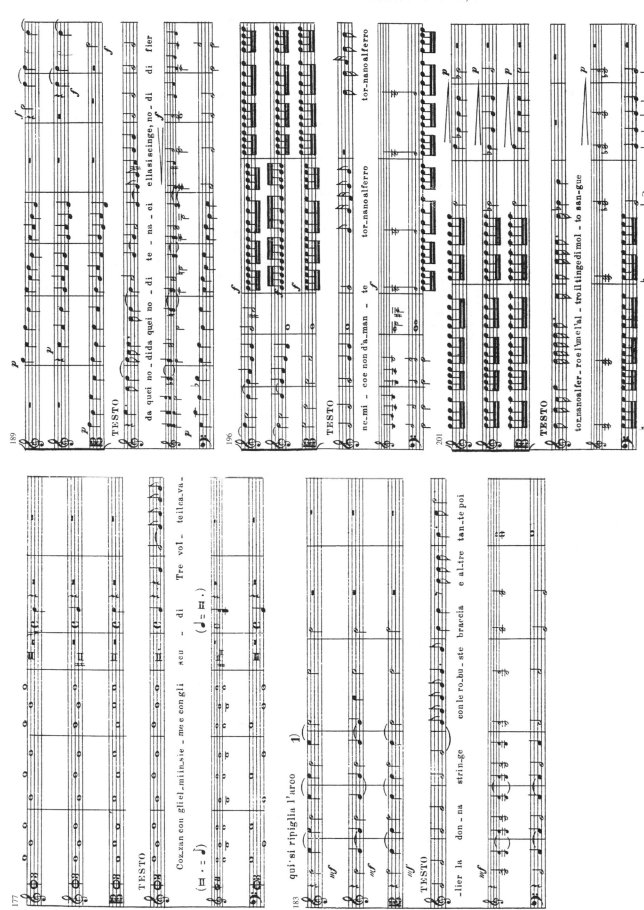

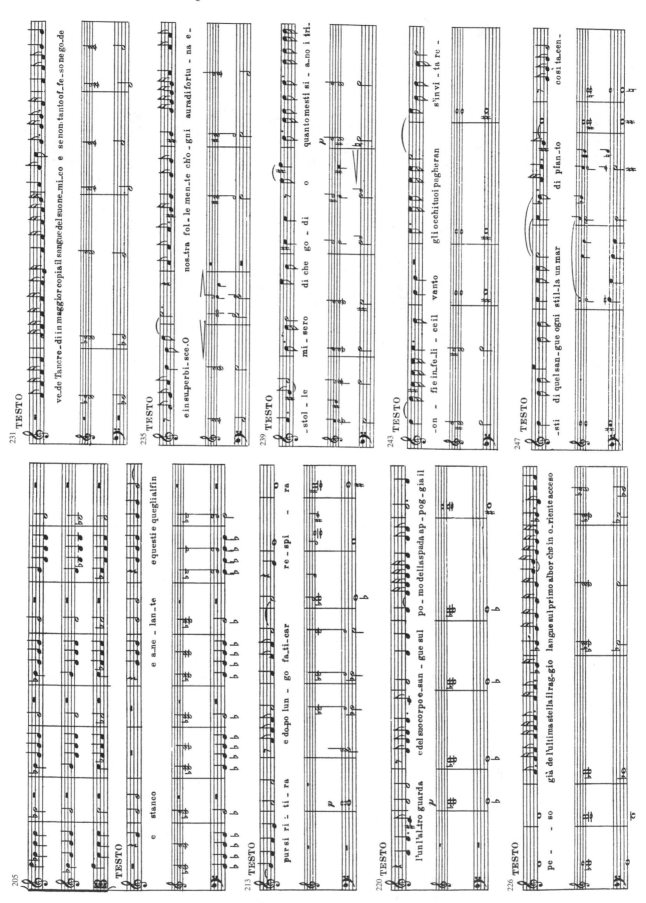

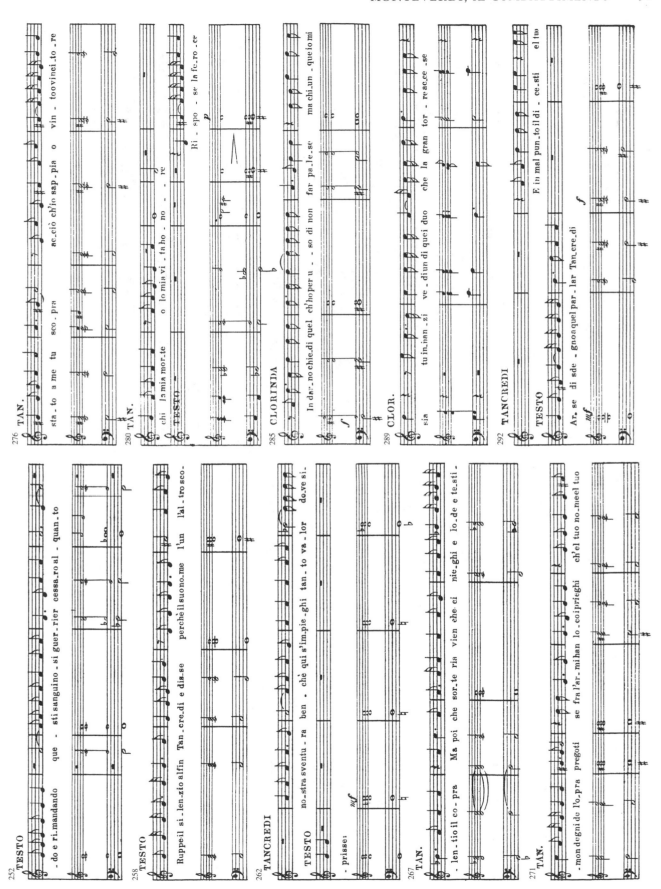

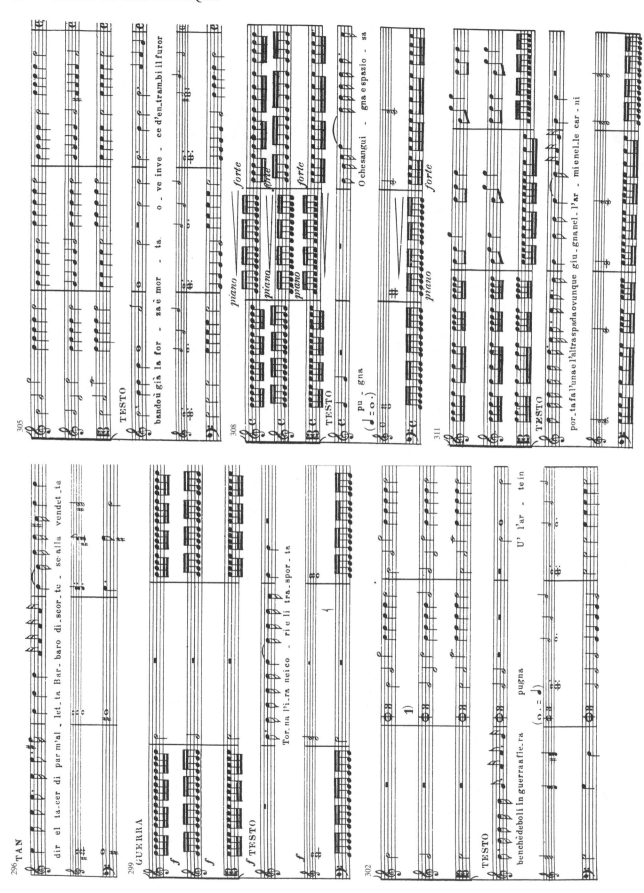

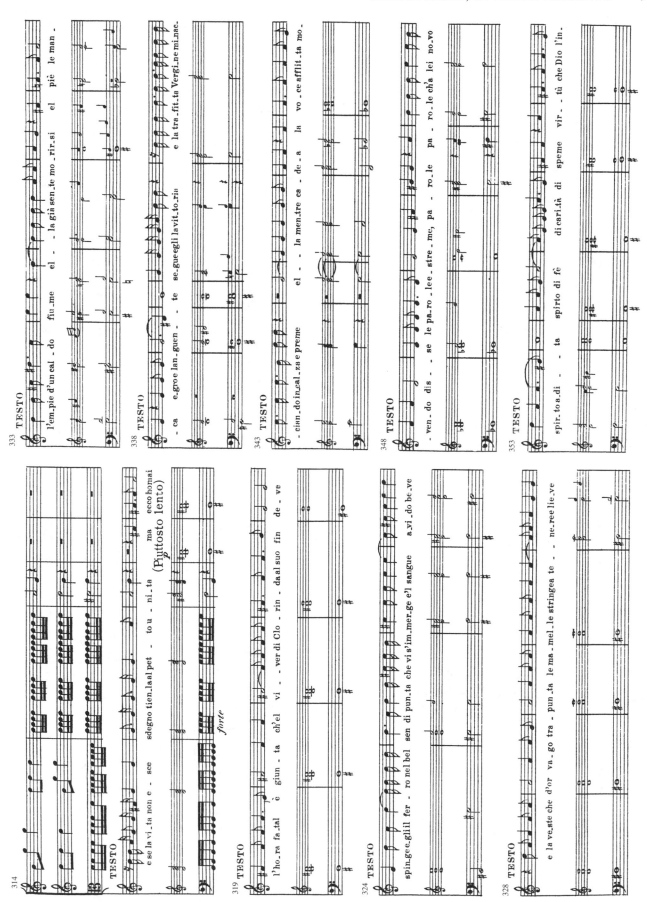

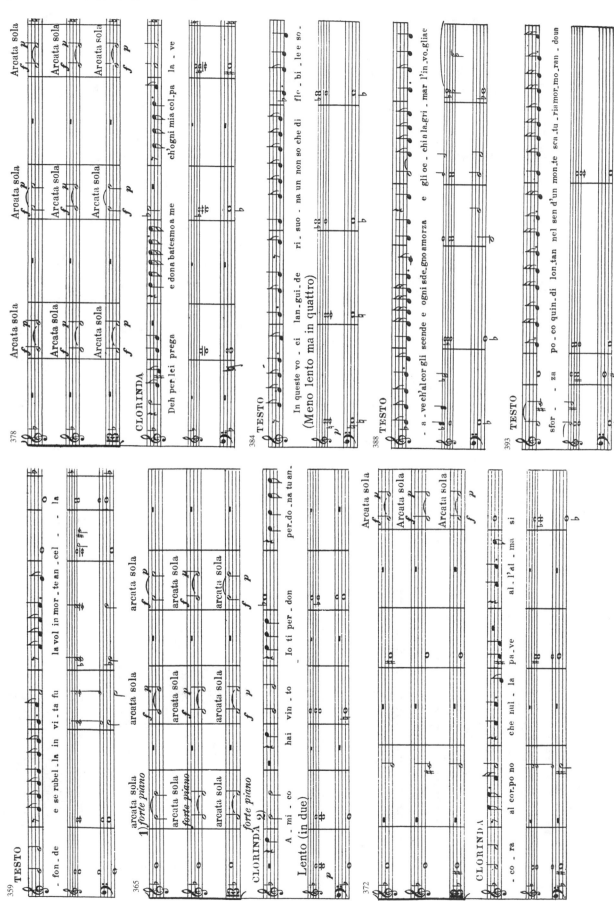

Il fine del Tancredi

# TEXT AND TRANSLATION

*1.*

Tancredi, che Clorinda un uomo stima,
Vol ne l'armi provarla al paragone.
Va girando colei l'alpestre cima
Ver altra porta ove d'entrar dispone.
Segue egli impetuoso onde assai prima
Che giunga in guisa avvien che d'armi suone,

Ch'ella si volge e grida: "O tu, che porte
Correndo sì?" Rispose: "E guerra e morte."

*2.*

"Guerra e mort'havrai," disse.
  "Io non rifiuto
Darlati se la cerchi," e fermo attende.

Nè vol Tancredi, ch'ebbe a piè veduto
Il suo nemico, usar cavallo, e scende;
E impugna l'uno e l'altro il ferro acuto
Ed aguzza l'orgoglio e l'ira accende.
E vansi incontro a passi tardi e lenti

Quai due tori gelosi e d'ira ardenti.

*{Sinfonia}*

*3.*

Notte, che nel profondo oscuro seno
Chiudesti e nell'oblio fatto sì grande,
Degno d'un chiaro sol, degno d'un pieno
Teatro opre sarian sì memorande,
Piacciati ch'indi il tragga e 'n bel sereno

Alle future età lo spieghi e mande
Viva la fama lor e tra lor gloria
Splenda del fosco tuo l'alta memoria.

---

Tancredi, thinking Clorinda to be a man,
Wishes to test her in combat.
She wanders about the rocky peak
Toward another gate that she may enter.
He follows her so impetuously that before
He reaches her his armor clatters,

So that she turns and cries: "You, what do you bring,
Running so?" He replies: "War and death!"

"War and death you will have," she says.
  "I do not refuse
To give it to you, if you seek it," and stopping, she waits.

Tancredi does not wish, seeing his enemy
On foot, to use his horse; he dismounts,
And each seizes his sharp sword,
Whetting his pride, his anger igniting.
And they advance upon one another with steps slow and heavy,

Like two bulls jeaous and with anger burning.

Night, you who within your deep dark breast
Conceal in oblivion a feat so great
—Worthy of clear daylight, of a full
Theater, would be events so memorable—
May it please you that I bring it forth and, in the open,

To future ages reveal and proclaim it.
Long live their fame and, in their glory,
Let shine the lofty memory of your darkness!

**4.**

Non schivar, non parar, non pur ritrarsi
Voglion costor nè qui destrezza ha parte.
Non danno i colpi hor finti hor pieni
    hor scarsi;
Toglie l'ombra e'l furor l'uso dell'arte.

Odi le spade orribilimente urtarsi
A mezzo il ferro e'l piè d'orma non parte.

Sempre il piè fermo e la man sempre
    in moto
Nè scende taglio in van nè punta a voto.

**5.**

L'onta irrita lo sdegno alla vendetta

E la vendetta poi l'onta rinnova,
Onde sempre al ferir, sempre alla fretta
Stimol novo s'aggiunge e piaga nova.
D'hor in hor più si mesce e più ristretta
Si fa la pugna e spada oprar non giova;
Dansi coi pomi e infelloniti e crudi,

Cozzan con gli elmi insieme e con gli
    scudi.

**6.**

Tre volte il cavalier la donna stringe
Con le robuste braccia ed altre tante,
Poi da quei nodi tenaci ella si scinge,
Nodi di fier nemico e non d'amante.

Tornano al ferro e l'un e l'altro il tinge
Di molto sangue, e stanco ed anelante
E questi e quegli alfin pur si ritira
E dopo lungo faticar respira.

---

They neither flinch, nor parry, nor retreat,
Nor does dexterity here play a role.
They do not give blows now feigned,
    now full, now weak;
The darkness and their rage prevent the use
of strategy.

Hear their swords clashing horribly
In the middle of the blades—and their feet
remain planted.

Their feet always firm, hands always in
    motion,
No stroke falls in vain, nor any swordpoint
astray.

Dishonor [when one is struck] spurs anger
to revenge,

And revenge then renews dishonor;
Thus constantly to wounding and to haste
New stimulation is added, and new wounds.
Closer and closer they mingle, and closer
Grows the fight, so that swords are useless;
They strike with their pommels, roughly
    and cruelly,

They butt each other with their helmets and
    shields.

Three times the knight squeezes the lady
With strong arms, and each time
From that tenacious embrace she frees herself
—The embrace of a fierce enemy, not a
    lover.

They return to the sword, and each stains it
With much blood; exhausted and breathless,
Each finally retreats
And after long struggles breathes.

7.

The one regards the other, the weight of his pale
Body resting on the pommel of his sword.
By now the rays of the last star are languishing

In the first dawn that has risen in the east.
Tancredi sees the greater quantity of blood
Shed by his enemy and that he himself is not so badly hurt;

In this he rejoices and is proud. Oh, our foolish

Mind, that praises every breath of fortune!

8.

Wretched man, in what do you rejoice? How sad

Will be your triumphs, how unhappy your boasting!

Your eyes will pay, if living you remain,
For each drop of that blood with a sea of tears.
Thus, waiting silently, these
Bloody warriors stopped for a while.
Breaking the silence, finally, Tancredi spoke,
So that each might discover the other's name:

9.

"It is indeed our misfortune to be employing here

Such valor, when silence covers it.
But since an adverse fate denies us
Praise and witnesses worthy of our deed,
I pray you—if in war there is a place for prayers

—To reveal to me your name and station,

So that I may know, whether in defeat or victory,

Whom my death or my life honors."

7.

L'un l'altro guarda e del suo corpo esangue
Sul pomo della spada appoggia il peso.
Già de l'ultima stella il raggio langue

Sul primo albor ch'è in oriente acceso.
Vede Tancredi in maggior copia il sangue
Del suo nemico e sè non tanto offeso.

Ne gode e insuperbisce. O nostra folle

Mente ch'ogni aura di fortuna estolle!

8.

Misero, di che godi? O quanti mesti

Fiano i trionfi ed infelice il vanto!

Gli occhi tuoi pagheran, s'in vita resti,
Di quel sangue ogni stilla un mar di pianto.
Così tacendo e rimandando questi
Sanguinosi guerrier cessaro alquanto.
Ruppe il silenzio alfin Tancredi e disse,
Perchè il suo nome l'un l'altro scoprisse:

9.

"Nostra sventura è ben che qui s'impieghi

Tanto valor dove silenzio il copra.
Ma poi che sorte ria vien che ci nieghi
E lode e testimon degni de l'opra,
Pregoti, se fra l'armi han loco i prieghi,

Che'l tuo nome e'l tuo stato a me tu scopra,

Acciò ch'io sappia, o vinto o vincitore,

Chi la mia morte o la mia vita honore."

10.

Rispose la feroce: "Indarno chiedi
Quel ch'ho per uso di non far palese,
Ma, chiunque io mi sia, tu innanzi vedi
Un di quei duo che la gran torre accese."

Arse di sdegno a quel parlar Tancredi
E "In mal punto il dicesti," [indi riprese,]

"E'l tuo dir e'l tacer di par m'alletta,

Barbaro discortese, alla vendetta."

11.

Torna l'ira nei cori e li trasporta

Benche deboli in guerra a fiera pugna

U'l'arte in bando, u'già la forza è morta,

Ove invece d'entrami il furor pugna!

Oh che sanguigna e spaziosa porta
Fa l'una e l'altra spada ovunque giugna
Nell'armi e nelle carni! e se la vita
Non esce, sdegno tienla al petto urita.

12.

Ma ecco homai l'hora fatal è giunta
Che'l viver di Clorinda al suo fin deve.

Spinge egli il ferro nel bel sen di punta

Che vi s'immerge e'l sangue avido beve,

E la veste che, d'or vago trapunta,

---

The fierce woman replied: "In vain you ask
That which I am not accustomed to reveal,
But, whoever I am, you see before you
One of the two who burned the great tower."[7]

Burning with rage at this speech, Tancredi
Replied: "It was poorly calculated to say that;

Both your speech and your silence equally invite me,

Ignoble barbarian, to vengeance."

Anger returns to their hearts and carries them,

Although weakened by war, to fierce combat,

Where art is abandoned and strength is already dead,

Where instead of these things, [only] rage fights.

Oh what a bloody and spacious gateway
Makes each sword wherever it reaches
Into armor or flesh! And if life
Does not depart, it is because anger holds it united to their breast.

But see, now the fatal hour has arrived
When the life of Clorinda to its end must come.

He thrusts the end of his sword into her beautiful breast,

So that it immerses itself and eagerly drinks the blood,

And the garment, with gold beautifully embroidered,

---

[7]Clorinda had been one of two Muslim warriors responsible for burning the siege tower that the Christians had been using in their attack on Jerusalem.

That clasps her tender, delicate breasts,
Fills with a hot stream. She already feels
Herself dying and her feet give out, weak
and collapsing.

13.

He follows up his victory, and the wounded
Maiden is menacingly pursued and pressed.
She, as she falls, her afflicted voice
Moving, speaks her final words,
Words spoken to her by a new spirit,
A spirit of faith, charity, and hope,
Virtues that God instills in her, for though
a rebel
In life was she, he wishes her in death his
servant.

14.

"Friend, you have won. I pardon you; pardon
Me as well—not my body, which fears
nothing—
But my soul. Pray for it, and give
Baptism to me, which all my sins washes."
In this dying voice there resounded
Something so mournful and soft
That it rose to his heart and all anger died,
And his eyes to tears were induced and
forced.

15.

Not far from there, in the hollow of the
mountain,
Gushed murmuring a little stream.
He ran to it and filled his helmet in the
spring,
And returned sadly to his great and pious
duty.
He felt his hand tremble as the face,
As yet unknown, was unmasked and
revealed.

Le mammelle stringea tenere e lieve,
L'empie d'un caldo fiume. Ella già sente
Morirsi e'l piè le manca egro e languente.

13.

Segue egli la vittoria, e la trafitta
Vergine minacciando incalza e preme.
Ella, mentre cadea, la voce afflitta
Movendo, disse le parole estreme,
Parole ch'a lei novo spirto ditta,
Spirto di fè, di carità, di speme,
Virtù che Dio l'infonde, e se rubella
In vita fu, la vol in morte ancella.

14.

"Amico, hai vinto. Io ti perdon, perdona
Tu ancora—al corpo no, che nulla pave—
All'alma sì. Deh per lei prega e dona
Battesmo a me, ch'ogni mia colpa lave."
In queste voci languide risuona
Un non so che di flebile e soave
Ch'al cor gli scende ed ogni sdegno
ammorza
E gli occhi a lagrimar l'invoglia e sforza.

15.

Poco quindi lontan, ne sen del monte,
Scaturia mormorando un picciol rio.
Egli v'accorse e l'elmo empiè nel fonte,
E tornò mesto al grande ufficio e pio.
Tremar sentì la man mentre la fronte
Non conosciuta ancor sciolse e scoprio.

La vide e la conobbe e restò senza

E voce e moto. Ahi vista! ahi conoscenza!

*16.*

Non morì già che sue virtuti accolse

Tutte in quel punto e in guardia al cor le mise;

E premendo il suo affanno a dar si volse

Vita con l'acqua a chi col ferro uccise.

Mentre egli il suon de' sacri detti sciolse,

Colei di gioia trasmutossi e rise,

E in atto di morir lieta e vivace

Dir parea: "S'apre il ciel, io vado in pace."

—Torquato Tasso (*Gerusalemme liberata*, Canto 12, stanzas 52–62 and 64–68)

He saw her and recognized her and was struck

Voiceless and motionless. What vision! What revelation!

He did not yet die, for gathering his strength

Together in one place, he set it to guard his heart,

And putting aside his anguish turned to give

Life with water to her whom with iron he had killed.

While he unfurled the sound of the sacred words,

She, with joy transformed, smiled,

And, at the moment of death, happy and full of life,

Seemed to say: "Heaven opens; I go in peace."

## EDITION

Our edition is, as in Selection 4, an earlier twentieth-century one. Although largely true to the original part books of Monteverdi's Eighth Book of Madrigals, the editor has added indications of dynamics and tempo as well as a realization of the figured bass. Monteverdi's original dynamics are spelled out in italics, as in measures 171–72, where the word *piano* is closely followed by *forte*.[8] Also original are a number of other indications given in regular type, translated below:

m. 18: *motto del cavallo* = "motion of the horse"
m. 73: *sinfonia* = "instrumental passage"
mm. 80 and 106: *passeggio* probably refers to what would later be called a ritornello
m. 174: *qui si lascia l'arco, e si strappano le corde con duoi ditti* = "here the bow is put down and the strings are pulled with two fingers" —that is, a strong pizzicato

---

[8]The editor's suggestion to play a crescendo here is surely a correct interpretation of Monteverdi's intention.

m. 183: *qui si ripiglia l'arco* = "here the bow is taken up again"

mm. 366ff.: *arcata sola* = "in one bow," that is, go from *forte* to *piano* in a single bow

m. 445 (strings): *queste ultima nota va in arcata morendo* = this last note is bowed [so as to] die away"

m. 445 (Clorinda): *lunga voce in piano* = long note, becoming soft

Omitted from this edition is another indication at measure 133: *principio della guerra* = "beginning of the battle."

The archaic triple-time signatures at measure 18 and elsewhere probably imply a specific tempo relationship with the preceding common-time sections. The editor suggests equating each half-measure of this triple time with a quarter note in the preceding section (see m. 38). But this and other editorial tempo equations in the score probably assume too slow a tempo for the common-time sections, whose beat might fall instead on the half note.

In measures 130–32 the tenor partbook contains an embellished version of the line given in our edition:

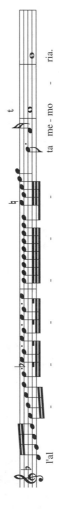

## PERFORMANCE ISSUES

Monteverdi's foreword specifies that the accompanying instruments were to be what we would call a string quartet—two violins, viola, and an instrument resembling the cello—plus a contrabass viola da gamba and harpsichord. Many aspects of violin construction and technique at this date differed from those of modern instruments but can be reconstructed from surviving instruments, pictures, and written accounts. By the same token, the nature of early-Baroque Italian harpsichords is fairly well understood, although the precise manner of realizing the figured bass is more difficult to ascertain. The editorial continuo realization in our edition was intended for the piano and omits the arpeggiation and other ornaments that a harpsichordist of Monteverdi's day would probably have employed.

Monteverdi directs that the playing reflect the changing emotional character of the text, implying changes of tempo and dynamics beyond those indicated in the score. Similarly, the narrator is enjoined to sing in a way that reflects the "emotions of the oration" and not to add any embellishments except in Stanza 3, the invocation of Night.

The composer's foreword also describes an early staged performance in which the two characters sang in costume as they acted out the scene; Tancredi even made his entrance on some sort of hobby horse (a *cavallo mariano*)! Presumably this stage machine, as well as the stage action, was stylized rather than realistic; Monteverdi's foreword suggests that the action was choreographed so that the actors moved and struck their blows in time with the music. Today this work is usually performed in concert, without staging, but one wonders how the musical effects might be enhanced by appropriate lighting, scenery, costume, and action.

## 8. Pier Francesco Cavalli (1602–1676), *Giasone* (opera: selections)

a. Act 1, scene 14 ("Dell'antro magico")

Medea.

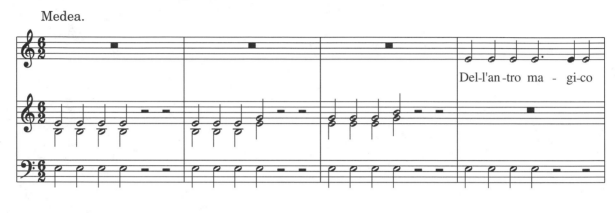

Del-l'an -tro ma - gi-co

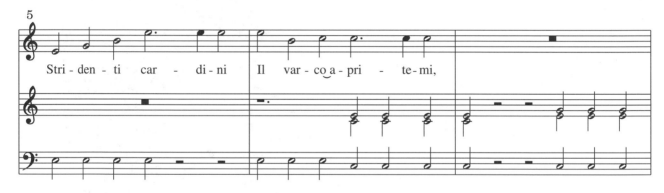

Stri - den - ti car - di - ni    Il var - co a - pri - te-mi,

E frà le te - ne-bre    Del ne-gro o-spi-ti-o Las - sa - te    mè.

Sù l'a - ra or-ri - bi - le

Del la - go sti - gi - o I fo - chi splen - di - no,

E sù ne man - di - no Fu - mi, che tur - bi - no La lu - ce al

sol.

Dal - l'ab - bru - cia - te gle - be Gran mo - nar - ca del - l'om - bre in - ten - to a - scol - ta - mi,

[6]

E se i dar - di d'A - mor già mai ti pun - se - ro, A - dem - pi ò Rè de' sot - te - ra - nei

6
#

31
po - po - li L'a-mo-ro-so de - sio, che'l cor mi sti - - mo - la,    E tut-to, tut-to A-
6                    [6]            7    #6

35
ver - no,        e tut-to, tut-to A-ver-no al-la bell' op - ra u - ni - sca -
                        #

39
si.            I mo-stri for-mi - da - bi-li,    Del bel vel-lo di

42
Fris - so, Sen-ti-nel-le fe-ro-ci in-fa-ti - ca - bi - li,    Per po-ten-za d'a-

44
bis - so Si ren-do-no a Gia - son    og - gi do - ma - bi - li.

47
Dall' ar - sa Di - te (Quan-te por-ta - te Ser-pi al-la fron-te) Fu-rie ve-
5#

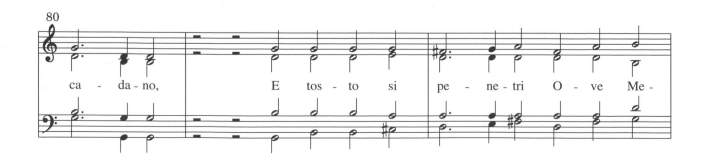

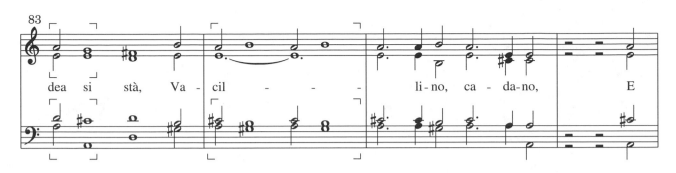

dea si stà, Va - cil - - - li - no, ca - da - no, E

tos - to si pe - ne - tri O - ve Me - dea si stà.

*Volano.*

Spirito

Del gran du - ce tar - ta - re - o Le tue pre - ci o Me - dea, Gl'ar - bi - tri

le - ga - no E i nu - mi in - fer - ni a cen - ni tuoi si pie - ga - no, Plu - to le tue

vo - ci u - dì. In que - sto cer - chio d'or Si ra - chiu - d'il va -

[4    #]

lor.    Che di Gia - son il    cor    Ar - me - rà    que - sto    dì.

Medea.

Si,  si,  si,  Vin-ce - rà  Il  mio re,  Si,  si,  si,  Vin-ce - rà,  vin - ce -

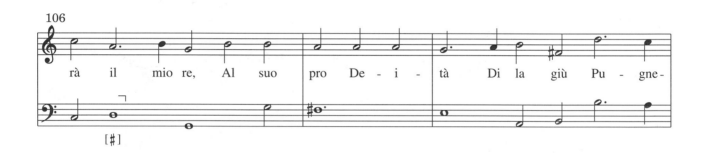

rà  il  mio re,  Al  suo  pro  De - i - tà  Di  la  giù  Pu - gne -

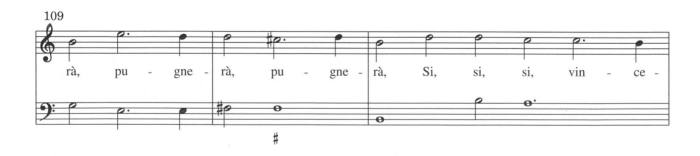

rà,    pu - gne - rà,    pu - gne - rà,    Si,  si,  si,  vin - ce -

rà,  vin - ce - rà,  si,  si,  si,  vin - ce - rà,  vin - ce - rà.

b.  Act 3, scene 21 ("Infelice ch'ascolto?")

Isifile.

In - fe-li - ce ch'a - scol - to? Non t'af-fa-nar Gia - so - ne, Che se la vi - ta

mi - a Fu (co-me ben in - te - si) Un' a - bor - to d'er - ro - ri, Che pro-du - ce il tuo

duo - lo, Ven-go a sa-cri-fi - car-la a tuoi fu - ro - ri; S'io pe - ri - vo tra

l'ac - que, U - na mor - te si bre - ve For-se non ap-pa-ga-va i tuoi ri-go - ri:

Ma, se vi - va son i - o, Ral - le - gra-ti, ral - le - gra-ti ò cru -

de - le, Già che po - trai con re-pli-ca-te. mor - ti Sfo-gar, sfo - gar nel fie-ro cor

## TEXT AND TRANSLATION

### Medea

Dell'antro magico,
Stridenti cardini,
Il varco apritemi,
E frà le tenebre
Del negro ospitio
Lassate me.
Su l'ara orribile
Del lago stigio
I fochi splendino,
E sù ne mandino
Fumi, che turbino
La luce al sol.
    Dall'abbruciate glebe,
Gran monarca dell'ombre intento
  ascoltami,
E se i dardi d'Amor già mai ti punsero,
Adempi, ò Rè de' sotterranei popoli,
L'amoroso desio che'l cor mi stimola,
E tutto Averno alla bell'opra uniscasi.
I mostri formidabili,
Del bel vello di Frisso
Sentinelle feroci infaticabili,
Per potenza d'abisso
Si rendono a Giasone oggi domabili.
Dall'arsa Dite
(Quante portate
Serpi alla fronte),
Furie, venite,
E di Pluto gl'imperi a me svelate.
Già percoto
Il suol col piè:
    Orridi
Demoni,
Spiriti
D'Erebo,
Volate a me.
    Così indarno vi chiamo?
Quai strepiti,
Quai sibili,
Non lascian penetrar nel cieco baratro
Le mie voci terribili?
    Dalla sabbia
Di Cocito
Tutta rabbia
Quà v'invito
Al mio soglio,
Quà, vi voglio;
A che si tarda più?

### Medea

Creaking hinges,
Open for me the door
Of the magical cave,
And in the darkness
Of the black shelter
Let me in.
Above the horrible altar
Of the Stygian lake[9]
The flames sparkle
And send up
Smoke that clouds
The light of the sun.
    From your singed rocks,
Great monarch of the shades, hear me
  carefully,
And if the arrows of Love ever wounded you,
Fulfill, king of the underworld peoples,
The amorous desire that urges my heart
And let all Avernus join in the fair work.
Formidable monsters,
Fierce, tireless sentinels
Of Phrixos's beautiful fleece,
By the power of the abyss
Let you be tamed today by Jason.
From burning Dis [Hades]
—How many serpents
You carry on your face!—
Furies, come,
And show me the domain of Pluto.
Already the earth
Shakes at my feet.
    Horrid
Demons,
Spirits
Of Erebus,
Fly to me!
    In vain do I call you?
What noises,
What hissing
Prevent my terrible words from
Penetrating the blind abyss?
    From the sands
Of Cocytus [another lake of the Underworld],
Enraged
I summon you
To my throne;
I demand you—
Why do you delay?

---

[9]In Classical mythology, the Styx was one of the rivers (here, a lake) of the underworld.

### Coro

Le mura si squarcino,
Le pietre si spezzino,
Le moli si franghino,
Vacillino, cadano
E tosto si penetri
Ove Medea si stà.
*Volano.*

### Spirito

Del gran duce tartareo
Le tue preci, o Medea,
Gl'arbitrii legano
Ei numi inferni ai cenni tuoi si piegano,
Pluto le tue voci udì.

In questo cerchio d'or
Si racchiude valor,
Che di Giasone il cor
Armerà questo dì.

### Medea

Si, si, si,
Vincerà
Il mio rè.
Al suo prò
Deità
Di la giù
Pugnerà.
Si, si, si,
Vincerà.

. . .

### Isifile

Infelice, che ascolto?
Non t'affannar, Giasone,
Che, se la vita mia
Fu (come ben intesi)
Un aborto d'errori
Che produce il tuo duolo,
Vengo a sacrificarla a'tuoi furori.
S'io perivo tra l'acque,
Una morte sì breve
Forse non appagava i tuoi rigori.
Ma, se viva son io,
Rallegrati, o crudele,
Già che potrai con replicate morti
Sfogar nel fiero cor l'empio desio.

Sì, sì, tiranno mio,
Ferisci a parte a parte
Queste membra aborrite,
Sbranami a poco a poco
Queste carni infelici,

### Chorus

Let the walls [of the city] be torn down,
Let the building stones be smashed,
Let the structures be broken.
Let them shake and fall
And soon be pierced
Where Medea wishes.
*They fly.*

### A spirit

The great leader of the underworld
Is bound, O Medea
By your will,
And the infernal spirits yield to your command.
Pluto has heard your voice.
*{Handing her a large magic ring}*
This golden ring
Possesses power
That today will arm
Jason's heart.

### Medea

Yes, yes, yes,
He will win,
My king.
For him
The god
Of below
Will fight.
Yes, yes, yes,
He will win.

. . .

### Hypsipyle

Unfortunate me, whom do I hear?
Do not worry, Jason,
For, if my life
Has been (as I well have understood)
A monstrosity of errors
Producing your grief,
I come to sacrifice it to your anger.
Had I perished in the water,
A death so quick
Might not have satisfied your harshness.
But, since I am alive,
Be glad, cruel one,
For you can, through repeated deaths,
Satisfy in your fierce heart your wicked
  desire.
Yes, yes, my tyrant,
Dismember into pieces
These hated limbs,
Tear, little by little,
This unfortunate flesh,

Anatomizza il seno,
Straziami a tuo piacere,
Martirizami i sensi,
E'l mio lento morire
Prolunghi a me'l tormento, a te'l gioire.
Ma se d'esser marito
L'adorate memorie alfin perdesti,
Fa ch'il nome di padre
Fra le tue crudeltadi intatto resti.
Non ti scordar, Giason, che padre sei,
E che son di te parte i parti miei.
Se legge di natura
Obliga agl'alimenti anco le fiere,
Fa che mano pietosa
Gli sominstri almen vitto mendico,
E non soffrir ch'i tuoi scettrati figli
Per la fame languenti
Spirin l'alme innocenti.
    Regina, Egeo, amici,
Supplicate per me questo crudele,
Ch nel ferir mi lasci
Queste mammelle da'suoi colpi intatte,
Acciò nutrisca almen i figli miei
Dal morto sen materno un freddo latte.
    Pregatelo pietosi
Che quegl'angeli infanti
Assistino ai martiri
Della madre tradita,
E ch'ad ogni ferita
Ch'imprimerà nel mio pudico petto
Bevino quelli il sangue mio stillante,
Acciò ch'ei, trapassando
Nelle lor pure vene, in lor s'incarni,
Ond'il lor seno in qualche parte sia
Tomba innocente, all'innocenza mia.
Addio terra, addio sole,
Addio regina amica, amici, addio;
Addio scettri, addio patria, addio mia
   prole.
    Scolta la madre vostra
Dal suo terrestre velo
Attenderà di rivedervi in cielo.
Venite, cari pegni,
Temp'è che vi consegni
All'adorato mostro,
Ch'è carnefice mio, e padre vostro.
    Figli, v'attendo e moro,
E te, Giason, benchè omicida, adoro.

—Giacinto Andrea Cicognini

Dissect my breast,
Destroy me to your pleasure,
Torment my senses,
And prolong my slow death
To my torment and your enjoyment.
But if you already have lost
The adored memory of being a husband,
Let the name of "father"
Remain untouched by your cruelties.
Do not forget, Jason, that you are a father,
And that your children are also mine.
If a law of nature
Makes even wild animals feed them,[10]
Let your pitying hand
Give them at least a beggar's diet
And let not your sceptered sons,
Weak from hunger,
Give up their innocent souls.
    Queen [Medea], [King] Aegeus, friends,
Plead for me with this cruel one
That in striking me he leave
My breasts untouched by his blows,
So that at least my sons may be nourished
By cold milk from a dead maternal breast.
    Beg of him pitiably
That these angelic children
Be present at the martyrdom
Of their betrayed mother,
And that with every wound
That strikes my chaste breast
They may drink my dripping blood,
Which, passing
Into their pure veins, will become theirs,
And their breasts will in some part be
An innocent tomb for my innocence.
Farewell, earth; farewell, sun;
Farewell, queen, my friend; friends, farewell;
Farewell, scepter; farewell, country; farewell,
  my children.
    Your mother, released
From her earthly form
Will look forward to seeing you in heaven.
Come, dear children,
It is time that I consign you
To the beloved monster
Who is my killer and your father.
    Children, I keep you and I die,
And you, Jason, though a murderer, I adore.

---

[10]This might refer to the Roman myth of Remus and Romulus, who as infants were nourished by a she-wolf.

## EDITION

Our edition reflects the surviving manuscript scores of the work. The barlines are placed irregularly, following a characteristic source (see below).

## PERFORMANCE ISSUES

Unlike the printed score of *Orfeo*, the manuscripts of *Giasone* provide few details of performance. Although the precise instrumentation must have varied, most performances were probably scored quite economically, using an ensemble similar to that of Monteverdi's *Combattimento*: a few bowed strings and a small continuo group. Good acting and stagecraft, rather than overblown orchestration, must have been important to the work's effect, alongside singing that employed a certain amount of rhythmic freedom and virtuoso embellishment but was above all always sensitive to Cavalli's musical rhetoric.

## SOURCE

The present edition has been newly prepared after consultation with the manuscript Venice, Biblioteca Nazionale Marciana, IV, 363 (9887).

# 9. Jean-Baptiste Lully (1632–1687), *Armide* (opera: selections)

a. Overture

**b.** Act 2, scene 5 (recitative "Enfin, il est en ma puissance" and air "Venez seconder mes désirs")

## TEXT AND TRANSLATION

**Armide,** *tenant un dard à la main*

Enfin il est en ma puissance,
Ce fatal ennemi, ce superbe vanqueur.
La charme du sommeil le livre à ma
    vengeance;
Je vais percer son invincible coeur.
Par lui, tous mes captifs sont sortis
    d'esclavage;
Qu'il éprouve toute ma rage.
*Armide va pour frapper Renaud et ne peut*
*exécuter le dessein qu'elle a de lui ôter*
*la vie.*
Quel trouble me saisit? qui me fait
    hésiter?
Qu'est-ce qu'en sa faveur la pitié me
    veut dire?
Frappons . . . Ciel! qui peut m'arrêter?

Achevons . . . je frémis! Vengeons-nous
  . . . je soupire!
. . .
Venez, secondez mes désirs,
Démons, transformez-vous en
    d'aimables zéphirs.
Je cède à ce vainqueur, la pitié me
    surmonte;
Cachez ma faiblesse et ma honte
Dans les plus reculés déserts;
Volez, conduisez-nous au bout de
    l'univers.

—Philippe Quinault

**Armide,** *holding a dart in her hand*

At last he is in my power,
This fatal enemy, this proud conqueror.
The charm of sleep surrenders him to my
    vengeance;
I shall pierce his invincible heart.
By him were all my captives freed from
    slavery;
Let him feel all my rage.
*Armide goes to strike Renaud but is unable to*
*execute her plan of depriving him of his life.*

What disturbance seizes me? what makes
    me hesitate?
What, in his [Renaud's] favor, can pity say
    to me?
[Let me] strike [Renaud] . . . Heavens! what
    could be stopping me?
Let us finish it . . . I tremble! Let us take
    revenge . . . I sigh!
. . .
Come, do as I wish,
Demons, transform yourselves into
    pleasant breezes.
I surrender to this conqueror, pity overcomes
    me;
Hide my weakness and my disgrace
In the most faraway deserts;
Fly, lead us to the ends of the world.

## EDITION

The overture is reproduced from a nineteenth-century edition which, in turn, closely reflects Lully's own published score. Although the C clefs used for the three inner parts will be unfamiliar to most readers, the editor has provided a literal transcription for keyboard, labeled "Kl.-Ausz."

    The recitative from Act 2, scene 5, immediately follows an orchestral introduction in dotted-overture style (not reproduced here). The latter portion of this recitative is omitted, as is the orchestra's version of the air, which immediately precedes the vocal version shown here.

## PERFORMANCE ISSUES

French Baroque instrumentation, rhythm, ornamentation, and other aspects of performance involve conventions developed, in part, under Lully's direction.[11]

---

[11]These are discussed at length in Chapter 5 of the text volume.

The editorial keyboard reduction in the score of the overture should not be confused with a figured bass realization. Indeed, in the absence of figures in the overture, it is not certain that the basso continuo part (*basse-continue*) here was originally meant to include a realization. On the other hand, the recitative and air for the soprano role of Armide were certainly meant to be accompanied by a realized continuo part, played by harpsichord (or perhaps lute), possibly with viola da gamba doubling the bass line.[12]

The changing time signatures of the recitative have strict proportional significance, a holdover from Renaissance notation. Most likely the quarter note remains constant through all changes of meter, except in measures written in cut time (or with the time signature "2"). There the beat shifts to the half note, which is equal in value to the quarter note of the surrounding measures.

## SOURCES

The chief source for our score is the first edition, *Armide, tragédie mise en musique par Monsieur de Lully. . . .* [13]The overture is reproduced from *Publikationen älterer praktischer und theoretischer Musikwerke*, vol. 14, ed. Robert Eitner (Leipzig: Breitkopf und Härtel, 1885).

---

[12]See the edition cited below for a realization of the figured bass.
[13]Paris: Ballard, 1686. This was compared with a reduced score published as the *seconde edition* (Paris: Ballard, 1713; facs., Beziers: Société de musicologie de Languedoc, [1980]).

**10.** Barbara Strozzi (1619–1677), *Ardo in tacito foco* (cantata or strophic aria)

## TEXT AND TRANSLATION

**Cuore che reprime alla lingua di manifestare il nome della sua cara**

**A heart that prevents the tongue from revealing the name of its beloved**

*Prima parte*

1  Ardo in tacito foco,
2  Neppure m'è concesso
3  Dal geloso cor mio
4  Far palese a me stesso
5  Il nome di colei ch'è 'l mio desio
6  Ma nel carcer del seno
7  Racchiuso tien l'ardore
8  Carcerier di se stesso, il proprio core,
9  E appena sia contento
10 Con aliti e sospiri
11 Far palese a la lingua i suoi martiri.

*Stanza 1*

I burn in silent fire,
For I am even prevented
By my own jealous heart
From revealing to myself
The name of her who is my desire.
But in the prison of my breast
My ardor holds bound
My own heart as its prisoner,
And it is barely content
Through breaths and sighs
To reveal to the tongue its suffering.

*Seconda parte*

12 Se pur, per mio ristoro,
13 Con tributi di pianto
14 Mostrar voglio con fede
15 A quella ch'amo tanto
16 Che son d'Amor le lagrime mercede,
17 Ecco'l cor, ch'esalando
18 Di più sospiri il vento
19 Assorbe il pianto e quel umor n'ha spento.
20 E con mio duol m'addita
21 Che gl'occhi lagrimanti
22 Sono muto le lingue ne gl'amanti.

*Stanza 2*

Even if, for my consolation,
Through payments in tears
I were to show, in truth,
To her whom I love so much,
That tears are the payment for [my] love,
Then, as the heart exhaled
Even more sighs, the wind would
Soak up the tears and the latter would be all spent.
And, to my grief, it shows
That weeping eyes
Are the silent tongues of lovers.

*Terza & ultima parte*

23 Qual sia l'aspro mio stato
24 Ridir nol ponno i venti,
25 Ne pur le selve o l'onde
26 Udiro i miei lamenti,
27 Ma solo il duol entro al mio cor s'asconde.
28 E quale in chiuso specco
29 Disfassi pietra al foco
30 Tal'io m'incenerisco a poco a poco,
31 E s'ad'altri la lingua
32 È scorta alla lor sorte
33 A me la lingua è sol cagion di morte.

*Stanza 3*

How bitter my state is
Cannot be recounted by the winds,
Nor have the woods or the waves
Heard my complaints;
Only sadness hides itself within my heart.

And as beneath a concave mirror
A stone melts in the fire,
So am I reduced to ashes, little by little,
And if for others the tongue
Guides them to their fortune,
To me the tongue is only the cause of death.

—Giovanni Francesco Loredano (?)

## EDITION

Our score is based on the original edition. The rhythmic notation has been modernized: barlines have been regularized and note values in the triple-time sections are half those of the original. Half-brackets in the triple-time sections indicate so-called colored notation in the original, used to mark short-long rhythms (as in m. 35) and hemiolas (mm. 54–55).

The text underlay of the edition reproduced here is faulty in measures 40–43, where the first syllable of *proprio* should fall on b♭′ in measure 40 and continue as a melisma through the f′ in measures 42–43. In measure 113 the first syllable of *amante* should be elided to the preceding word, *negli*, and sung with the second syllable of the latter. In measures 132–33 the indicated elision between *onde* and *udiro* is incorrect; instead, the second syllable of *udiro* should fall on the downbeat of measure 133 and its last syllable should elide with the next word, *i* (and similarly in m. 146).

A few small rhythmic errors also require correction. In measures 47 and 48 the first syllable of *sospiri*, shown here as an eighth note, should actually be a sixteenth note preceded by a sixteenth rest—an expressive bit of word painting on the word "sighs." A sixteenth rest is also missing on the fourth beat of measure 81, which should have the same rhythm as the second beat of the following measure.

In addition, many slurs have been omitted, especially on the chromatic line in measures 67–69 and on many two-note figures spanning a half step, as in measures 29–30, where the slur on the syllable "-o" marked an ornamental figure known as *anticipazione della syllaba*. In the original, these two-note slurs appear to be signals to the singer for particularly expressive performance (perhaps using an intense vibrato or tremolo on the first note).

## PERFORMANCE ISSUES

The vocal part is presumably to be performed with considerable dynamic contrast and freedom of tempo and rhythm, reflecting the words. The triple-time sections should probably flow relatively smoothly; the tempo marks *adagio* and *presto* probably signify relatively small differences in speed, far less than the words suggest today (despite the notation in large note values, even in the *adagio* sections the $\frac{6}{2}$ measures should probably be "in two," the beat falling on the dotted whole note).

Strozzi provides virtually no clues to the realization of the continuo part (there are only a few figures, as in m. 31). Whether played on a form of lute or harpsichord, it should surely be simple, never distracting attention from the voice.

## SOURCES AND ACKNOWLEDGMENTS

The score given here is based on Strozzi's *Cantate ariete à una, due, e tre voci*, op. 3 (Venice, 1654) and is reproduced with kind permission of A-R Editions.[14]

---

[14]For a facsimile of the original edition, see the bibliography in the text volume.

## 11. Alessandro Scarlatti (1660–1725), *Correa nel seno amato* (cantata: selections)

a. Aria "Fresche brine"

*Second time: end here, then repeat measures 1–20.

*Dal Segno*

b.  Aria "Onde belle"

mor - mo - ri - o,    mor - mo - ri - o,    deh    pian - ge -

- - te    al    pian - to

mi - - o,    deh    pian - ge -

-  -  - te          al    pian  -  -

6    6        6      #6
              4

-  -  -  - to    mi  -  -

♮        ♭7              #        ♭5        4    3

-  -  o.

♭6  5  6  4  3  ♮      ♭          ♭                    #    4 3

## TEXT AND TRANSLATION

| | | |
|---|---|---|
| 1 | Fresche brine che pietose | Fresh frost so merciful, |
| 2 | Ravvivate queste rose | Revive these roses |
| 3 | E baciate il lembo ai fior, | And kiss the tips of the flowers. |
| 4 | Deh, cadete e pallidette, | Ah, fallen and pale, |
| 5 | Trasformate in lagrimette, | Transformed into little tears |
| 6 | Sol piangete al mio dolor. | You weep alone at my sorrow. |

. . .                                                  . . .

| | | |
|---|---|---|
| 1 | Onde belle, che pietose | Waves, lovely and merciful, |
| 2 | Questi prati rinfrescate, | Who refresh these meadows, |
| 3 | Ascoltate, e dolorose, | Listen [to me], and, saddened, |
| 4 | Con lugubre mormorio, | With lugubrious murmurings, |
| 5 | Deh, piangete al pianto mio. | Ah, weep with my weeping. |

## PERFORMANCE ISSUES

The manuscript scores preserving Scarlatti's cantatas leave open the questions of what type of voice—female or male castrato—sang them and whether the violin parts were played by soloists or multiple players. The instrumentation of the continuo part is likewise left open, although by this date both harpsichord and cello are likely to have participated (Scarlatti was himself a keyboard player, and two other movements of this cantata are exceptional in including short passages in which the right-hand part is written out for the harpsichordist). No doubt the singer was expected to add a certain amount of improvised ornamentation, but the elaborate decoration of da capo arias that would become standard practice in the eighteenth century was probably not yet a regular feature and would seem inappropriate to the relatively simple style of "Fresche brine."

## SOURCE

The cantata is preserved in several eighteenth-century manuscripts. For a realization of the continuo part, see the modern edition of the complete work.[15]

---

[15]Alessandro Scarlatti, *Correa nel seno amato*, ed. Otto Drechsler (Kassel: Bärenreiter, 1974).

**12.** Henry Purcell (1659–95), *From Rosy Bowers*
(song or cantata)

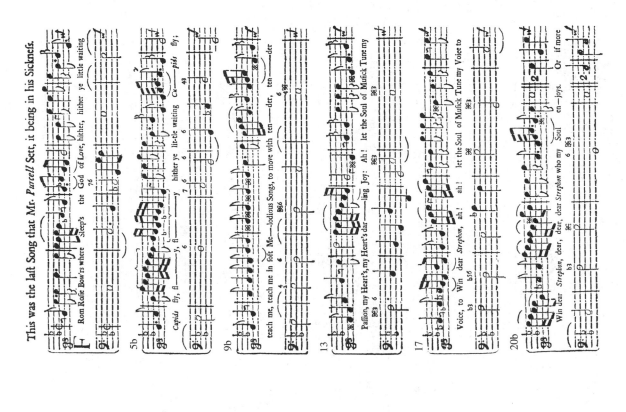

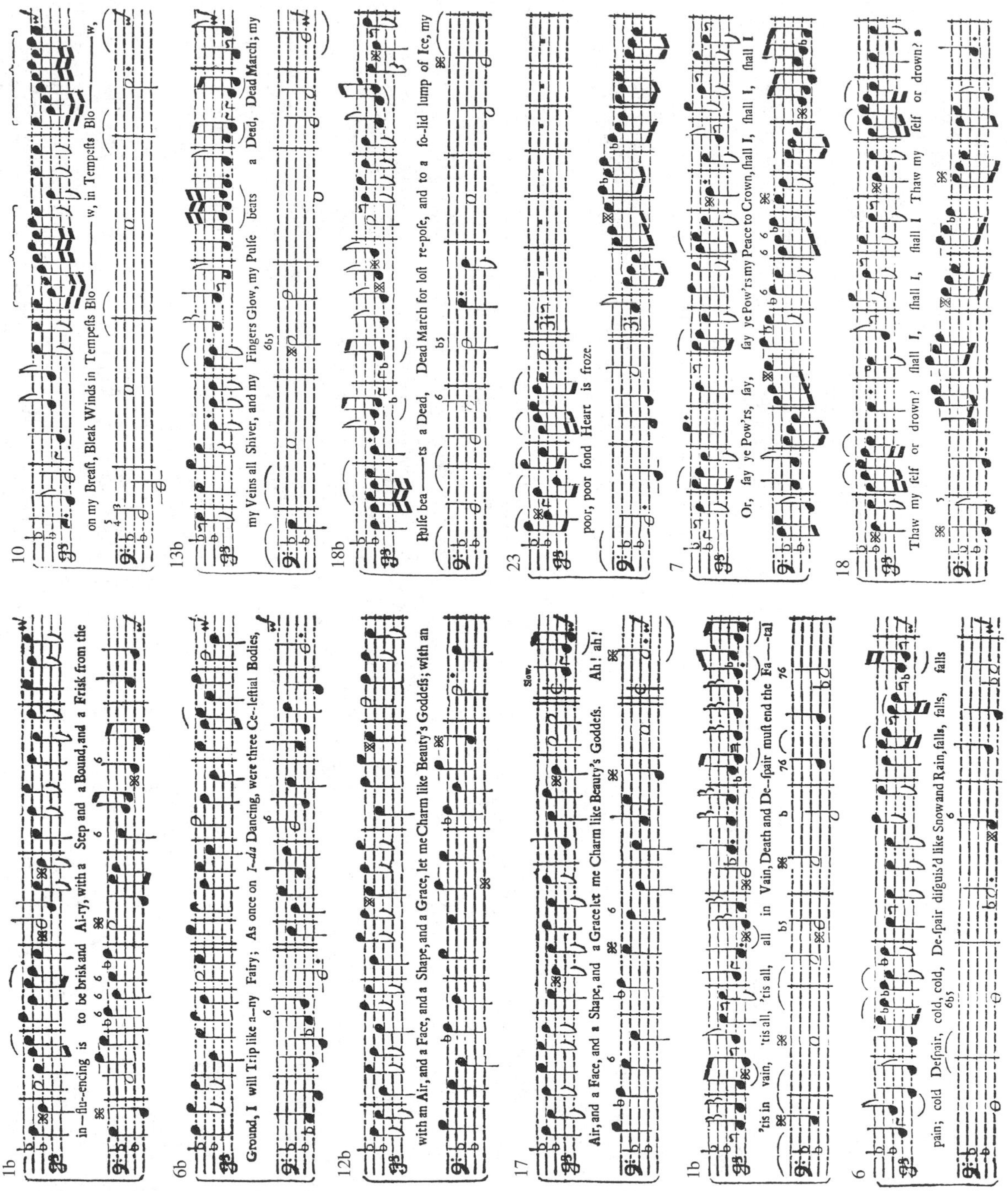
in-flu-encing is to be brisk and Ai-ry, with a Step and a Bound, and a Frisk from the
Ground, I will Trip like a-ny Fairy; As once on I-da Dancing, were three Ce-lestial Bodies,
with an Air, and a Face, and a Shape, and a Grace, let me Charm like Beauty's Goddess; with an
Slow.
Air, and a Face, and a Shape, and a Grace let me Charm like Beauty's Goddess. Ah! ah!
'tis in vain, 'tis all, 'tis all, all in Vain, Death and De-spair must end the Fa-tal
pain; cold Despair, cold, cold, De-spair disguis'd like Snow and Rain, falls, falls, falls, falls
on my Breast, Bleak Winds in Tempests Blo—w, in Tempests Blo—w,
my Veins all Shiver, and my Fingers Glow, my Pulse beats a Dead, Dead March; my
Pulse bea—ts a Dead, Dead March for lost re-pose, and to a so-lid lump of Ice, my
poor, poor fond Heart is froze.
Or, say ye Pow'rs, say, say ye Pow'rs my Peace to Crown, shall I, shall I, shall I
Thaw my self or drown? shall I, shall I, shall I Thaw my self or drown?

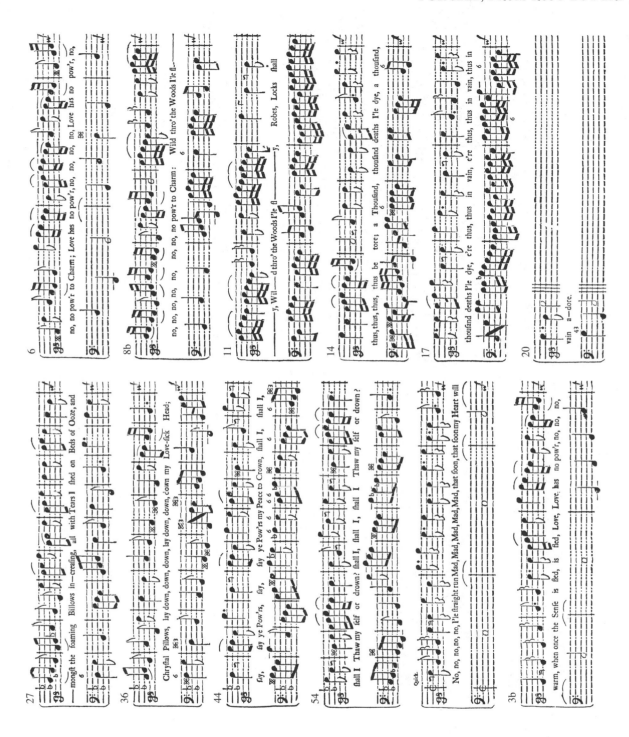

# TEXT

*{I. Recitative}*

1 From rosy bowers where sleeps the god of love,
2 Hither, ye little waiting Cupids, fly;
3 Teach me in soft melodious songs to move
4 With tender passion my heart's darling joy:
5 Ah! let the soul of music tune my voice,
6 To win dear Strephon,* who my soul enjoys.          *Don Quixote

*{II. Air}*

1 Or if more influencing
2 Is to be brisk and airy,
3 With a step and a bound
4 And a frisk* from the ground                        *a playful leap (?)
5 I will trip* like any fairy;                         *dance lightly
6 As once on Ida* dancing                             *mountain near ancient Troy
7 Were three celestial bodies,*                       *the Graces, minor female deities
8 With an air, and a face,
9 And a shape, and a grace,
10 Let me charm like beauty's goddess.*               *Venus

*{III. Recitative}*

1 Ah! 'tis in vain, 'tis all, 'tis all in vain,
2 Death and despair must end the fatal pain;
3 Cold despair, disguis'd like snow and rain,
4 Falls on my breast; bleak winds in tempests blow,
5 My veins all shiver, and my fingers glow;
6 My pulse beats a dead march* for lost repose,      *funeral march
7 And to a solid lump of ice my poor fond heart is
  froze.

*{IV. Air}*

1 Or say, ye powers, my peace to crown,
2 Shall I thaw myself or drown?
3   Amongst the foaming billows,
4   Increasing all with tears I shed,
5   On beds of ooze, and crystal pillows,
6   Lay down, lay down my lovesick head.

{*V. Recitative*}

1 No, no, I'll straight run mad,
2 That soon my heart will warm;
3 When once the sense is fled,
4 Love has no power to charm.
5    Wild through the woods I'll fly;
6    Robes, locks shall thus be tore.
7    A thousand deaths I'll die
8    Ere* thus in vain adore.    *before

—Thomas D'Urfey

## EDITION

Our edition is a facsimile from an early printed collection of Purcell's songs in which it bears the heading "The last song the author set, it being in his sickness." This claim that Purcell wrote the music while suffering from his final illness has not been confirmed.

The notation is essentially that used today except for a few readily understood differences. For example, the clefs at the opening have a slightly different appearance from their modern counterparts, but they are the treble G clef and bass F clef of today. The little squiggle at the end of each line is a *custos* that points to the next pitch at the beginning of the following line or page. There are also some differences in the use of accidentals. Some flats are placed under, rather than in front of, the notes to which they apply (as in m. 6). What we would call the sharp sign is used to indicate B natural (as in m. 11).

The time signature "2" used for the second section ("Or if more influencing") probably stands for a quick form of duple time (modern $\frac{2}{2}$). In the fourth section, the time signature "3 1" is equivalent to modern $\frac{3}{8}$; it too probably implies a relatively quick tempo.[16]

At measure 4 of the third section, another early printed source gives an alternate version, accentuating the word *death* through the unusual upward leap of a diminished octave:

---

[16]For an edition in modern notation, see *The Works of Henry Purcell*, vol. 16, *Dramatic Music: Part 1*, ed. by the Purcell Society (London: Novello, 1906), 181–93.

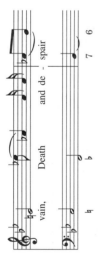

## PERFORMANCE ISSUES

This composition was written as a musical scene for a larger theatrical work, Part 3 of an English adaptation of Cervantes's *Don Quixote*. But its publication as a self-contained "song" within a few years of Purcell's death shows that, like most of Purcell's stage music, it was also performed on its own, often no doubt by amateurs in domestic settings. The two parts are unlabeled, but the upper is certainly for a female soprano, the lower a continuo part that would often have been realized by harpsichord with an optional viola da gamba or cello doubling the bass line.[17]

Only the third and the fifth sections bear tempo marks—in English, suggesting that Purcell's readers were as yet unfamiliar with what are now commonly understood Italian tempo words. Some of the original "time signatures" have implications for tempo as well. There is a single ornament sign, in measure 8 of the opening section (probably a trill), but performers would have added numerous ornaments elsewhere, particularly at cadences.

The double bar in the middle of the second section is probably an indication that at least the first half of this section is to be repeated.

## SOURCES

Our facsimile is from *Orpheus Britannicus* (The British Orpheus; London, 1698; 2nd. ed., 1721).[18] The alternate version reproduced above is from *New Songs in the Third Part of the Comical History of Don Quixote Written by Mr. Durfey* (London, 1696).[19]

---

[17] For a realization of the continuo part, see the modern edition mentioned in the previous note.

[18] For the complete two-volume work, see the facsimiles published by Broude (New York, 1965) and Gregg Press (Ridgewood, N.J., 1965).

[19] Facsimile in *Don Quixote: The Music in the Three Plays of Thomas Durfey*, ed. Curtis Price, Music for London Entertainment 1660–1800, ser. A, vol. 2 (Turnbridge Wells: Richard MacNutt, 1984), 14–15.

# 13. Giovanni Gabrieli (ca. 1553/6–1612), *In ecclesiis*
## (*concertato motet*)

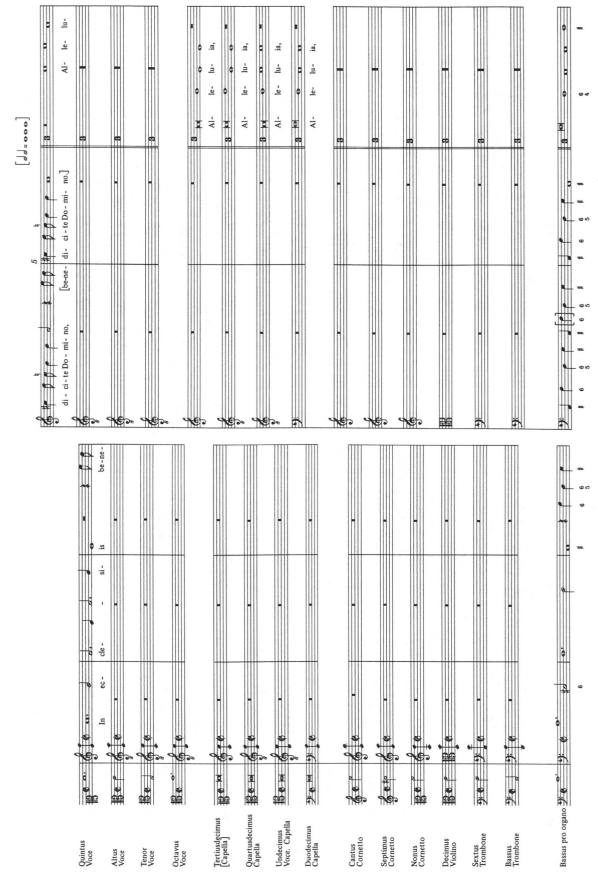

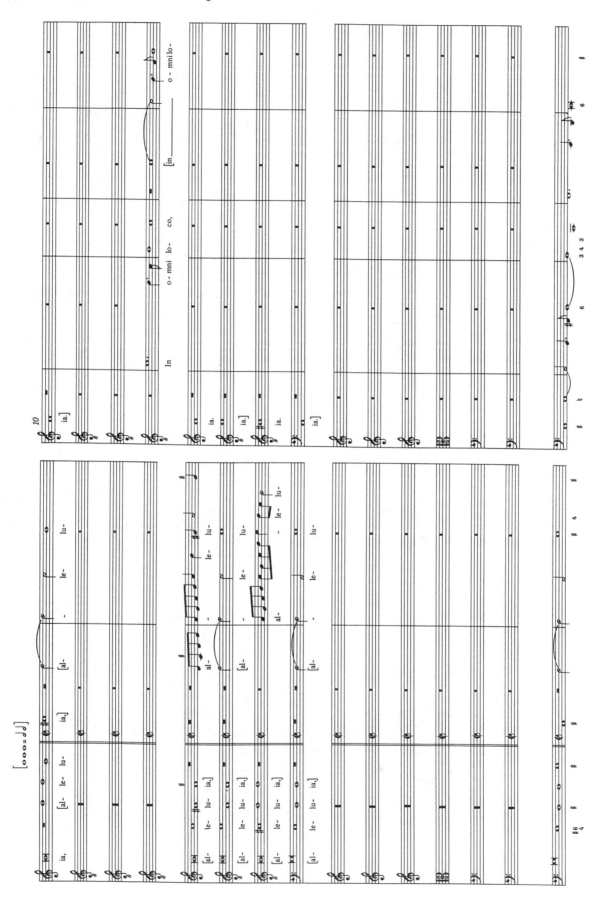

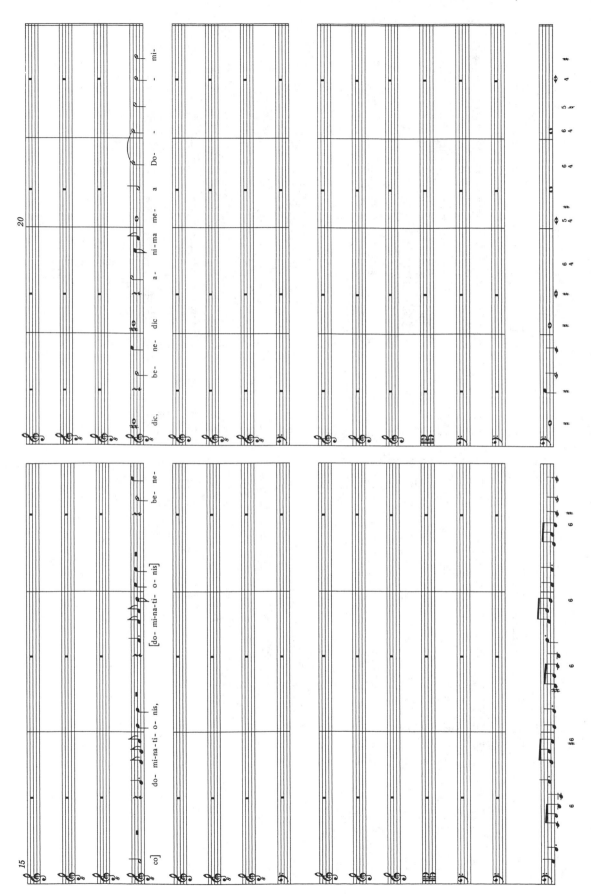

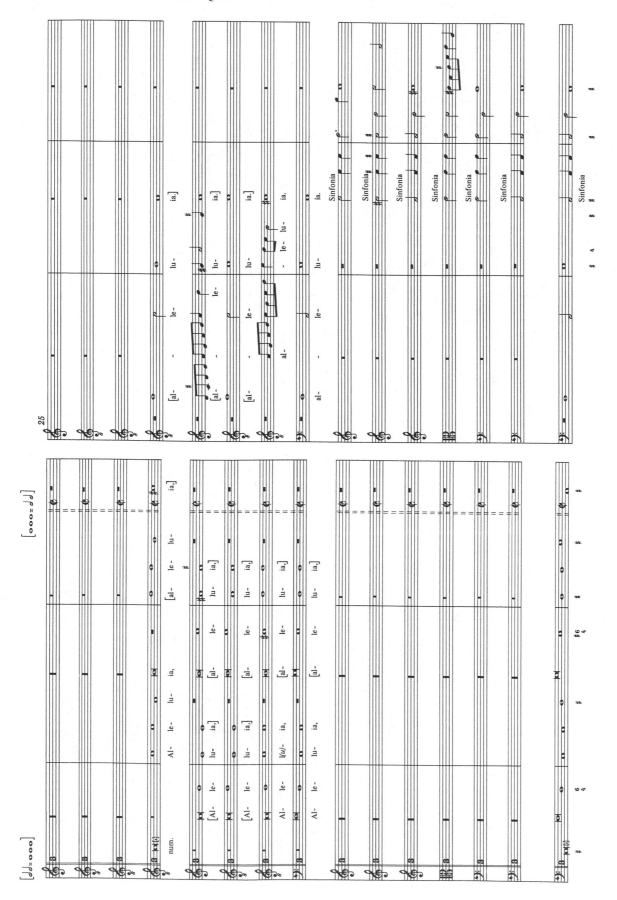

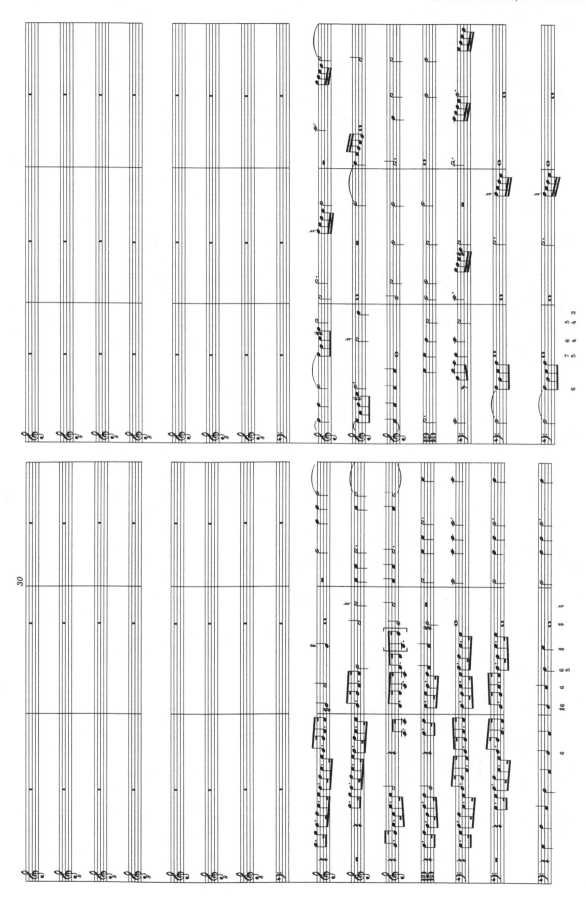

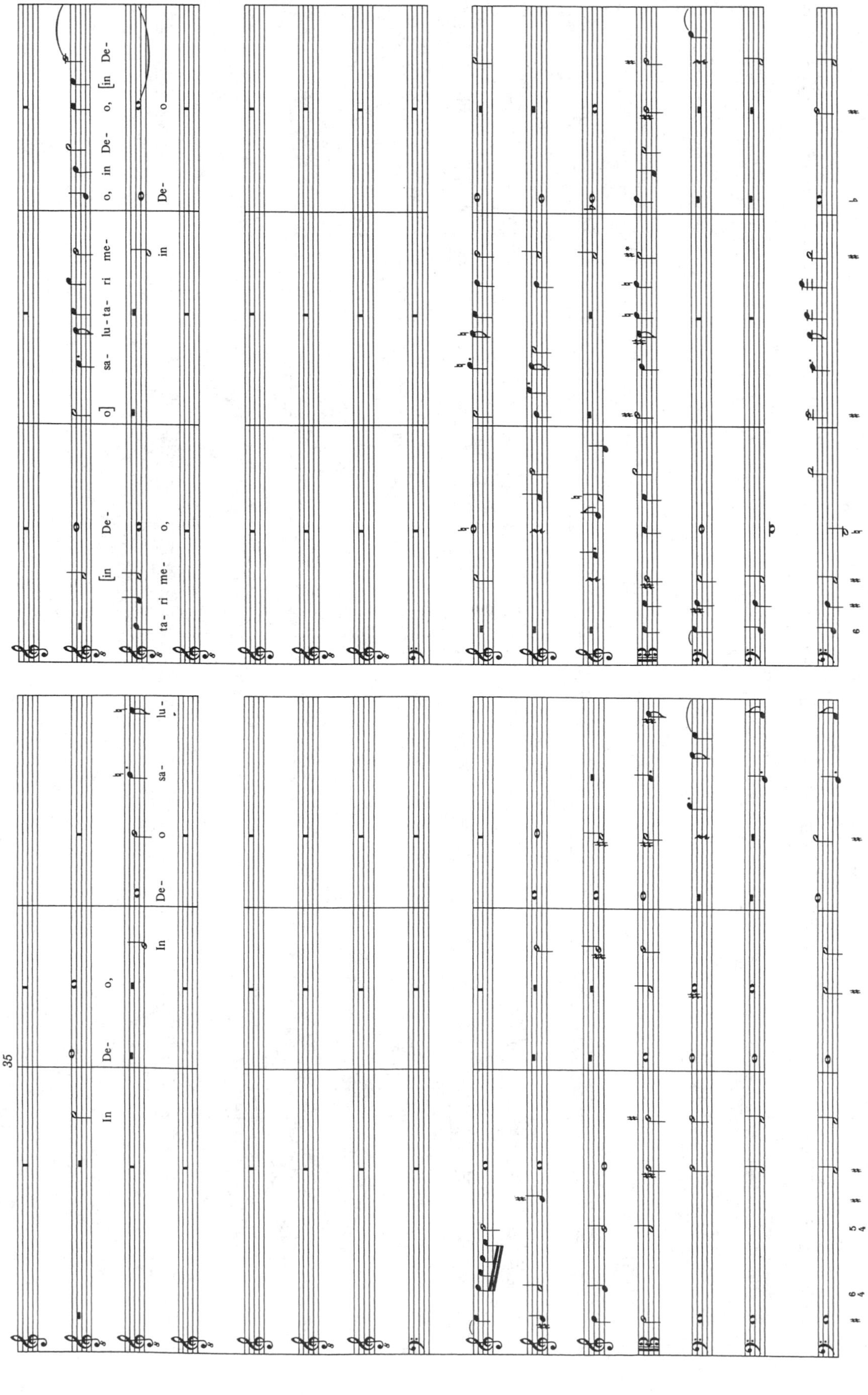
35
In De- o,
In De- o sa- lu-
[in De- o] sa- lu-ta- ri me- o, in De- o, [in De-
ta- ri me- o, In De- o

40
- o]
sa- lu-ta-ri me- o, [sa- lu-ta- - ri me-
sa- lu-ta-ri me- o et
45
o] et glo- ri- a, glo- ri-a me- a. De-
glo- ri- a, et glo- - ri- a me- a.

De- us au - xi- li-um me- - um et spes
us au - xi - li-um me- - - um
50
me- a in De - o est, [in De - o est,] et spes
et spes me- a in De - o est, [in De - o est,]

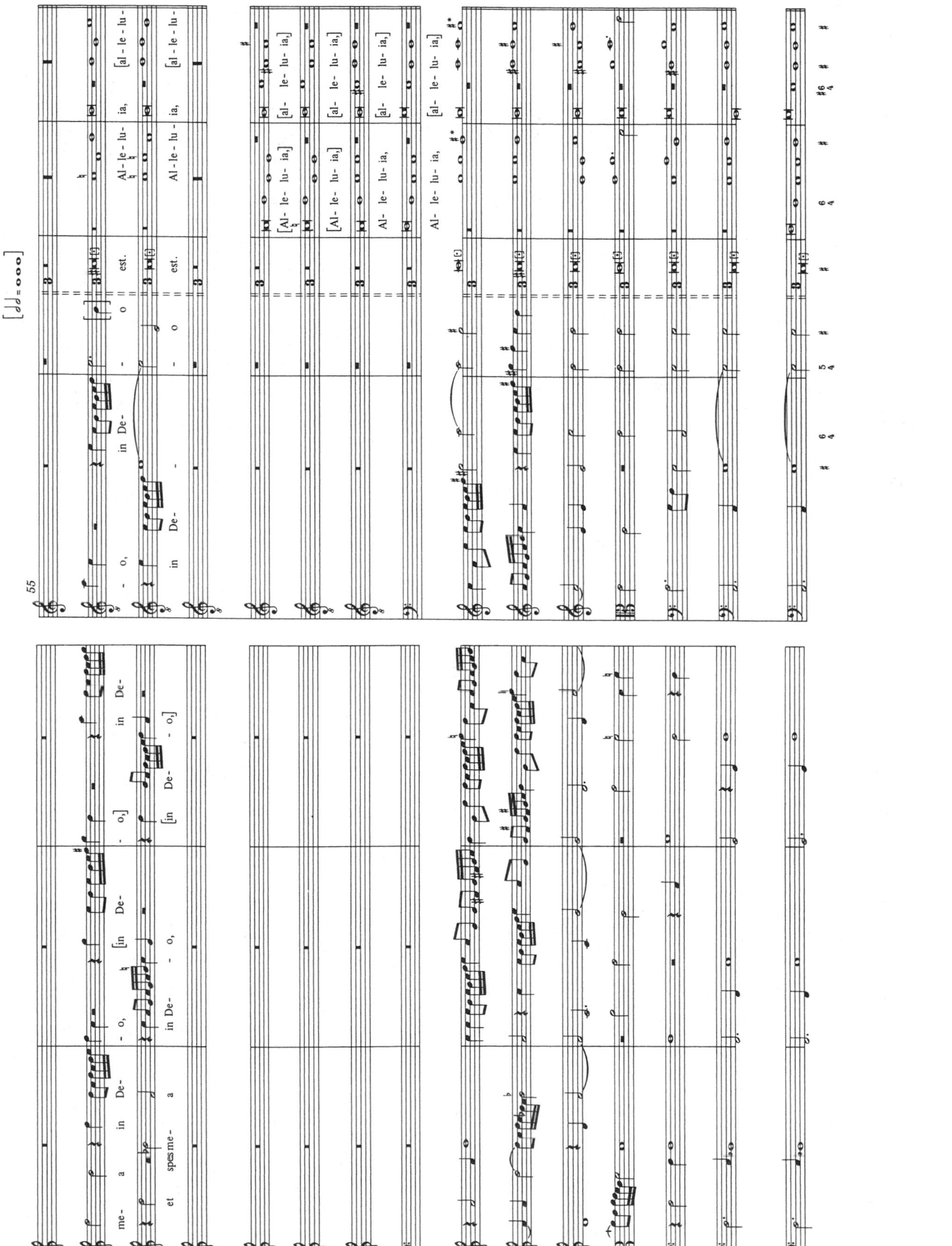
me- a in De- - o, [in De- - o,] in De-
et spes me- a in De- - o, [in De- - o,]
55
- o, in De- - o est. Al - le - lu - ia, [al - le - lu -
in De- - o est. Al - le - lu - ia, [al - le - lu -
[Al- le- lu- ia,] [al- le- lu- ia,]
[Al- le- lu- ia,] [al- le- lu- ia,]
Al- le- lu- ia, [al- le- lu- ia,]
Al- le- lu- ia, [al- le- lu- ia,]

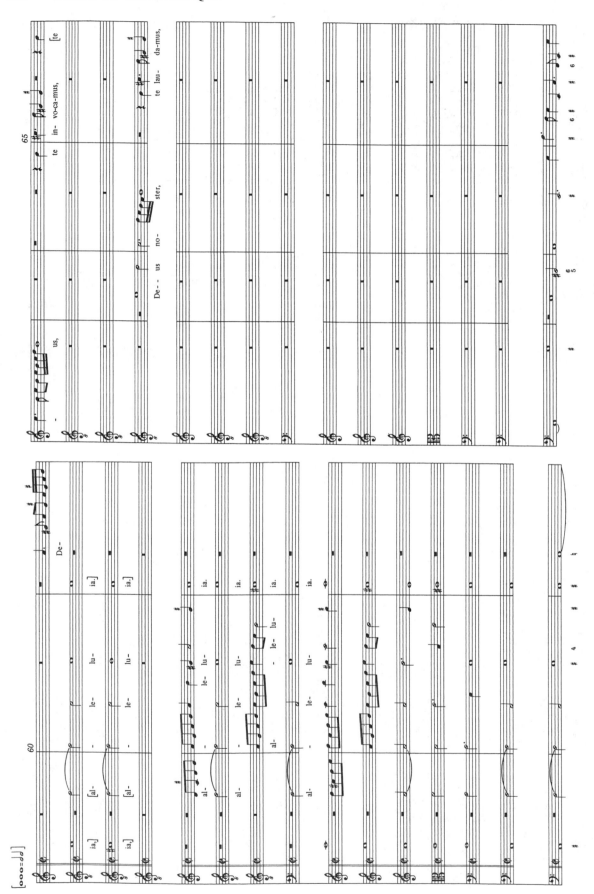

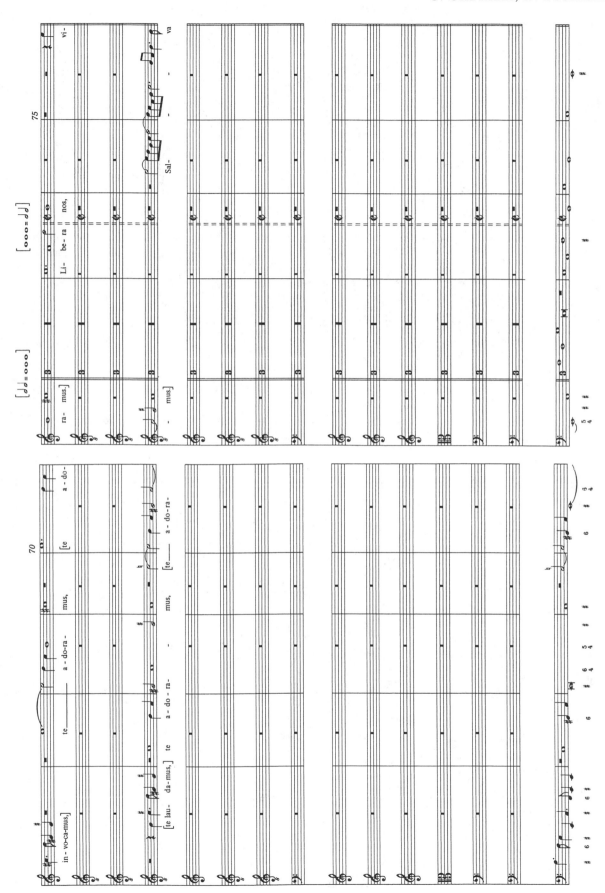

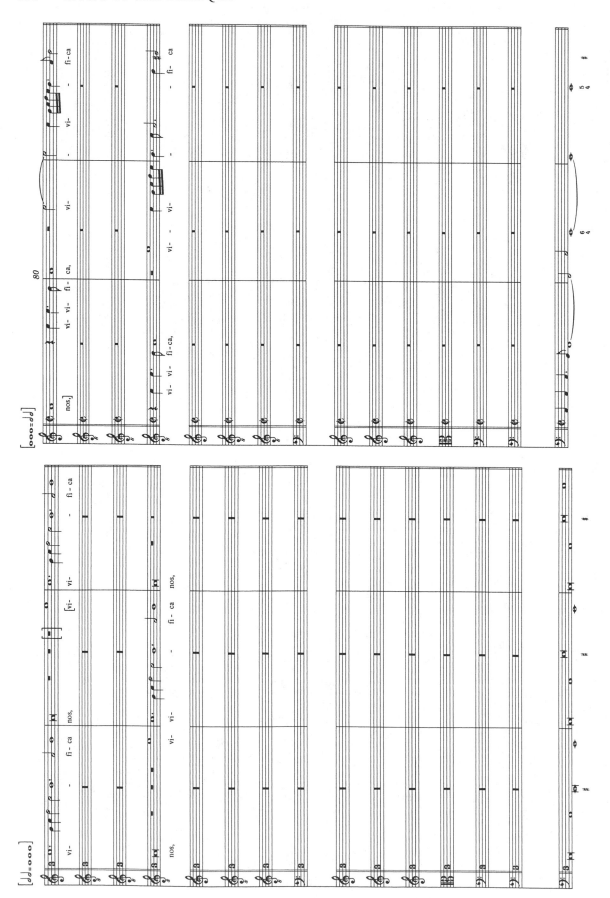

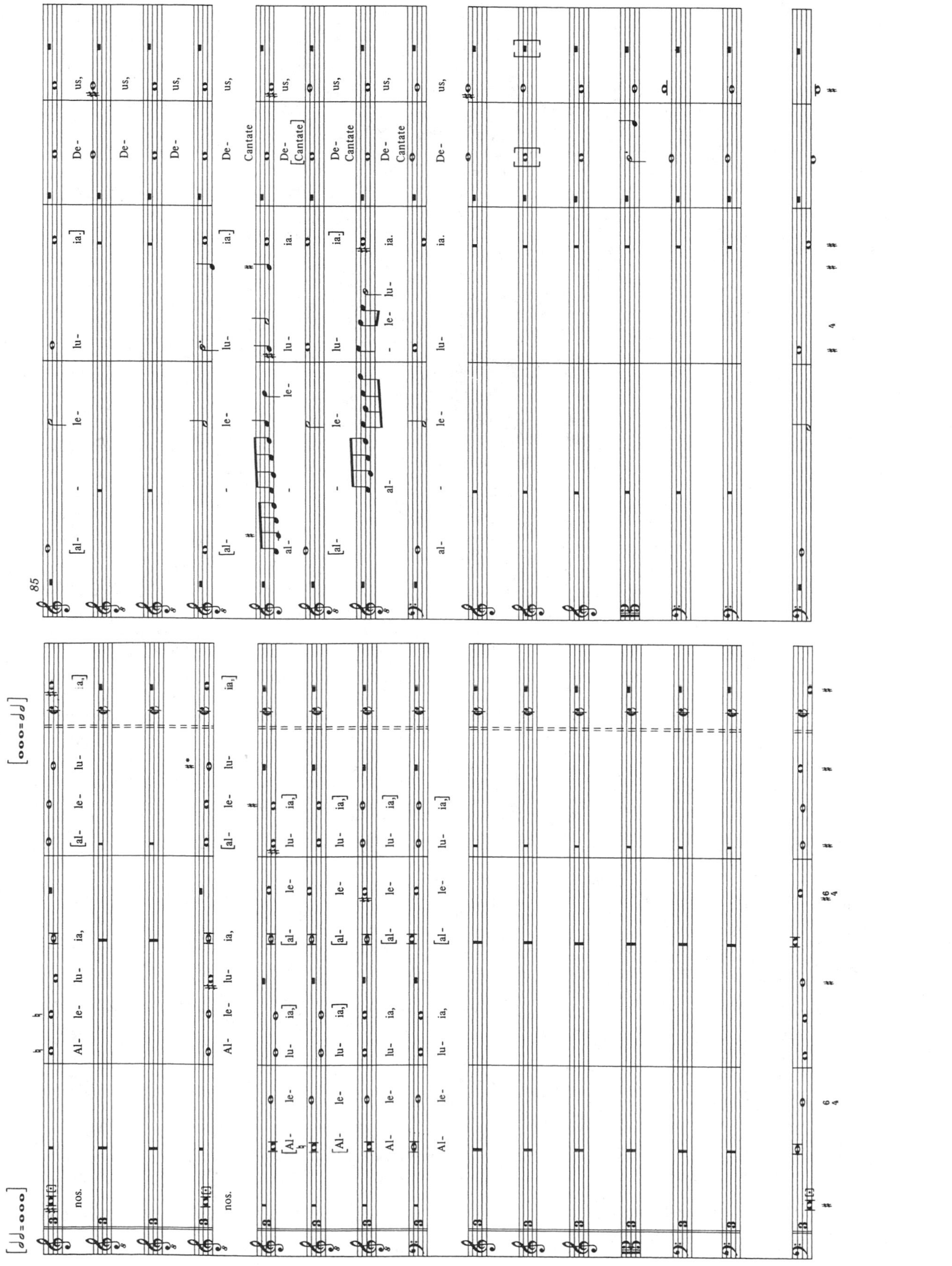
[♩♩=ooo]
[ooo=♩♩]
nos. Al- le- lu- ia, [al- le- lu- ia.]
nos. Al- le- lu- ia, [al- le- lu- ia.]
[Al- le- lu- ia,] [al- le- lu- ia,]
[Al- le- lu- ia,] [al- le- lu- ia,]
Al- le- lu- ia, [al- le- lu- ia,]
Al- le- lu- ia, [al- le- lu- ia,]
85
[al- - le- lu- ia.] De- us,
[al- - le- lu- ia.] De- us,
De- us,
De- us,
al- - le- lu- ia. Cantate
De- us,
[al- - le- lu- ia.] [Cantate] De- us,
al- - le- lu- ia. Cantate De- us,
al- - le- lu- ia. De- us,
6 4
♯6 4
♯ 4

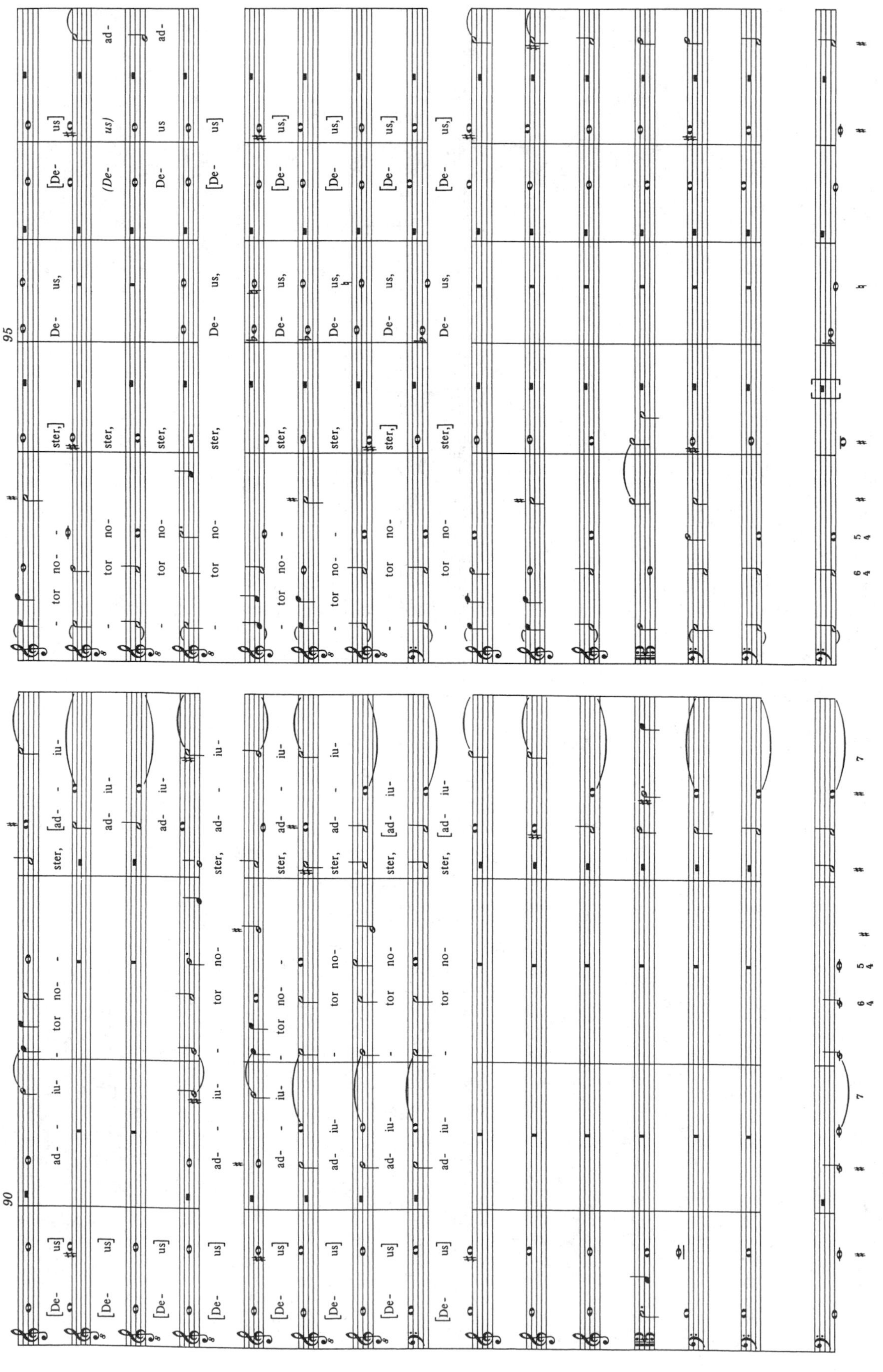
90
95
[De- us] ad- - iu- - tor no- - ster, [ad- - iu-
- tor no- - ster,] De- us, [De- us] ad-
[De- us] ad- iu- tor no- ster, ad- iu-
- tor no- ster, De- us, [De- us,]

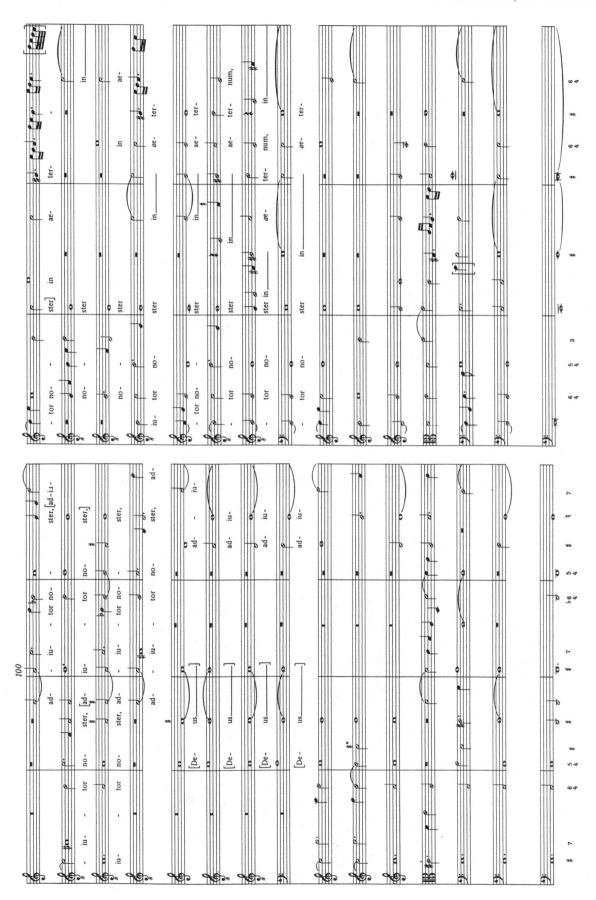

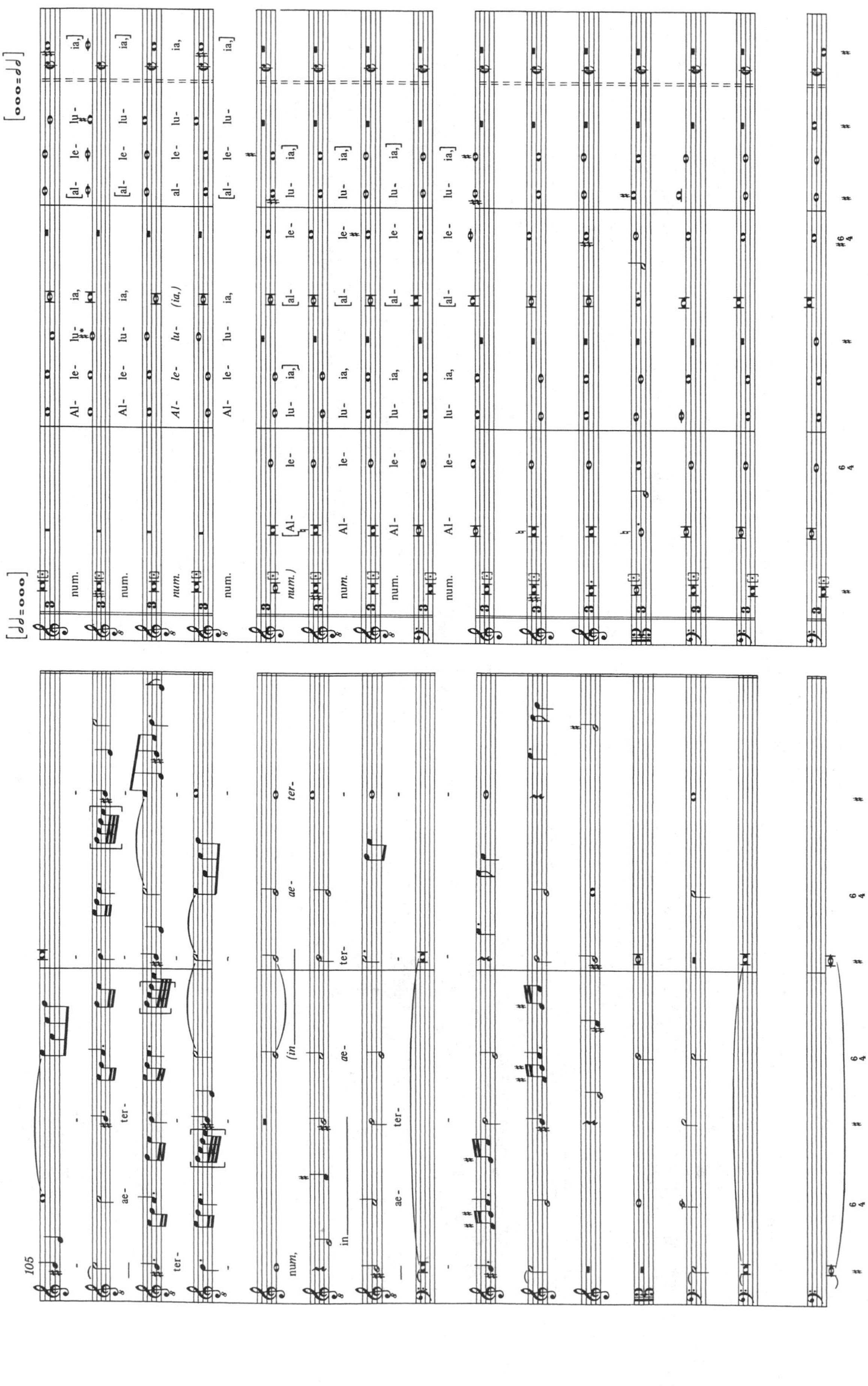
105
ae- ter- num,
(in ae- ter-
in ae- ter-
[𝅗𝅥𝅗𝅥=𝅝𝅝𝅝]
num.
Al- le- lu- ia,
[al- le- lu- ia,]
[𝅝𝅝𝅝=𝅗𝅥𝅗𝅥]
6 4

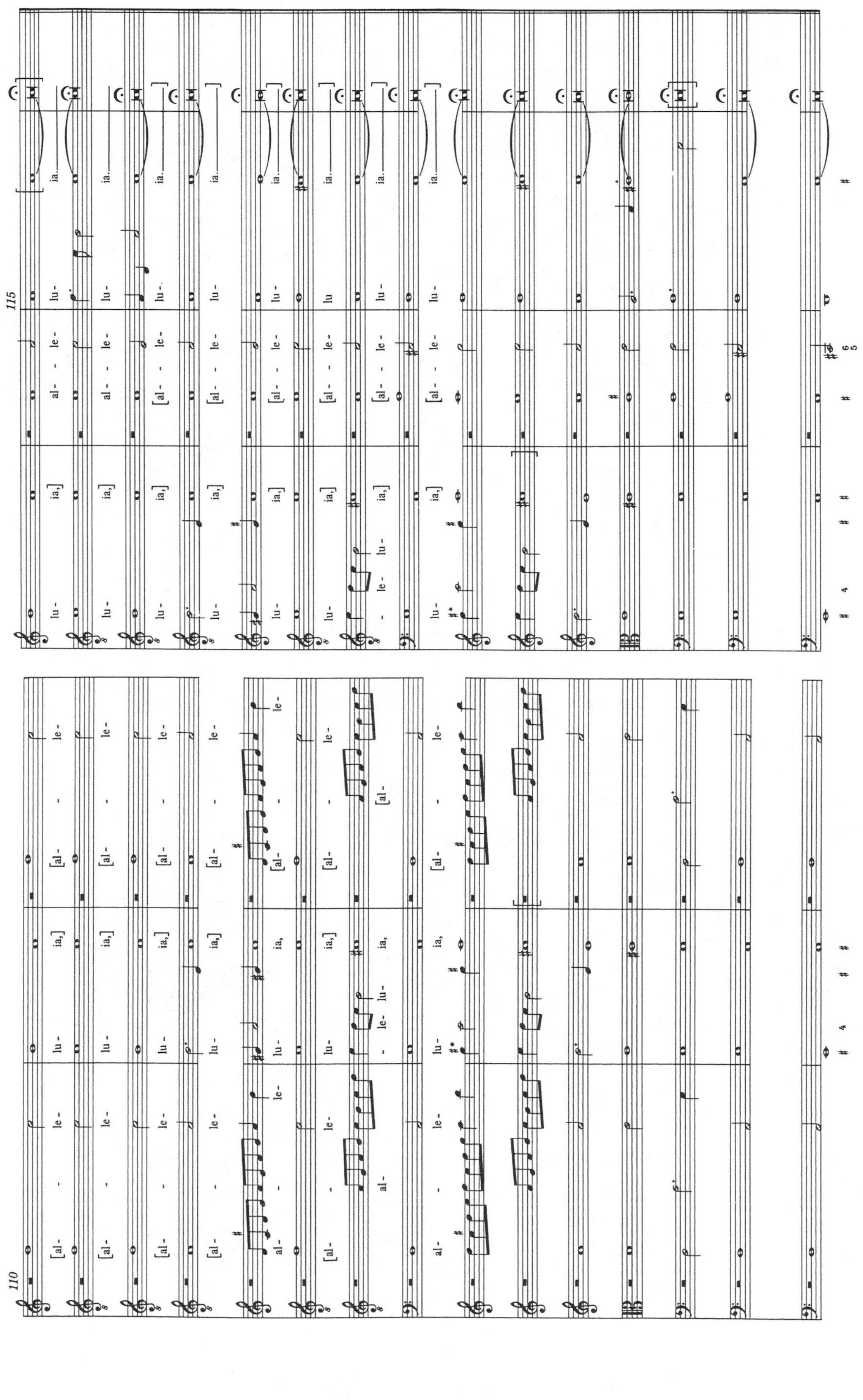

## TEXT AND TRANSLATION

1 In ecclesiis benedicite Domino.
2 Alleluia.
3 In omni loco dominationis benedic anima mea Dominum.
4 Alleluia.
5 In Deo salutari meo et gloria mea,
6 Deus auxilium meum et spes mea in Deo est.
7 Alleluia.
8 Deus noster te invocamus, te laudamus, te adoramus.
9 Libera nos, salva nos, vivifica nos.
10 Alleluia.
11 Deus adjutor noster in aeternum.
12 Alleluia.

1 In the churches, bless the Lord.
2 Hallelujah.
3 In every place of [his] power bless, my soul, the Lord.
4 Hallelujah.
5 In God [is] my salvation and my glory,
6 God [is] my help and my hope is in God.
7 Hallelujah.
8 Our God, we invoke you, we praise you, we praise you, we adore you.
9 Free us, save us, give us life.
10 Hallelujah.
11 God is our hope forever.
12 Hallelujah.

## EDITION

Our score is based on the individual performing parts that constituted the original edition (Venice, 1615). Each part bears one of the traditional Latin headings inherited from the sixteenth century (*cantus*, *altus*, *quintus*, etc.). In addition, each is also assigned to a solo vocal part (*voce*), a member of the *capella*, or a specific instrument. The editor has gathered the fourteen main parts into three groups or choirs; at the top are the solo voices, and at the bottom is a *bassus pro organo* ("bass for the organ"), which today would be called a basso continuo part. The continuo figures included in this part are editorial, and although they are occasionally anachronistic it is difficult to imagine the organist's improvising a realization without some such guide to the correct harmonies.

Just to the left of the opening time signature, the editor has also indicated the range of each of the main parts. From this one can observe that Gabrieli has kept the voices largely within the traditional range of an octave while exploiting the much wider ranges of the instruments. Among the latter, the three cornettos include both soprano and alto types; the two trombones (or sackbuts) also fall within distinct tenor and bass ranges, respectively. The part labeled *violino* is actually for what we would call a viola, as the range and clef make clear.

## PERFORMANCE ISSUES

There is no indication that the four *capella* parts should be doubled, nor is there any reason to think that Gabrieli expected a lute, violone, or other stringed instrument to join the organ. These have become common modern practices, based on German accounts of the performance of polychoral music in the early Baroque. Nevertheless, this Venetian work could be satisfactorily performed by fifteen musicians.

The higher vocal parts originally may have been performed by male castratos. Although boys or falsetto voices might also have been used, women's voices would not have been heard in a Venetian church of the period. The four solo parts might well have been sung with a certain amount of improvised embellishment, perhaps including some of the ornaments described in Caccini's *Nuove musiche*.

There are no tempo indications as such, but as in works by Monteverdi, Lully, and others, what we would call time signatures are also indications for proportional tempo relationships, signified by the editor in brackets. Despite the large note values, the basic tempo remains relatively brisk, as in sixteenth-century polyphony; in the sections in "cut time," the beat should probably be on the whole note.

## SOURCES AND ACKNOWLEDGMENTS

Our score is taken from Giovanni Gabrieli, *Opera omnia*, vol. 5, *Motets in "Symphoniae sacrae"* (*Venice, 1615*), *III*, ed. Richard Charteris, Corpus Musicae Mensurabilis 12/5 (Neustadt-Stuttgart: Hänssler, 1996). It is reproduced by kind permission of the publisher.

## 14. Heinrich Schütz (1585–1672), *Herr, neige deine Himmel*, SWV 361 (*concertato* motet)

# TEXT AND TRANSLATION

| | |
|---|---|
| 1 Herr, neige deine Himmel und fahr herab; | Lord, bow thy heavens and come down, |
| 2 Taste die Berge an, so rauchen sie, | Touch the mountains so that they smoke. |
| 3 Lass blitzen und zerstreuen sie; | Send forth lightning and scatter them; |
| 4 Wirf deine Strahlen und schrecke sie. | Shoot your arrows and destroy them. |
| 5 Sende deine Hand aus der Höhe | Send your hand from the heights |
| 6 Und erlöse mich von grossen Wassern, | And save me from great waters, |
| 7 Und errette mich von der Hand der fremden Kinder. | And preserve me from the hand of foreign peoples. |
| 8 Gott, ich will dir ein neues Lied singen, | God, I will sing you a new song, |
| 9 Ich will dir spielen auf dem Psalter von zehen Saiten. | I will play to you on a psaltery with ten strings. |

—Psalm 144:5–7, 9

# PERFORMANCE ISSUES

Unlike his teacher Gabrieli, Schütz specified the addition of a bowed string instrument to the continuo part: a "violone," the term here probably signifying a bass viola da gamba (not a double bass). Although both the violins and the voices might add occasional trills and other ornaments, there is little opportunity for the more elaborate types of improvised embellishment described in contemporary treatises, for Schütz has written out all the necessary melodic figuration. The relatively plain style and the rather sparse original figures of the continuo part imply a simple chordal realization.

As in the previous work, the time signatures also signify tempo proportions. Thus the whole note in the opening section is worth three whole notes in the triple-time section that begins at measure 43.

# SOURCES

The score is reproduced from Heinrich Schütz, *Symphoniae sacrae: Zweiter Theil*, ed. Philipp Spitta, *Sämmtliche Werke* 7 (Leipzig: Breitkopf und Härtel, 1888), 127–33.[20] This edition is based closely on the work's original printed source, Schütz's *Symphonarum sacrarum secunda pars, opus 10* (Sacred symphonies, part 2, Dresden, 1647).

---

[20]For a more recent edition including a basso continuo realization, unfortunately transposed to the key of E minor, see Heinrich Schütz, *Symphoniae sacrae II 1647 Nr. 13–22*, ed. Werner Bittinger, *Neue Ausgabe sämtlicher Werke* 16 (Kassel: Bärenreiter, 1965), 83–92.

**15.** Heinrich Schütz (1585–1672), *Saul, Saul, Saul, was verfolgst du mich?*, SWV 415 (*concertato* motet)

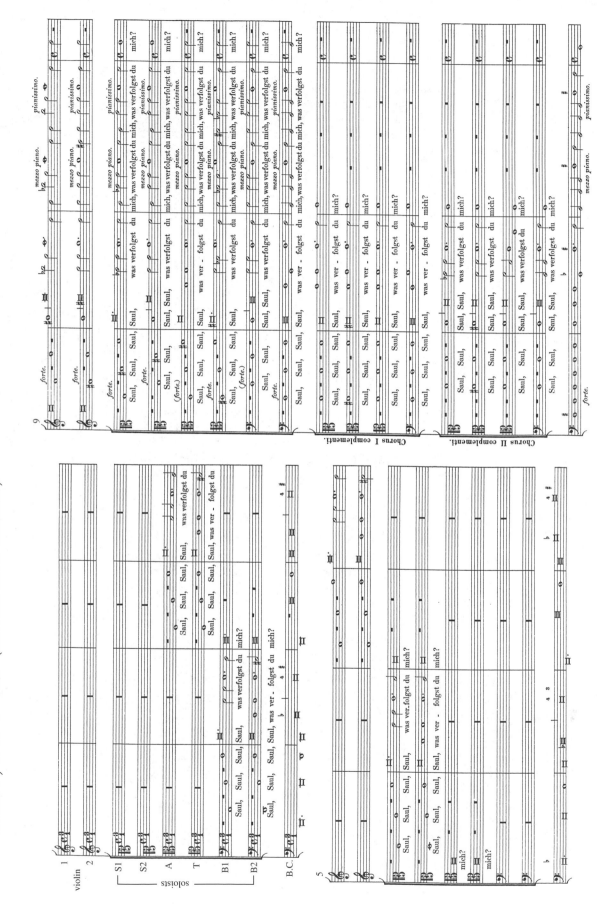

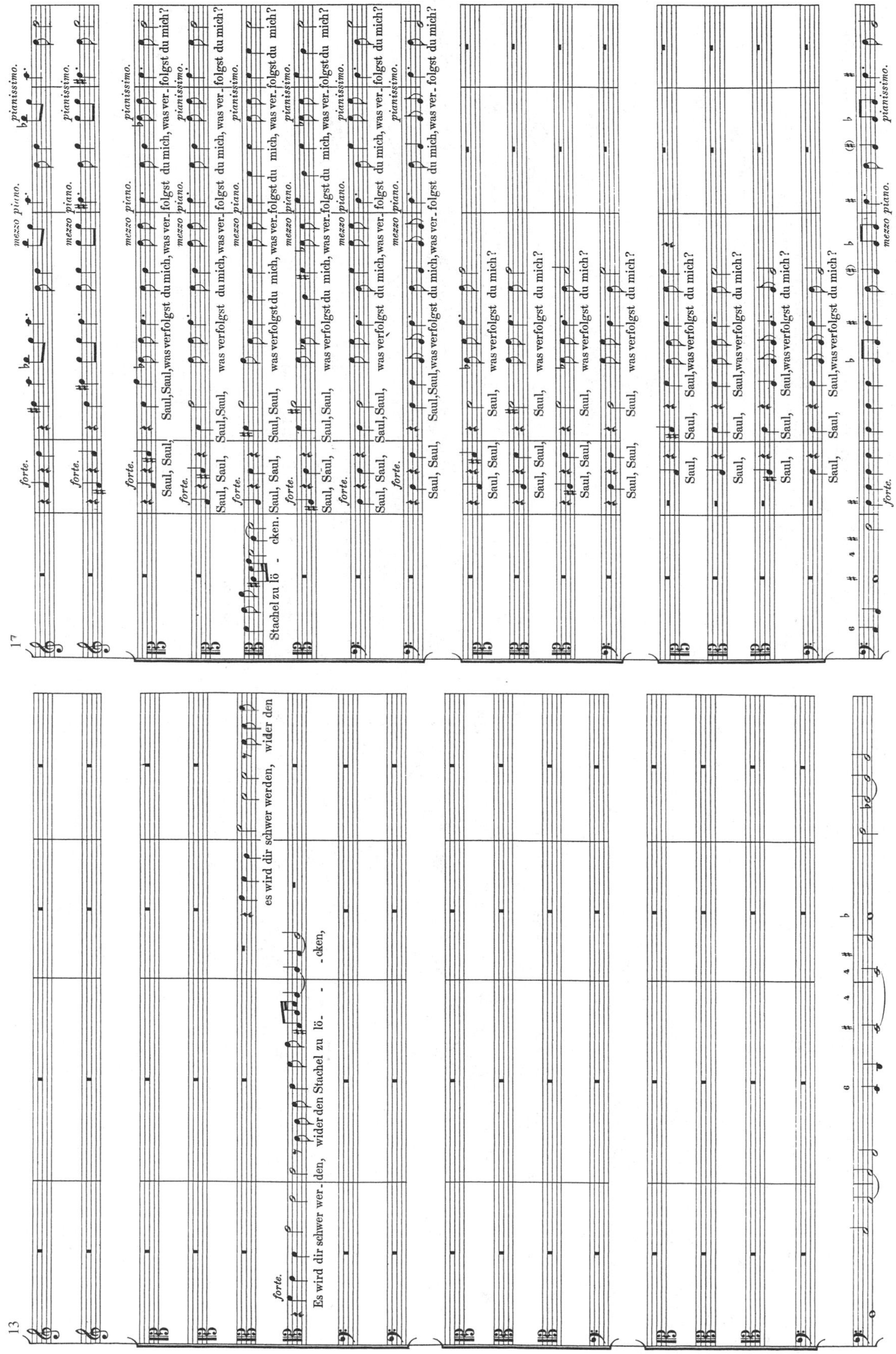
13
forte.
Es wird dir schwer wer-den, wider den Stachel zu lö - -cken,
es wird dir schwer werden, wider den
17
Stachel zu lö - cken.
forte.
mezzo piano.
pianissimo.
Saul, Saul, Saul, Saul, was verfolgst du mich, was ver-folgst du mich, was ver-folgst du mich?
Saul, Saul, was verfolgst du mich?
Saul, Saul, was verfolgst du mich?

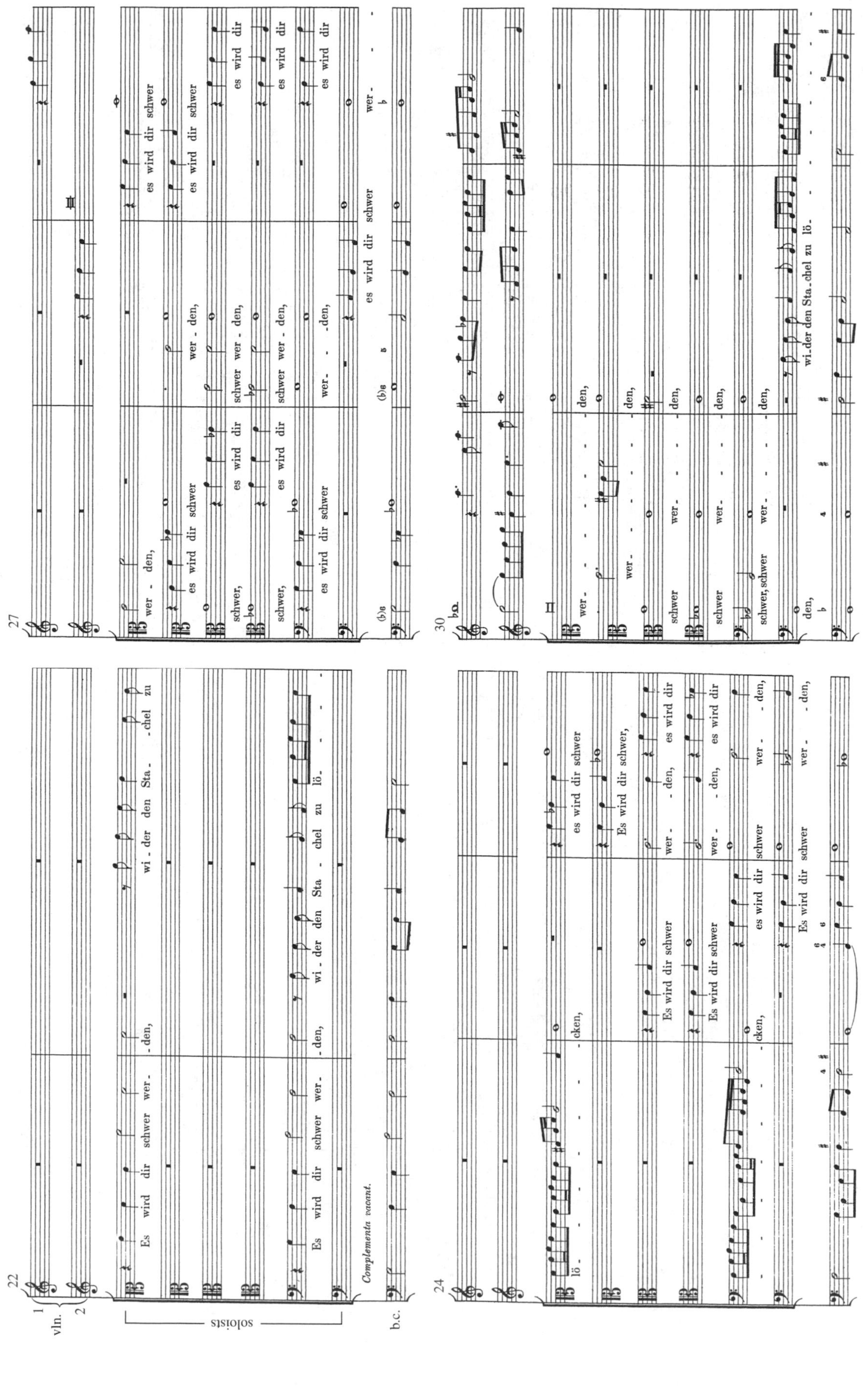
vln. 1
2
soloists
b.c.
Complementa vacant.
22
24
27
30
Es wird dir schwer wer - den, wi - der den Sta - chel zu
Es wird dir schwer wer - den, wi - der den Sta - chel zu lö - - -
lö - - - - cken,
Es wird dir schwer
es wird dir schwer
Es wird dir schwer, es wird dir
wer - den, es wird dir schwer
wer - den, es wird dir schwer
Es wird dir schwer wer - den,
wer - den, es wird dir schwer
schwer, es wird dir schwer wer - den,
wer - - - - den,
schwer wer - den,
schwer, schwer wer - - - - den,
den, wi - der den Sta - chel zu lö - - - -

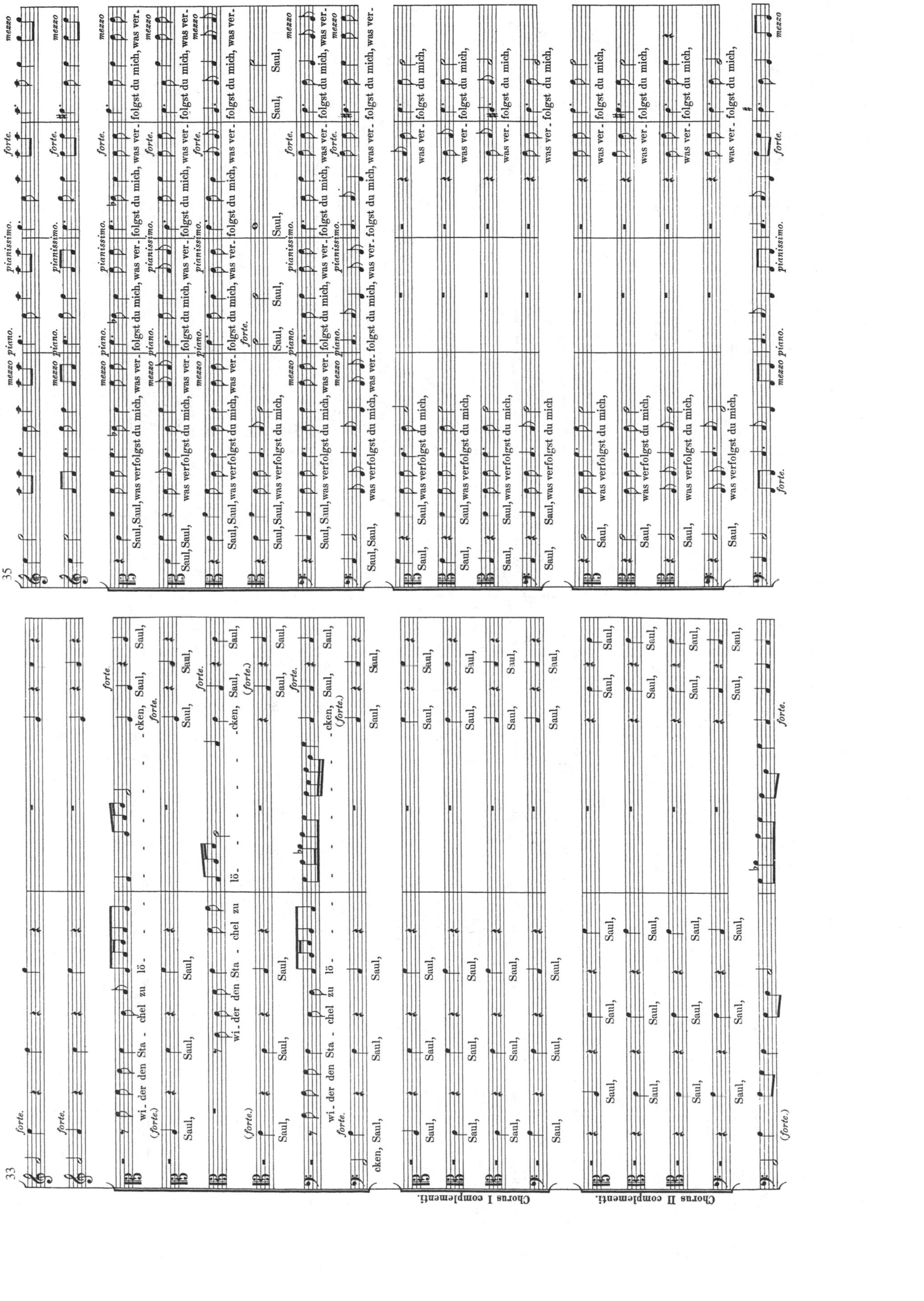
33
35
forte.
wi - der den Sta - chel zu lö - - - - - cken, Saul, Saul,
Saul, Saul, Saul, Saul, Saul,
cken, Saul, Saul, Saul,
Chorus I complementi.
Chorus II complementi.
Saul, Saul, was verfolgst du mich, was ver - folgst du mich, was ver - folgst du mich, was ver - folgst du mich, was ver -
mezzo piano.
pianissimo.
forte.
mezzo
Saul, was verfolgst du mich,
was ver - folgst du mich,

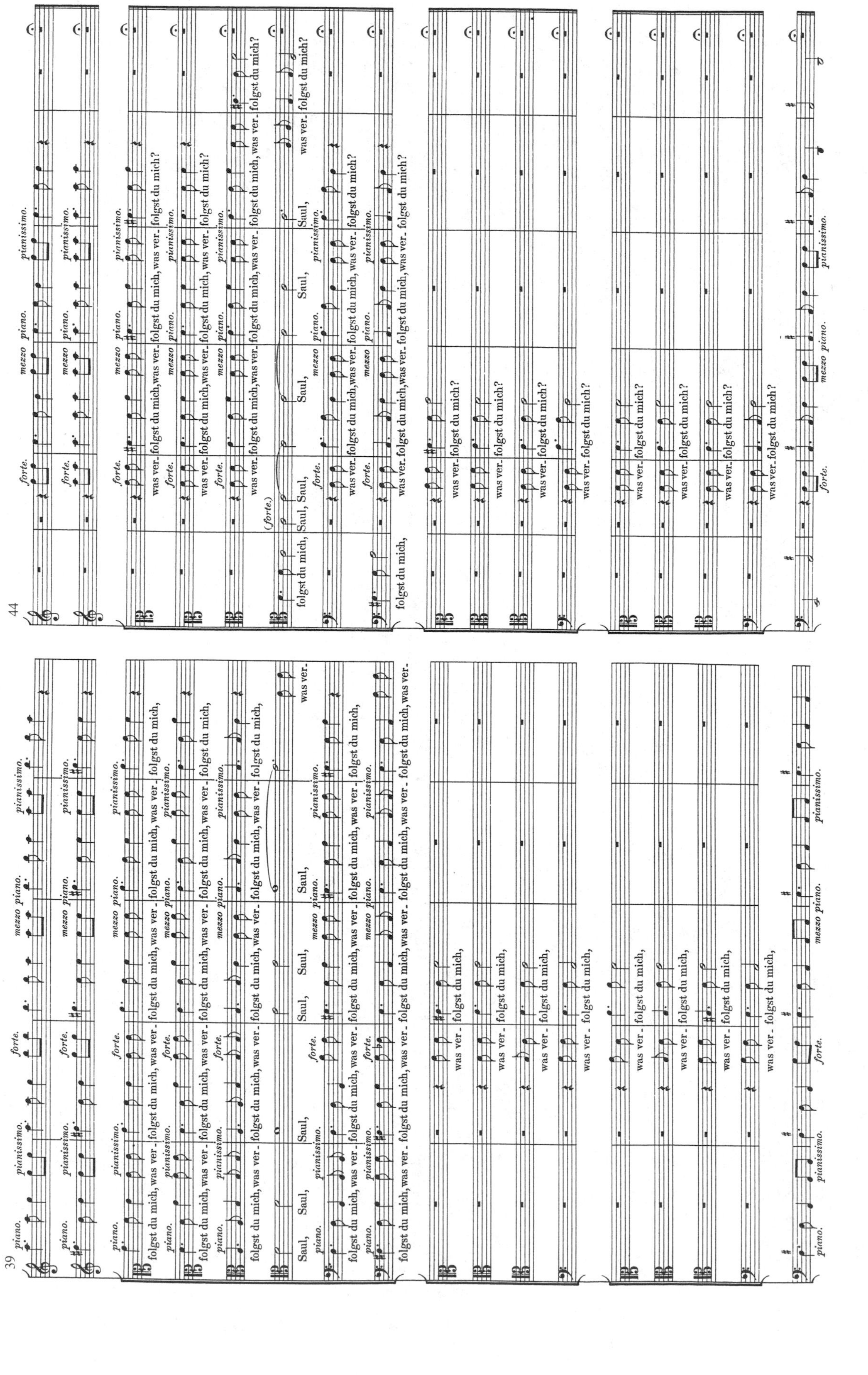
39
44
piano.
pianissimo.
forte.
mezzo piano.
(forte.)
Saul, Saul,
folgst du mich, was ver-
folgst du mich?
was ver-folgst du mich?

## TEXT AND TRANSLATION

1 Saul, Saul, was verfolgst du mich?
2 Es wird dir schwer werden, wider
   den Stachel zu lökken.

—Acts 26:14

Saul, why do you persecute me?
It will be difficult for you to kick against the
   prods.

## EDITION

This score, like Selection 14, is reproduced from a nineteenth-century edition that, like other scholarly editions of the period, retained the original clefs and labels for the individual parts. The broad outlines of Schütz's polychoral score are nevertheless perfectly clear. The six principal vocal parts are joined by two violins (top two staves) and by two optional or *capella* choirs of four voices each, here designated *chori complementi* ("complementary choirs"). At the bottom of each system is the basso continuo.

## PERFORMANCE ISSUES

As in Selection 13, the vocal and instrumental parts were probably not meant to be doubled, although Schütz again directs the use of "violone" together with organ on the basso continuo part. Modern performances often include trombones and other instruments that double or substitute for the voices of the capella choruses.

The two instrumental parts might be played not only by violins but by other "similar" instruments, by which Schütz might have had cornettos in mind. The time signatures again imply tempo relationships; three whole notes in the opening triple-time section were probably meant to be worth one whole note in the duple-time section beginning at measure 16. The dynamic markings are original; a series of closely spaced diminishing dynamics (as in mm. 11–12) seems to signify a decrescendo. Note that from measure 36 to the end the tenor soloist remains *forte* while the other parts have repeated diminuendos from *forte* to *pianissimo*.

## SOURCE

The score is reproduced from Heinrich Schütz: *Symphoniae sacrae: Dritter Theil, Zweite Abtheilung*, ed. Philipp Spitta, *Sämmtliche Werke* 11 (Leipzig: Breitkopf und Härtel, 1891), which derives from Schütz's *Symphonarum sacrarum tertia pars, opus 12* (Sacred symphonies, part 3, Dresden, 1650).

## 16. Giacomo Carissimi (1605–1674), *Jephte* (oratorio: selections)

Filia

[Sop. 1]

Can - ta - te me - cum Do - mi - no, can - ta - te om - nes

[B.c.]

3

po - pu - li, lau - da - te bel - li prin - ci - pem, qui no - bis de - dit glo - ri - am et Is - ra - el vi -

6    7

6

cto - ri - am, lau - da - te bel - li prin - ci - pem, qui no - bis de - dit glo - ri - am et

4   3[♯]                                                                                                    6

9

Is - ra - el vi - cto - ri - am et Is - ra - el vi - cto - ri - am,

4 3[♯]        6    7  6

12

et Is - ra - el, et Is - ra - el vi - cto - ri - am.

♯                                                                          4        3[♯]

4   3[♯]

## TEXT AND TRANSLATION

**Historicus**

Cum autem victor Jephte
in domum suam reverteretur,
occurrens ei unigenita filia sua
cum tympanis et choris praecinebat:

**Filia**

Incipite in tympanis
Et psallite in cymbalis.
Hymnum cantemus Domino,
Et modulemur canticum.
Laudemus regem coelitum,
Laudemus belli principem,
Qui filiorum Israel
Victorem ducem reddidit.


Hymnum cantemus Domino,
Et modulemur canticum,
Qui dedit nobis gloriam
Et Israel victoriam.

**Filia**

Cantate mecum Domino,
Cantate omnes populi,
Laudate belli principem,
Qui nobis dedit gloriam
Et Israel victoriam.


Cantemus omnes Domino,
Laudemus belli principem
Qui dedit nobis gloriam
Et Israel victoriam.

**Historicus**

Cum videsset Jephte,
qui votum Domino voverat,
filiam suam venientem in occursum,
in dolore et lachrimis scidit
vestimenta sua et ait:

**Jephte**

Heu mihi! filia mea, heu
decepisti me, filia unigenita,
et tu pariter, heu filia mea
decepta es.

**Filia**

Cur ego te pater decepi,
et cur ego filia tua unigenita
decepta sum?

**Narrator [bass]**

When Jephtha had returned
victorious to his house,
running to him his only daughter
sang to him with timbrels and dances:

**Daughter [soprano 1]**

Take up the timbrels
And sound the cymbals.
We shall sing a hymn to the Lord
And make a song.
We shall praise the heavenly king,
We shall praise the prince of war
Who to the children of Israel
Has restored their victorious leader.

**[Sopranos 2 and 3]**

We shall sing a hymn
And make a song to the Lord,
Who has given us glory
And to Israel victory.

**Daughter**

Sing with me to the Lord,
Let all the people sing,
Praise the prince of war
Who has given us glory
And to Israel victory.

**[Chorus: all 6 voices]**

Let us all sing to the Lord,
Let us praise the prince of war
Who has given us glory
And to Israel victory.

**Narrator [alto]**

When Jephtha,
who had sworn an oath to the Lord,
saw his daughter running to meet him,
with sadness and tears he tore
his clothes and said:

**Jephtha [tenor]**

Woe is me! my daughter, alas,
you have undone me, my only daughter,
and yourself as well; alas, my daughter,
you are undone.

**Daughter**

How, father, have I undone you,
and how am I, your only daughter,
undone?

CARISSIMI, *JEPHTE*   157

**Jephte**

Aperui os meum ad Dominum,
ut quicumque primus de domo mea
occurrerit mihi offeram illum
Domino in holocaustum.
Heu mihi! filia mea, heu
decepisti me, filia unigenita,
et tu pariter, heu filia mea
decepta es.

—anonymous, after Judges 11:34–35

**Jephtha**

I have opened my mouth to the Lord,
that whoever first from my house
should run to me, I will offer him
to the Lord as a burnt offering.
Woe is me! my daughter, alas,
you have undone me, my only daughter,
and yourself as well; alas, my daughter,
you are undone.

## PERFORMANCE ISSUES

The sopranos were probably adult male castrati, and the same voices that sang the solo parts of the Historicus, Jephtha, and his daughter also sang in the chorus; even in the choral sections, the parts were probably not doubled. Most likely the continuo was played by organ alone, although in modern performances viola da gamba and chittarone are often included. Modern performances often use additional instruments to double the choral parts, which may be sung by multiple voices, but this is unlikely to have been Carissimi's intention.

## SOURCE

Our score is based on *Carissimi's Werke: Erste Abtheilung*, ed. Friedrich Chrysander, Denkmäler der Tonkunst, vol. 2 (Bergedorf, ca. 1869), corrected by consultation with the critical edition by Janet Beat (London: Novello, 1974), which follows a manuscript copy by the composer Marc-Antoine Charpentier as its principal source.

## 17. Marc-Antoine Charpentier (ca. 1645/50–1704), *Frigidae noctis umbra*, H. 414 (oratorio: selections)

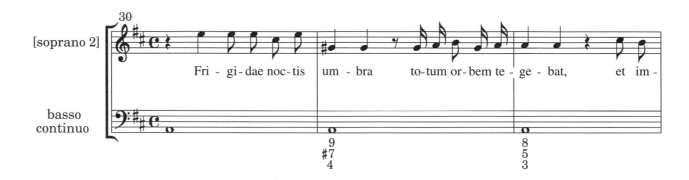

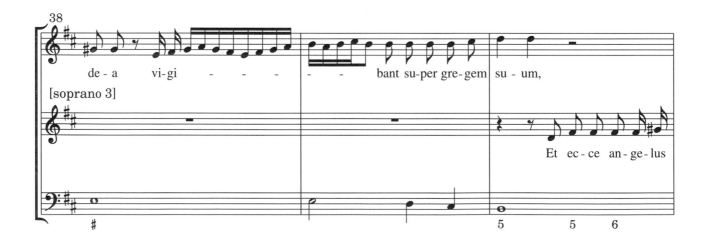

## TEXT AND TRANSLATION

### Récit de l'historien

Frigidae noctis umbra totum
orbem tegebat, et immersi iacebant
omnes in somno profundo.
Pastores autem Iudeae vigilabant
super gregem suum. Et ecce
angelus Domini stetit iuxta eos,
et claritas Dei circumfulsit eos.
Timuerunt autem pastores timore magno;
et dixit illis angelus:

### Angelus

Nolite timere, pastores.
Ecce enim annuntio vobis
gaudium magnum quod erit
omni populo; quia natus est hodie
salvator vester in civitate David;
et hoc erit vobis signum:
invenietis pannis involutum
et reclinatum in praesepio.
Ite, pastores, et adorate illum.

—anonymous, derived from Luke 2:8–16

### The evangelist's account

The shadow of cold night covered
the whole world, and all those immersed
in it lay in a deep sleep.
But shepherds of Judea were watching
over their flock. And behold,
an angel of the Lord stood by them,
and the glory of God surrounded them.
The shepherds feared with a great fear;
and the angel said to them:

### Angel

Fear not, shepherds.
For behold, I announce to you
a great joy that will be
to all people; for born today is
your savior in the city of David;
and this will be a sign to you:
you will find [him] wrapped in
swaddling clothes, lying in a stable.
Go, shepherds, and adore him.

## PERFORMANCE ISSUES

Like Selection 16, the oratorio from which this excerpt is taken was probably intended to be a fairly intimate work performed with one voice or one instrument on a part. The bass line might have been doubled by viola da gamba, but organ would probably have sufficed. In keeping with French practice, the three soprano parts heard in this selection would have been sung by women; the original singers are named in Charpentier's manuscript. Actually, the second and third parts are best described as mezzo-sopranos, and as pitch levels in seventeenth-century France were about a whole step below today's, all three parts would have been relatively low.[21]

The score contains no ornaments, but numerous trills, appoggiaturas, and other figures would have been added by the singers as well as the violinists, according to French conventions (e.g., a trill on f♯′ in the cadential formula in m. 35; an appoggiatura or *port de voix* c♯″ before the d″ on the downbeat of m. 40). In the angel's solo, eighth notes would probably have been performed as *notes inégales* (unequal notes). Charpentier, like Carissimi, probably expected the work to be performed without breaks between sections; his score employs the same tempo conventions as did Lully (note the single bar of cut time at m. 51).

## SOURCE

Our edition has been newly prepared from the composer's manuscript, which has been published in facsimile.[22]

---

[21]Only the first soprano was originally notated in treble clef; the other two are in the lower soprano clef in Charpentier's manuscript.

[22]Paris, Biblothèque National, Rés. Vm¹ 259, reproduced in Marc-Antoine Charpentier, *Œuvres complètes*, 1/6, *Meslanges autographes* (Paris: Minkoff, 1996), 171–82. A modern edition of the complete work includes realized basso continuo but is transposed a tone lower and includes suggested scoring for soloists and chorus, now thought to be anachronistic; see Marc-Antoine Charpentier, *Song of the Birth of Our Lord Jesus Christ*, Marc-Antoine Charpentier, ed. H. Wiley Hitchcock (St. Louis: Concordia, 1959).

## 18. George Frideric Handel (1685–1759), *Orlando* (opera: selections)

a. Act 1, scene 8 (recitative and aria "Oh care parolette")

b. Act 1, scene 9 (recitative and aria "Se fedel vuoi")

6

c. Act 1, scene 10 (recitative and aria "Fammi combattere")

## TEXT AND TRANSLATION

*Act 1, scene 8*

DORINDA SOLA

**Dorinda**

Povera me! Ben vedo che m'alletta
Con un parlar fallace;
Ma così ancor mi piace,
E ogni sua paroletta
Mi fa all'udito certa consonanza
Che accorda col desio pur la speranza.

DORINDA ALONE

**Dorinda**

Poor me! I know I am allured
By his deceptive speech;
But thusly he still pleases me,
And each of his little words
Makes, when I hear it, a certain harmony
That tunes my hopes to my desires.

[ARIA]

| | |
|---|---|
| 1  Oh care parolette, o dolci sguardi, | Oh, dear words, sweet looks, |
| 2  Sebben siete bugiardi | Though you are liars, |
| 3  Tanto vi crederò. | I shall still believe you! |
| 4      Ma poi che far potrò, | But then what shall I do, |
| 5      Allor ch troppo tardi | When, too late, |
| 6      Io vi concoscerò. | I see through you? |
| *Parte.* | *She leaves.* |

*Act 1, scene 9*

ZOROASTRO, ANGELICA, E POI
  ORLANDO

ZOROASTER AND ANGELICA, THEN
  ORLANDO

**Zoroastro**

Noti a me sono i tuoi fatali amori
Con Medoro; e non temi
La vendetta d'Orlando?

**Zoraster**

I am aware of your fatal love
For Medoro; don't you fear
Orlando's vengeance?

**Angelica**

      É ver, che devo
Molto all'eroe, ma—

**Angelica**

      It's true that I owe
Much to the hero, yet—

**Zoroastro**

      Già sen vien! Celato
Mi terrò per vegliar d'ognuno al fato.

**Zoroastro**

      But he's coming! Concealed,
I shall keep watching over each one's
  destiny.

*Si ritira a parte.*

*He withdraws.*

**Orlando** *in disparte*

Quando mai troverò l'orme fugaci
D'Angelica la bella?

**Orlando** *(aside)*

Whenever shall I find the fleeting traces
Of fair Angelica?

**Angelica**

Oh Dei, se vien Medoro,
Che quì attendea per partir seco! Eh
  forse,
Se Orlando qua conduce il novo amore
Per quella ch'ei salvò da man nemica,

Non sarà così grande il mio timore.
Vo' fingermi gelosa
Per meglio discoprire il suo pensiero.
*Si presenta ad Orlando.*
Orlando, ed è pur vero
Ch'io qui ti veda!

**Angelica**

Oh Gods, if Medoro should come,
He whom I was awaiting here to leave with
  him! If only
A new love were to conduct Orlando
Toward her whom he saved from an enemy
  hand,
My fear would be less great.
I shall feign jealousy,
The better to discover his thoughts.
*She stands before Orlando.*
Orlando, is it true
That I see you here?

**Orlando**

      Oh Cieli! Oh cara, e come
Potevo mai sperar sì lieta sorte!
Angelica, mio bene.

**Orlando**

      Oh heavens! my dear, how
Could I ever hope for such good fortune?
Angelica, my love.

**Angelica**

      Erri nel nome,
Isabella vuoi dir, che là t'attende.

**Angelica**

      You err in the name;
You mean Isabella, who awaits you here.

**Orlando**

Son della principessa
Difensor, non amante.

**Angelica**

Ma per tale ti pubblicò Dorinda
Allora, e quando—

**Orlando**

Un'Angelica sol può amare Orlando.

**Angelica**

*vedendo Medoro da lontano*
(Ma, oh dei! vedo Medor!
Convien che Orlando allontani di qua.)
*Esce il mago facendo segno colla verga, sorge
di sotterra una gran fontana, che copre
Medoro, la scena cangiandosi in un
delizioso giardino.*

**Orlando**

Chiedimi o bella
Nuove prove d'amore.

**Angelica**

(O soccorso opportun!) Sentimi Orlando
Se pur vuoi, ch'io ti creda
A me fedel; pronto da te allontana

La dama, che a color di mano hai tolto,
O non vedrai d'Angelica più il volto.

[ARIA]

1 Se fedel vuoi, ch'io ti creda
2 Fa che veda
3 La tua fedeltà.
4　Finchè regni nel mio petto
5　Il sospetto,
6　Mai l'amor vi regnerà.
*Parte.*

*Act 1, scene 10*

ORLANDO SOLO

**Orlando**

T'ubbidirò, crudele,
E vedrai in questo istante,
Che della principessa
Fui solo difensor, ma non amante.

[ARIA]

1 Fammi combattere
2 Mostri e tifei,
3 Novi trofei
4 Se vuoi dal mio valor.

**Orlando**

I am that princess's
Defender, not her lover.

**Angelica**

But that is what Dorinda called you,
Then, and when—

**Orlando**

Orlando can love only Angelica.

**Angelica**

*seeing Medoro in the distance*
(But, oh gods, I see Medoro!
It is necessary that Orlando leave from here.)
*The magician comes forth waving his wand, and
a great fountain rises from beneath the earth,
concealing Medoro as the scene changes to a
delightful garden.*

**Orlando**

Ask, my dear,
For new proofs of my love

**Angelica**

(What good luck!) Hear me, Orlando,
If you would like me to think you are
Faithful to me, immediately separate
　yourself from
That lady whom you once took from them,
Or you shall never again see Angelica.

If you want me to trust in your faith,
Do something to show
Your faithfulness.
　　As long as my thoughts are ruled by
　　Suspicion,
　　Love shall never rule.
*She leaves.*

ORLANDO ALONE

**Orlando**

I will obey you, cruel one,
And you shall see in this instant
That of the princess
I was the defender, not the lover.

Make me combat
Monsters and demons,
If new trophies
You want of my valor.

| | | |
|---|---|---|
| 5 | Muraglie abbattere | Obstacles must be demolished, |
| 6 | Disfare incanti, | I must defeat enchantments, |
| 7 | Se vuoi ch'io vanti | If you want me to boast |
| 8 | Darti prove d'amor. | That I have given you proofs of my love. |
| | *Parte.* | *He leaves.* |

—after Carlo Sigismondo Capeci

## EDITION

Our score is taken from a nineteenth-century edition that closely reflects Handel's manuscript. Thus, as in many eighteenth-century composers' scores, the rather sketchy information about instrumentation given in the heading of each movement must be supplemented from clues within the body of the music.

In Dorinda's aria, the label *tutti unisoni* (literally, "all in unison") actually means violins 1 and 2, doubled by oboes. The oboes are silent in the *piano* passages, reentering in the *forte* passages marked *Tutti*. Similarly, the *bassi* (bass instruments) include, besides cellos, a double bass and perhaps one or two bassoons that drop out when the part is notated in tenor clef or where *pianissimo* is indicated. Possibly one of the two harpsichords often employed in opera seria dropped out at these points as well.

Handel left no indications of scoring for Angelica's aria, but the editor's parenthesized suggestions are surely correct. The continuo part in the recitatives was probably intended for a single harpsichord, possibly with a cello doubling the bass line.

## PERFORMANCE ISSUES

Some of the basic conventions of late Baroque Italian vocal performance, such as the interpretation of recitative and the decoration of da capo arias, are explained in the text volume. In the recitatives, the notes of the bass line would not have been held out as written but rather released after a beat or two. The harpsichordist might have emphasized certain words by decorating the accompanying chords with arpeggios.

Orlando's part was written for the alto castrato Senesino. Modern performances generally choose between an adult male falsetto singer or a female mezzo-soprano. Transposing the part an octave downward, for a baritone, would cause it to pass close to and even beneath the bass line in several passages. This would muddy the texture and dull the brilliance of the coloratura.

The tempo marking *Largo* (literally, "broad") for Angelica's aria does not necessarily indicate a particularly slow tempo. It may allude rather to a spacious, sustained style for both the singer and the string orchestra. The word *adagio* in measure 15 is probably a suggestion not only for a ritard but also for some improvised embellishment by the singer.

## SOURCE

The edition is that of Georg Friedrich Händel, *Werke*, vol. 82, *Orlando*, ed. Friedrich Chrysander (Leipzig: Deutsche Händelgesellschaft, 1881), which was based primarily on the autograph score (London, British Library, R.M. 20.b.8).

# 19. Jean-Philippe Rameau (1683–1764), *Les indes galantes* (*opéra-ballet*: selections)

On entend un prélude qui annonce la fête.

## TEXT AND TRANSLATION

*Nouvelle entrée, scene 4 {conclusion}*

ON ENTEND UN PRÉLUDE QUI ANNONCE     A PRELUDE IS HEARD, ANNOUNCING
LA FÊTE                              THE FESTIVITIES.

**Damon**

Déjà, dans les bois d'alentour,             Already, in the surrounding woods,
J'entends de nos guerriers les bruyantes    I hear the loud trumpets of our warriors.
   trompettes.
Leurs sons n'effrayent plus ces aimables    Their sounds no longer terrify these pleasant
   retraites;                                   retreats;
Des charmes de la paix ils marquent le      They mark the return of the charms of
   retour.                                      peace.
*(à Alvar)*                                  *(to Alvar)*
À vos tristes regrets dérobez ce beau jour! Rescue this beautiful day from your sad
                                               regrets!
Que le plaisir avec nous vous arrête!       Let pleasure hold you here with us!

**Alvar**

*(s'éloignant)*                             *(leaving)*
Hélas! Je vais cacher un malheureux amour.  Alas, I go to conceal an unfortunate love.

### Damon

*(le suivant)*
Venez plutôt l'amuser à la fête!

*(following him)*
Come instead to amuse it at the festivities!

*SCENE 5: ADARIO, ZIMA*

### Adario

Je ne vous peindrai point les transports
  de mon cœur,
Belle Zima, jugez-en par le vôtre!
En comblant mon bonheur
Vous montrez qu'une égale ardeur
Nous enflamme l'un et l'autre.

I shall not describe to you the raptures of
  my heart,
Beautiful Zima; judge them by your own!
Redoubling my good fortune,
You show that equal ardor
Enflames us both.

### Zima

De l'amour le plus tendre éprouvez la
  douceur!
Je vous dois la préférence.
De vous à vos rivaux je vois la différence:

L'un s'abandonne à la fureur,
Et l'autre perd mon cœur avec
  indifférence.
Nous ignorons ce calme et cette violence.

Feel the sweetness of the most tender love!

To you I owe my preference.
Between you and your rivals I see the
  difference:
The one abandons himself to passion,
And the other loses my heart with
  indifference.
We do not know this calmness nor this
  violence.

### {AIR}

1 Sur nos bords l'amour vole et prévient
  nos désirs.
2 Dans notre paisible retraite
3 On n'entend murmurer que l'onde et
  les zéphyrs;
4 Jamais l'écho n'y répête
5 De nos regrets ni de soupirs.

Above our shores, love flies and anticipates
  our desires.
In our peaceable retreat
One hears murmuring only the wave and
  the breezes;
Never does an echo there repeat
Either our regrets or our sighs.

### Adario

Viens, Hymen, hâte-toi, suis l'amour qui
  t'appelle.

Come, Hymen,[23] make haste, follow Love,
  who calls you.

### Zima, Adario

*{Duet}*
Hymen, viens nous unir d'une chaîne
  éternelle!
Viens encore de la paix embellir les
  beaux jours!
Viens! je te promets d'être fidèle.
Tu sais nous enchaîner et nous plaire
  toujours.
Viens! je te promets d'être fidèle.

Hymen, come join us with an eternal bond!

Come again to embellish with peace these
  fair days!
Come; I promise you I will be faithful.
You know how to bind us and to delight us
  forever.
Come; I promise you I will be faithful.

—Louis Fuzelier

---

[23]In ancient Greek religion, Hymen was the god of marriage.

## EDITION

This score is from an early twentieth-century edition that includes an editorial reduction of the instrumental parts, intended for playing on the piano when an orchestra is not available. This piano reduction appears in small print on the bottom two staves of each system, except in the recitatives, where these staves contain an editorial realization of the figured bass. Slurs and ornaments are mostly original, as are tempo and dynamic indications. A number of indications for tempo and instrumentation appear in parentheses; they seem to derive from secondary manuscript sources (see below).

The names of the instruments and the singing characters are given in abbreviated form: *Fl.* = *flûte*, that is recorder; $H^b$ = *hautbois* (oboe); $B^{ons}$ = bassoons; *Tromp.* = trumpet; *Timb.* = timpani; $V^{ons}$ = violins; *Alt.* = viola; *D.* = Damon; *A.* = first Alvar, then Adario; *Z.* = Zima.

## PERFORMANCE ISSUES

The brief *prélude* (mm. 1–4) is for the full orchestra of the French royal opera, which at this date included numerous players on the three upper string parts; the woodwind parts might have been doubled as well. The basso continuo would have been played by several cellos and one or two harpsichords, reinforced by double bass (the bassoon doubling is written out in our score). In Zima's air, a smaller group of violins probably played, and the continuo was probably more lightly scored here, as it certainly was in the recitatives and the closing duet.

Most of the ornamentation—trills and appoggiaturas of various types—has been written out, and there is little room for additional improvised decoration. The conventions that governed tempo in the older works of Lully and Charpentier must still have applied in the recitative sections, which show the changing time signatures typical of French Baroque vocal music. Thus the half note of the sections in "2" probably has the same value as a quarter note in the sections in "3" and in "C." But tempo in the *prélude* and in the duet is signified by verbal indications (in French), and that of Zima's aria is implied by its gavotte rhythm.

## SOURCE

The edition, by the composer Paul Dukas (1865–1935), was published as volume 7 of Jean-Philippe Rameau, *Oeuvres complètes* (Paris: Durand, 1902). Some of the individual volumes in this series are notoriously unreliable, adding inauthentic wind parts and other features, but the present score is derived closely from the first edition of the fourth *entrée*.[24]

---

[24]*Les indes galantes: Balet {sic} reduit a {sic} quatre grands concerts* (Paris: Boivin et al., 1736). As the title indicates, this print contained only selections from the work as a whole, but it included the complete fourth *entrée*, entitled *Les sauvages*.

**20.** Johann Sebastian Bach (1685–1750), *Herr Jesu Christ, wahr' Mensch und Gott*, BWV 127 (sacred cantata)

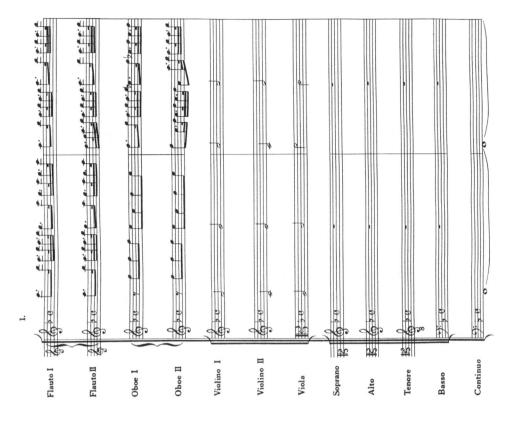

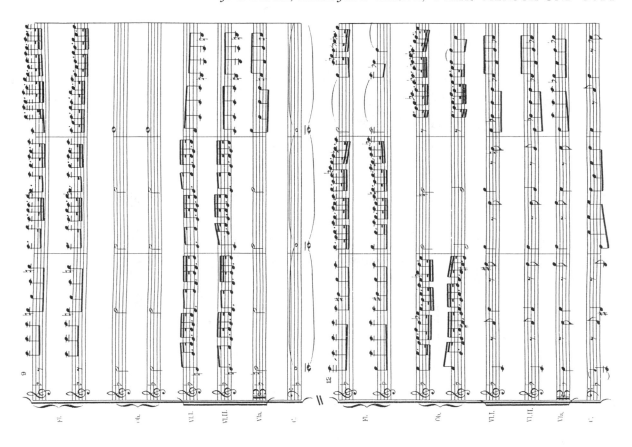

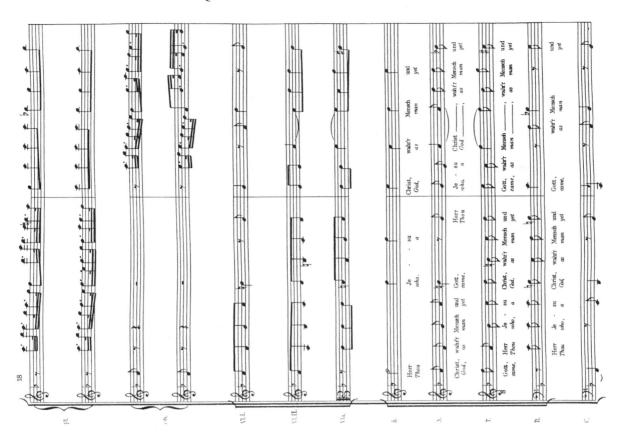

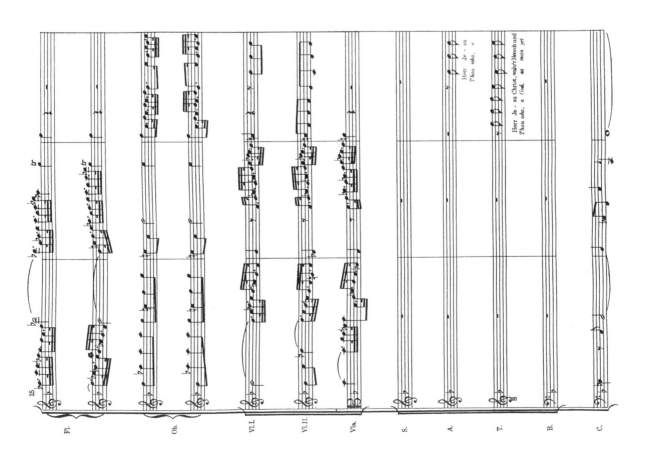

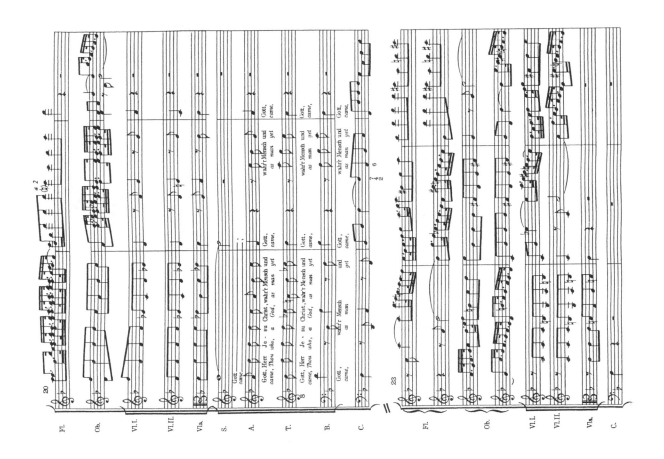

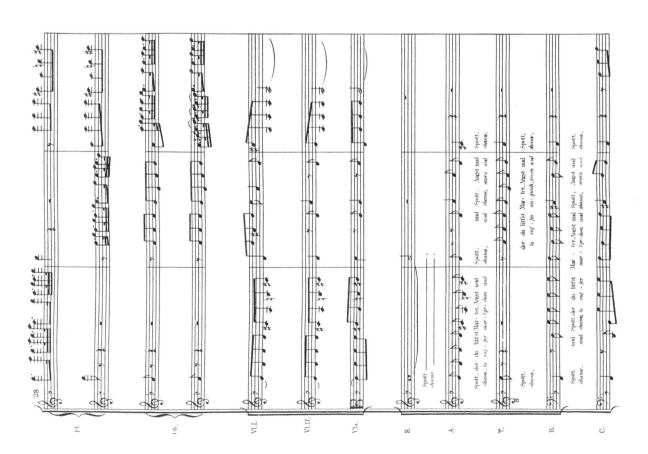

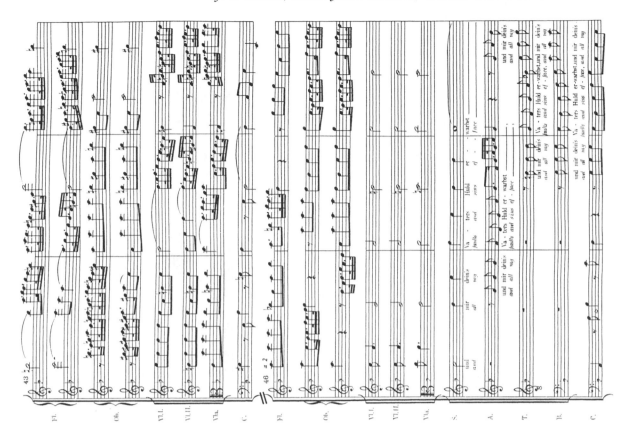

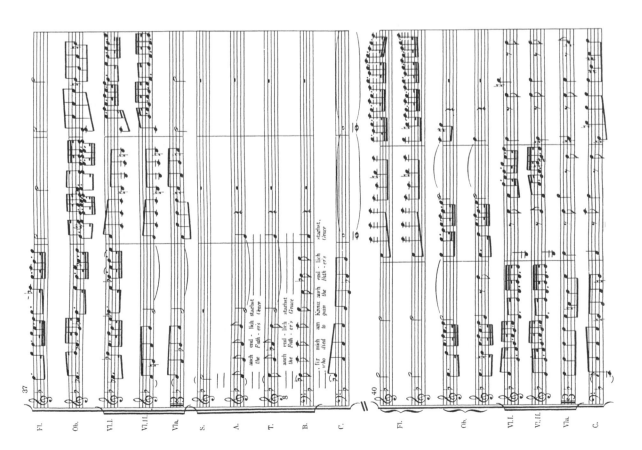

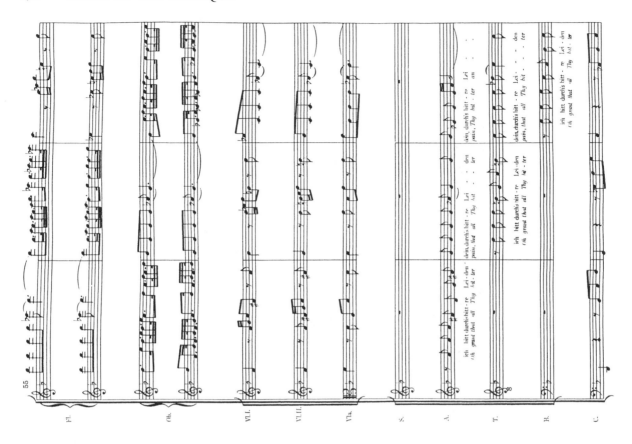

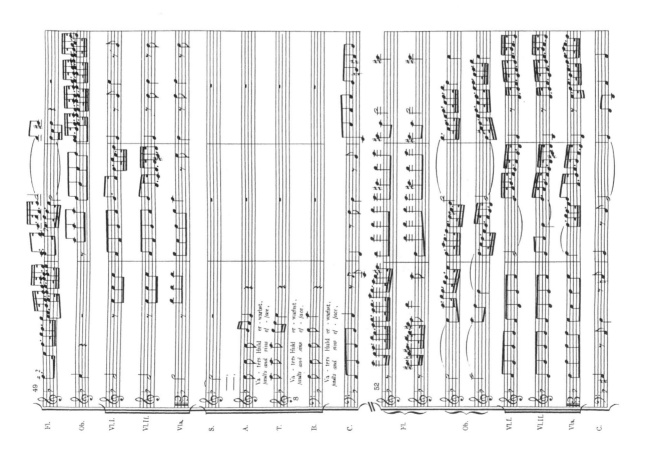

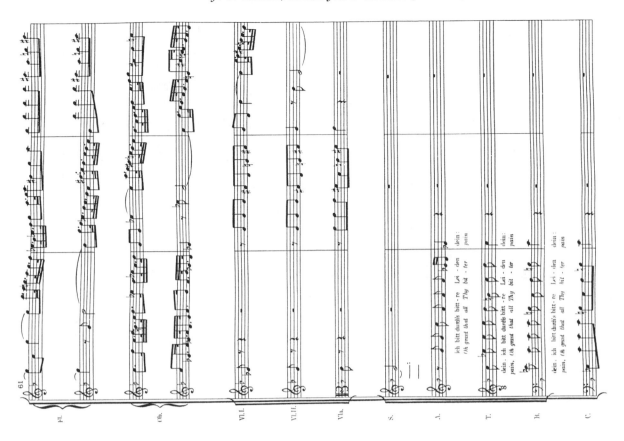

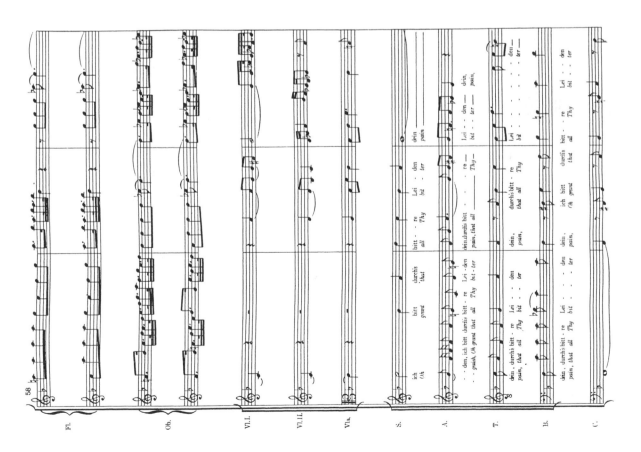

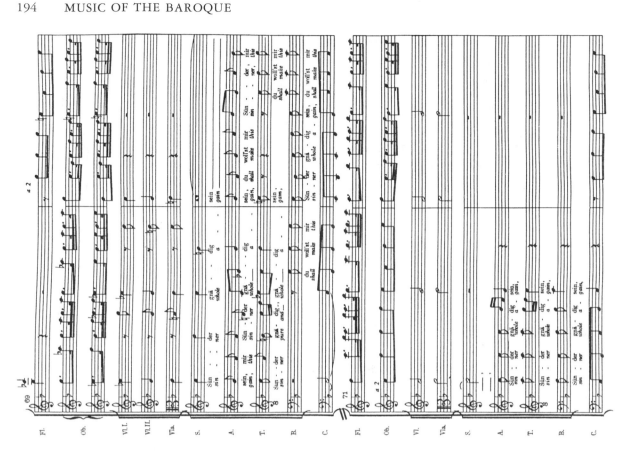

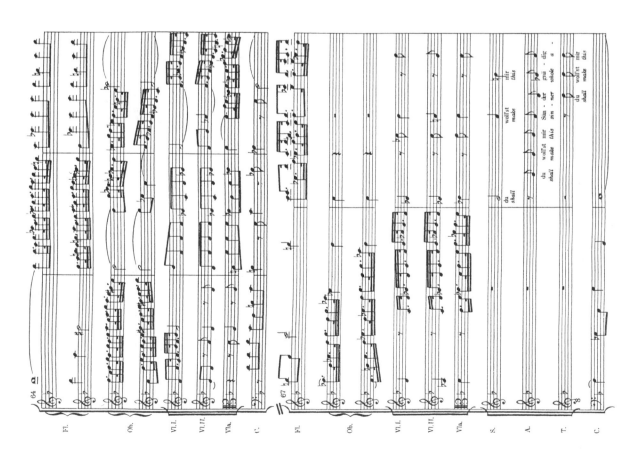

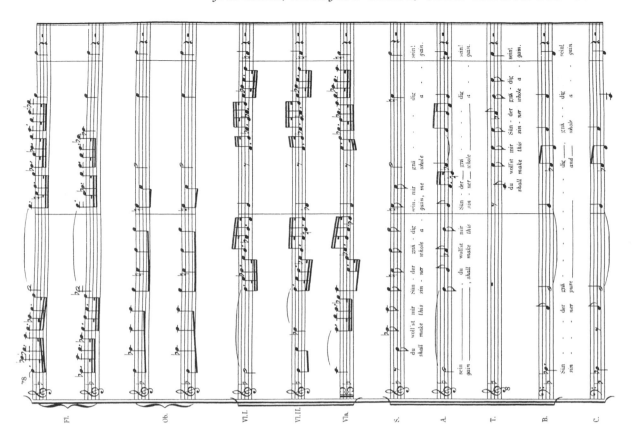

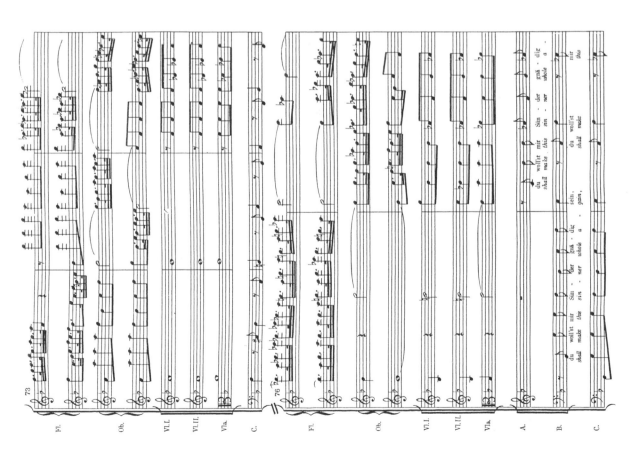

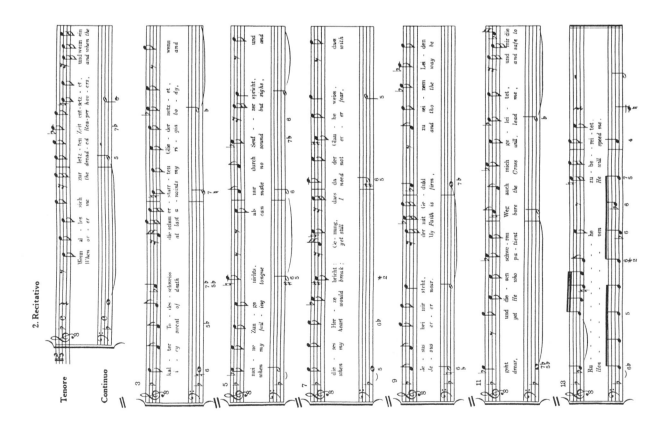

E.E. 6263

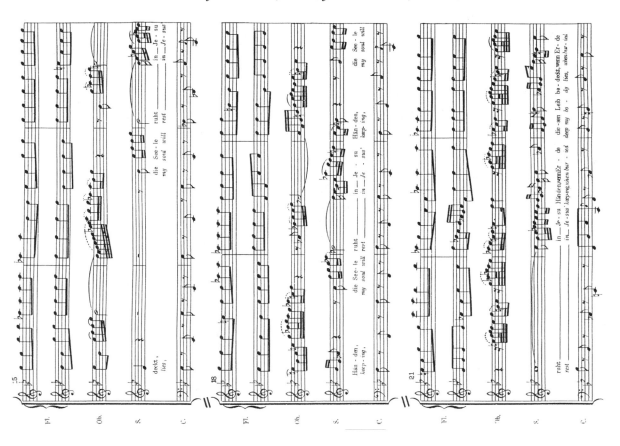

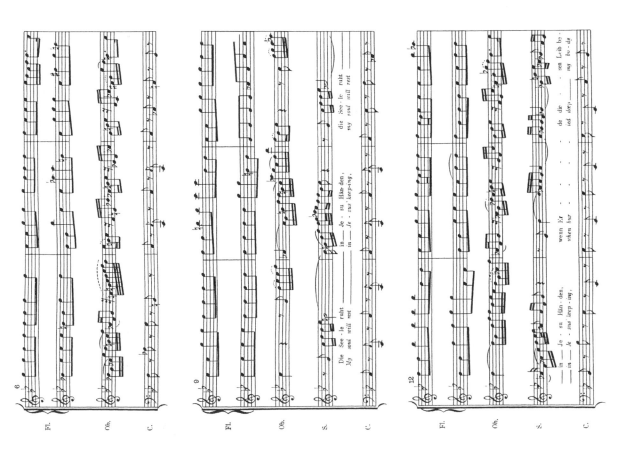

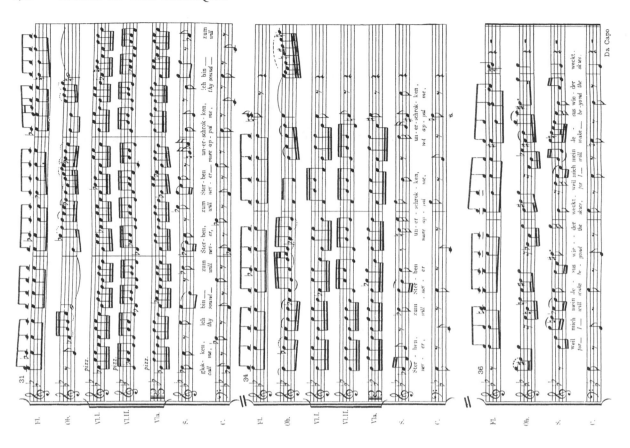

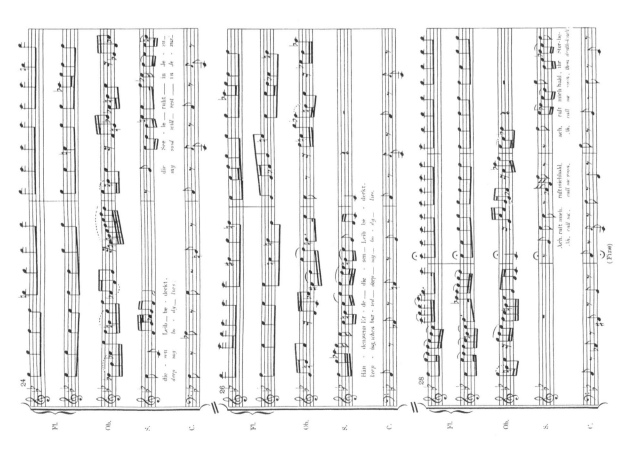

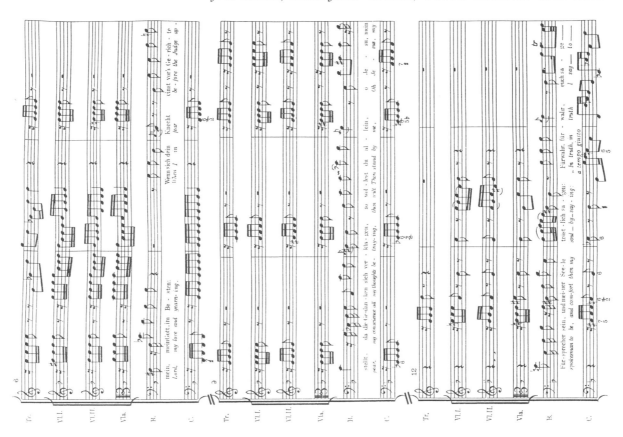

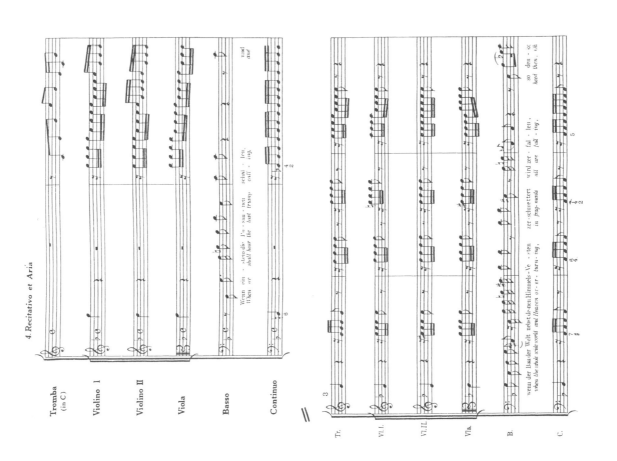

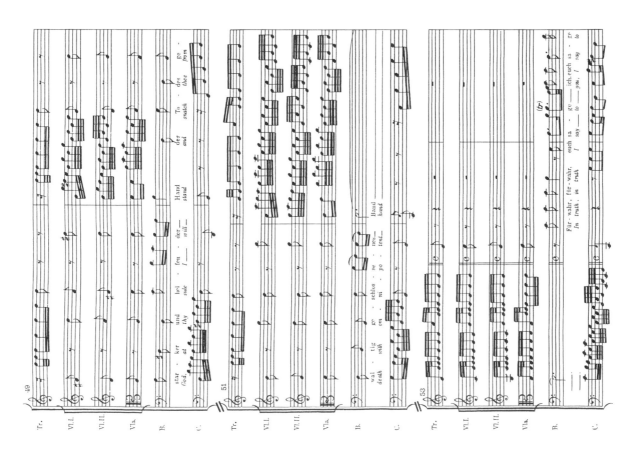

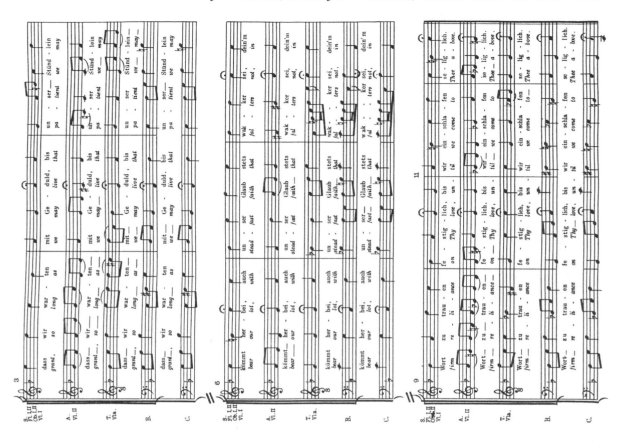

# TEXT AND TRANSLATION

## I.

| | |
|---|---|
| | {Chorus} |
| 1 Herr Jesu Christ, wahr'r Mensch und Gott | Lord Jesus Christ, true man and God, |
| 2 Der du litt'st Marter, Angst und Spott, | You who suffered martyrdom, pain, and scorn, |
| 3 Für mich am Kreuz auch endlich starbst, | [And who] for me on the cross finally died, |
| 4 Und mir dein's Vaters Huld erwarbst, | And for me your father's grace earned, |
| 5 Ich bitt' durch's bitt're Leiden dein: | I pray, by your bitter suffering: |
| 6 Du woll'st mir Sünder gnädig sein. | To me, a sinner, be merciful. |

## II. Recitativ

| | |
|---|---|
| | Recitative |
| 1 Wenn Alles sich zur letzten Zeit entsetzet, | When everything, in the final time, is destroyed, |
| 2 Und wenn ein kalter Todesschweiss | And when a cold deathly sweat |
| 3 Die schon erstarrten Glieder netzet, | The already stiff limbs enwraps, |
| 4 Wenn meine Zunge nichts, als nur durch Seufzer spricht, | When my tongue nothing but sighs speaks, |
| 5 Und dieses Herze bricht: | And this heart breaks: |
| 6 Genug, dass da der Glaube weiss, | [It is] enough that [my] belief knows |
| 7 Dass Jesus bei mir steht, | That Jesus by me stands, |
| 8 Der mit Geduld zu seinem Leiden geht | [He] who with patience to his suffering goes |
| 9 Und diesen schweren Weg auch mich geleitet, | And [along] this hard path leads even me, |
| 10 Und mir die *Ruhe zubereitet.* | And for me *rest prepares.* |

## III. Arie

| | |
|---|---|
| | Aria |
| 1 Die Seele ruht in Jesu Händen | The soul rests in Jesus' hands |
| 2 Wenn Erde diesen Leib bedeckt. | Though earth this body covers. |
| 3 Ach, ruft mich bald, ihr Sterbeglocken, | Ah, call me soon, you funeral bells, |
| 4 Ich bin zum Sterben unerschrocken | I am of death unafraid |
| 5 Weil mich mein Jesus wiederweckt. | So long as my Jesus reawakens me. |

## IV. Recitativ und Arie

| | |
|---|---|
| | Recitative and Aria |
| 1 Wenn einstens die Posaunen schallen, | When one day the trumpet sounds |
| 2 Und wenn der Bau der Welt | And when the span of the world, |
| 3 Nebst denen Himmels-Vesten | With its high solemnities |
| 4 Zerschmettert wird zerfallen, | Shattered, falls to pieces, |

5 Then think, my God, the best [of me]:
6 When your servant before the court of judgment stands,
7 When [his own] thoughts accuse him,
8 Then let you alone,
9 O Jesu, be my advocate,
10 And to my soul comfortingly say:
11 Behold, to you I say:
12 Though heaven and earth in fire [will] disappear
13 [Even] then will a believer forever stand.

14 He will not be condemned
15 And eternal death he will not taste;
16 Only, my child, hold fast to me.
17 I break, with a strong and merciful hand,
18 Of death the powerful encompassing bond.

*Chorale*

Oh Lord, forgive all our sin,
Help us to wait with patience
Until our time comes by,
Let our belief always be stronger,
In your word trusting firmly
Until we fall asleep blessedly.

5 So denke, mein Gott, im Bester:
6 Wenn sich dein Knecht einst vor's Gerichte stellt,
7 Da die Gedanken sich verklagen,
8 So wollest du allein,
9 O Jesu, mein Fürsprecher sein,
10 Und meiner Seele tröstlich sagen:
11 Fürwahr, euch sage ich:
12 Wenn Himmel und Erde im Feuer vergehen
13 So soll doch ein Gläubiger ewig stehen.

14 Er wird nicht kommen in's Gericht
15 Und den Tod ewig schmecken nicht,
16 Nur halte dich, mein Kind, an mich:
17 Ich breche mit starker und helfender Hand
18 Des Todes gewaltig geschlossenes Band.

Fürwahr, euch sage ich . . . .

*V. Choral*

1 Ach Herr, vergieb all' unsre Schuld,
2 Hilf, dass wir warten mit Geduld,
3 Bis unser Stündlein kömmt herbei,
4 Auch unser Glaub' stets wacker sei,
5 Dein'm Wort zu trauen festiglich,
6 Bis wir einschlafen seliglich.

## EDITION

Our edition closely follows Bach's original manuscript score, with the addition of an English text beneath the German This English version has been adapted for singing, and like any such text it is not an exact translation. *To understand the meaning of the German it is essential to use the literal translation given separately above.*

The score reproduces most of Bach's original designations for the instrumental and vocal parts. The two top lines, labeled "flauto," are actually for alto recorders in F; as the edition indicates, their parts were originally notated with a G clef set on the bottom line of the staff, the so-called French violin clef.[25]

---

[25]This was the usual clef for treble instrument parts in France at the time; Bach used it chiefly for recorder parts.

The continuo part includes a number of alternate notes in small notation, as in the opening measures of the third movement (the soprano aria). These alternate notes are for the organ, which at Leipzig in Bach's day was tuned higher than the other instruments. Its lowest note corresponded with low D of the cello, and thus any low Cs occurring in the music had to be played an octave higher, as shown.[26]

## PERFORMANCE ISSUES

The historical performance of Bach's cantatas has been investigated more thoroughly than that of perhaps any other early repertory, leading to discoveries that have provoked controversy in modern times, even though in most cases Bach's practices did not differ from those of his contemporaries. In particular, a strong case has been made for the view that most of these works were composed for vocal forces consisting of a single singer on each part. The instruments, too, were rarely doubled, with the exception of the violin and continuo parts.

Bach usually had an individual part copied out for each player and singer directly from his manuscript score. Often he added dynamics, slurs, and other performance markings to these parts. But because original parts do not survive for the present work, we lack many of Bach's specific performance markings. Nor do we know his exact intentions for such matters as the scoring of the continuo part. The latter generally was played by cello, double bass, and organ, but harpsichord or bassoon joined in certain works. It is possible that the trumpet, explicitly called for only in the fourth movement, also doubled the soprano part (the chorale melody) in the first and last movements. But in that case the player would probably have used a special slide mouthpiece in order to play the tones of the melody that were not normally available on the valveless "natural" brass instrument of Bach's day (f', a', and b').

Apart from issues of scoring, performers must also settle other issues that arise in Baroque works. For example, the dotted eighth notes of the first movement might be "overdotted." The written-out melodic embellishment of the soprano aria probably sounds best with some rhythmic freedom, suggesting improvisation, although this freedom might be applied only to the smaller values. There is little room for real improvisation, but ornaments such as trills might be added at conventionally appropriate places (e.g., movement 3, m. 26, oboe, b♮ on beat 4). The fermatas in the concluding chorale movement may have been merely a way of indicating the ends of phrases. But it is also possible that short pauses were taken at these points, and there was even a tradition of

---

[26]Bach's organist played from a transposing part; thus the organ part for the cantata would have shown the opening movement in E♭ instead of F.

organists' inserting cadenzas at these points during the congregational singing of chorales. The congregation probably would not, however, have joined in the singing of a chorale movement within a cantata.

## SOURCE AND ACKNOWLEDGMENTS

This edition is reproduced from Johann Sebastian Bach, *Herr Jesu Christ, wahr Mensch und Gott, BWV 127*, ed. Hans Grischkat, Die Kantate 10/221 (Hohenheim: Hänssler, 1966), with the kind permission of the publisher.

# 21. George Frideric Handel (1685–1759), *Jephtha*
## (English oratorio: selections)

a. From Part 2, scene 3

31

thy dark womb, and hide me,___ earth, in ___ thy dark womb, and hide me, earth,___ in
*schwar_zen Grund, und birg' mich,___ Erd', im ___ schwar_zen Grund, und birg'mich, Erd',___ im*

35

thy dark womb!
*schwar_zen Grund!*

40                                                                                Fine.

Ere I the name of fa_ther stain, and deep_est woe from con_quest gain,
*Eh' mir mein Va_ter_na_me Fluch, und bit_tres Weh der Sieg mir trug,*

44

ere I the name of fa_ther stain, and deep_est woe from con_quest gain, and deep_est woe from
*eh' mir mein Va_ter_na_me Fluch, und bit_tres Weh der Sieg mir trug, und bit_tres Weh der*

con _ quest gain,　ere　I the __ name of __　fa _ _ther stain,　and deepest woe from con _ quest gain.
*Sieg mir trug,*　*eh'*　*mir mein Va _ ter _*　*na _ _me Fluch,*　*und bit_tres Weh　der　Sieg mir trug.*

*Adagio.*

*Dal Segno.*

b. From Part 2, scene 4

## TEXT

*a. From Part 2, scene 3*

### Jephtha

Horror! confusion! harsh this music grates
Upon my tasteless* ears. —Be gone, my child,          *unable to sense anything pleasurable
Thou hast undone the father. Fly, be gone,
And leave me to the rack* of wild despair.          *torment

[ARIA]

1 Open thy marble jaws, O tomb,
2 And hide me, earth, in thy dark womb!
3     Ere I the name of father stain,
4     And deepest woe from conquest gain.

*b. From Part 2, scene 4*

### Chorus

  1 How dark, O Lord, are thy decrees!
  2 All hid from mortal sight!
  3 All our joys to sorrow turning,
  4 And our triumphs into mourning,
  5 As the night succeeds the day.
  6 No certain bliss,
  7 No solid peace,
  8 We mortals know
  9 On earth below.
 10 Yet on this maxim still obey:
 11 Whatever is, is right.

—Thomas Morell (with additions)

## EDITION

As with Handel's *Orlando* (Selection 18), our score is from the nineteenth-century edition of the composer's complete works. It is based on Handel's autograph manuscript, but the bottom two staves of each system contain the editor's piano arrangement of the orchestral parts; in the recitative these staves contain an editorial continuo realization. The dynamic indications in this part are also editorial.

In Jephtha's aria, *violini unisoni* means that the two violin parts play together at the beginning (but they divide in the B section). The staff designated "bassi" by the editor is the continuo part, but in the chorus the word *basso* refers to the bass voices of the choir. In the choral movement, the lower strings play along with the keyboard continuo on the part designated *organo* (organ).

## PERFORMANCE ISSUES

Handel would have directed the original performances of this work from the harpsichord, playing continuo throughout. The choir probably comprised a number of boy sopranos for the top part, plus several adult men on each of the three lower parts (altos singing the higher notes falsetto).[27] Continuo for the recitative was probably confined

---

[27]Although the top choral staff is labeled *Canto I. II.*, there is only one soprano part.

to harpsichord, perhaps joined by a single cello; the string orchestra employed in the aria probably included several players on each part, including a few violas that doubled the continuo an octave higher. An organ would have entered with the choir in the chorus.

The style and dramatic situation of Jephtha's aria clearly make improvisatory embellishment inappropriate. But at least a few cadential trills would surely have been heard (e.g., on f♯ in m. 53). Handel's tempo mark for the aria is unusually precise for a Baroque work ("With spirit, but not quick"). In the chorus, on the other hand, *largo*, which literally means "broad," might signify a spacious sort of performance but not necessarily a very slow one. *Larghetto* is probably somewhat faster; *a tempo ordinario* ("at a regular speed") refers to a moderate pace that was thought appropriate to solemn or weighty movements. In the final section, the repeated notes in the strings bear slurs (in mm. 114–15). These slurs, which should probably be extended to the entire section, signify a Baroque technique known as bow vibrato, in which the repetitions are produced by rhythmically pressing the stick (wood) of the bow with the first finger of the right hand, without any cessation of sound.

## SOURCE

The edition is reproduced from Georg Friedrich Händel, *Jephtha: Oratorium*, ed. Friedrich Chrysander, *Werke*, vol. 44 (Leipzig: Deutsche Händelgesellschaft, 1886), which is based primarily on the composer's autograph score.[28]

---

[28]London, British Library, R.M. 20.e.9; the editor Chrysander had published a now-rare facsimile edition in 1885 (Hamburg: Deutsche Händelgesellschaft).

## 22. Girolamo Frescobaldi (1583–1643), Toccata IX (from *Libro* 1)

Toccata Nona

## EDITION

This work was originally published in the standard Italian keyboard notation of the sixteenth and seventeenth centuries: two staves, as in modern notation, but with six and eight lines, respectively, on the upper and lower staves. This edition retains the original barlines, which correspond to what we would call $\frac{4}{2}$ time.

## PERFORMANCE ISSUES

The performing medium is specified by the title of the collection in which the toccata first appeared: harpsichord (or organ in later editions). The original publication included a preface by the composer that described a number of points about its performance. Among the most important points are the need for varying the tempo in accordance with the affect or expressive character of each passage, and the use of small pauses or ritards at cadences and at the ends of written-out embellishments. Other contemporary treatises describe such matters as fingering and the performance of ornaments such as trills, many of which were written out by the composer in this piece.

## SOURCE

The work was first published in Frescobaldi's *Toccate e partite d'intavolatura di cimbalo . . . libro primo* (Rome: Bordoni, 1615); a second edition appeared in 1616.[29] The choice of organ in place of harpsichord is offered in editions of 1628 and 1637.

---

[29]The edition reproduced here first appeared as Girolamo Frescobaldi, *Orgel- und Klavierwerke . . . Band III: Das erste Buch der Toccaten, Partiten usw. 1637 {sic}*, ed. Pierre Pidoux (Kassel: Bärenreiter, [1948]), 32–35.

# 23. Johann Jacob Froberger (1616–1667), Suite X in A minor

ALLEMANDE

## GIGUE

COURANTE

## SARABANDA

## EDITION

Froberger is thought to have been a student of Frescobaldi, and his toccatas employ the Italian keyboard notation of the latter, with its staves of six or more lines. Froberger's suites, however, are in the French style, in accordance with which Froberger used the modern five-line staff. The editor has converted the clefs to the modern treble and bass, but otherwise our edition is a very close transcription of the composer's manuscript (see below). The time signature "C3" used in the last three movements is the equivalent of modern $\frac{6}{4}$ or $\frac{3}{2}$.

## PERFORMANCE ISSUES

Like much Baroque keyboard music preserved only in manuscript, Froberger's suite lacks ornament signs. Precisely what ornaments would have been used in 1656, the date of the surviving manuscript, is uncertain, but they would have broadly resembled those indicated in later French-style keyboard music (see Selection 29 below). By the same token, the precise nature of the instruments for which Froberger conceived the piece is uncertain, but his first choice was probably a type of harpsichord fairly close to the French-style harpsichords of the eighteenth century that have been widely reproduced in our own time—as opposed to the more strident but less resonant Italian instruments of the seventeenth and eighteenth centuries.

Tempo was largely dictated by the traditional characteristics of each of the four dance movements. The allemande, however, was no longer a true dance during Froberger's lifetime and was probably played very freely, like an improvised prelude (see Selection 24). In the last four measures of the gigue, notated in "C," the half note is probably meant to be equal in duration to a dotted half in the preceding measures, although the equivalence should perhaps be treated freely.

## SOURCES AND ACKNOWLEDGMENTS

This edition is reproduced with the permission of the publisher from Johann Jakob Froberger, *Oeuvres complètes pour clavecin I: Livres de 1649, 1656 et 1658*, ed. Howard Schott, Le pupitre 57 (Paris: Heugel, 1979). The source for the edition was the composer's autograph manuscript of 1656 in Vienna, Österreichische Nationalbibliothek, Musiksammlung, Mus. Hs. 18707.[30]

---

[30]Facsimile in Robert Hill, ed., *Seventeenth Century Keyboard Music*, vol. 3/2 (New York: Garland, 1988).

## 24. Elizabeth-Claude Jacquet de La Guerre (1665–1729), *Prélude* from Suite III in A minor

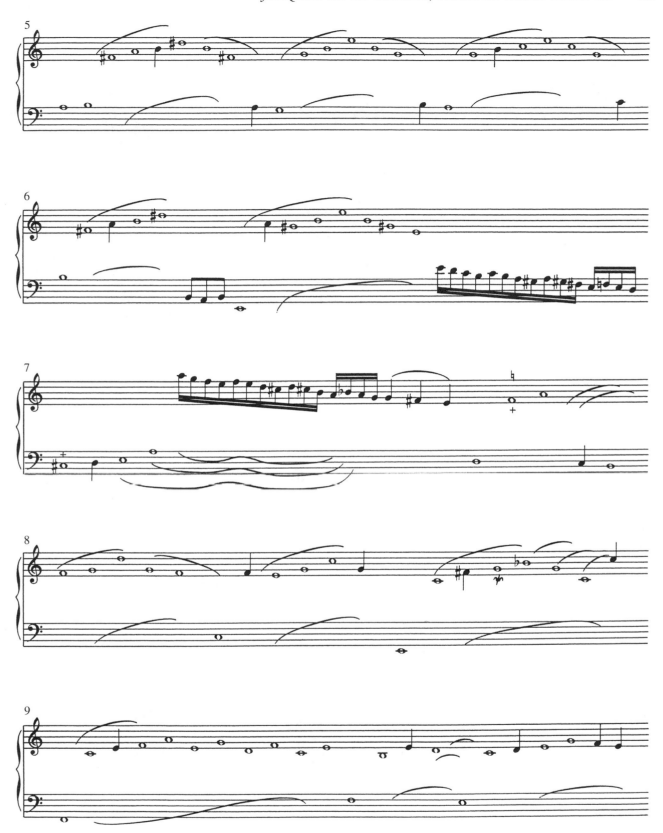

## PERFORMANCE ISSUES

This edition is a literal transcription of the original edition, which uses the unbarred notation characteristic of the unmeasured prelude. In this notation, what appear as whole notes are in fact notes of indeterminate value that might be played either quickly or slowly, depending on context and the performer's choice. A note followed by a slur is held for the length of the slur; similarly, notes drawn beneath a single slur are all sustained. In the latter case, the notes under the slur usually belong to a single harmony. Indeed, most of the piece consists of arpeggiated or broken chords, the "whole" notes representing chord tones and the other (smaller) note values serving as decorations. A few ornaments are indicated by symbols: the cross or plus sign (+) is an appoggiatura or *port de voix*, whereas the mordent or *pincé* is indicated by the customary squiggle cut by a slash (as on the second note of the lower staff; see Selection 29).

## SOURCES AND ACKNOWLEDGMENTS

This edition is reproduced with permission of the publisher from Elisabeth-Claude Jacquet de La Guerre, *Pièces de clavecin*, ed. Carol Henry Bates, Le pupitre 66 (Paris: Heugel, 1986). The latter is based on the first edition (long believed to have been lost): *Pièces de clavecin de Mad^elle de La Guerre . . . Premier Livre* (Paris, 1687).

**25.** Dietrich Buxtehude (ca. 1637–1707), *Nun bitten wir den heiligen Geist*, BuxWV 208 (chorale prelude)

## EDITION

Buxtehude's original notation for this piece was probably in the form of an organ *tablature*, in which notes and rhythms are indicated by letters and other symbols, without staff lines. The modern edition is based on an eighteenth-century manuscript in score notation, and the editor has distributed the notes onto three staves. The top staff is for the right hand, playing the decorated chorale cantus firmus on a solo manual; the middle staff is for the left hand, playing the two inner voices on a quieter accompanimental manual; and the feet play the bass, notated on the bottom staff, on the pedals.

## PERFORMANCE ISSUES

The chorale text is a prayer for deliverance and redemption (see Selection 26), suggesting a quiet registration overall. The three functional elements of the score would each have been played on a separate keyboard with its own registration: a relatively prominent soprano melody, quiet inner voices, and a distinct bass line. Although this score employs several French ornament signs, it is uncertain precisely how a German Baroque organist would have realized these signs or whether other contemporary French conventions, such as *notes inégales*, would have been applied. Fingering and pedal technique were probably quite different from those used today; in particular, Baroque organists rarely used the heels of the feet, confining their pedal technique to the toes and therefore using a primarily nonlegato type of articulation.

## SOURCE

The edition reproduced here is from *Dietrich Buxtehude: Werke für Orgel*, ed. Philipp Spitta, rev. Max Seiffert, vol. 2 (Leipzig: Breitkopf und Härtel, 1904); it is based on a manuscript copy by the German organist-composer Johann Gottfried Walther (1684–1748).[31]

---

[31]Berlin, Staatsbibliothek, Mus. ms. 22541/3.

## 26. Johann Sebastian Bach (1685–1750), *Nun bitten wir den heiligen Geist*, BWV 385 (four-part chorale setting)

### TEXT AND TRANSLATION

1 Nun bitten wir den heiligen Geist,      Now pray we to the Holy Spirit
2 Um den rechten Glauben allermeist,      For true belief above all,
3 Daß er uns behüte      That we should be protected
4 An unserm Ende      Until our end,
5 Wenn wir heimfahr'n aus diesen Elende.      When we come home from these miseries.
6 Kyrie eleis.      Lord have mercy.

—Martin Luther

## EDITION

This is one of the 371 Bach chorale settings published in 1784–87 by his son and student Carl Philipp Emanuel Bach.[32] Although many of these were drawn from Bach's cantatas and other sacred vocal works, this is one of about 185 whose source is unknown; some scholars believe that these settings come from lost cantatas. Among the earliest of Bach's vocal works to be printed, they were issued for study purposes, without their texts. This edition adds the first stanza of the text traditionally associated with this melody and transposes the entire setting down one step (from A major) for easier comparison with Buxtehude's setting (Selection 25).

---

[32] *Johann Sebastian Bachs vierstimmige Choralgesänge*, 4 vols. (Leipzig: Breitkopf). There have been many reprints; the most recent and most scholarly is Johann Sebastian Bach, *Choräle und Geistliche Lieder*, vol. 2, *Choräle: Der Sammlung C. P. E. Bach nach dem Druck von 1764–1787*, ed. Frieder Rempp, *Neue Ausgabe sämtlicher Werke*, III/2.2 (Kassel: Bärenreiter, 1996).

## 27. Dietrich Buxtehude (ca. 1637–1707), Praeludium in A minor, BuxWV 153

## EDITION

Like Selection 25, this work probably was first notated in tablature, but in the absence of surviving seventeenth-century manuscripts it has been edited from an eighteenth-century copy in staff notation. The latter employs just two staves, including the pedal part as the lowest voice on the bottom staff. This edition, like most modern editions of organ music, sets the bass apart on its own staff.

## PERFORMANCE ISSUES

A *praeludium* was traditionally played *cum organo pleno*, that is, using the full resources of the German Baroque organ to produce a massive sound. Contrast might have been produced by lightening the registration for one or more sections (e.g., the second fugue, mm. 67–104), but Baroque organs did not permit the frequent changes of timbre or dynamic level that are possible on many later instruments, nor does the music require them.

## SOURCE

The edition reproduced here is from Dietrich Buxtehude, *Werke für Orgel*, ed. Philipp Spitta, rev. Max Seiffert, vol. 1 (Leipzig: Breitkopf und Härtel, 1903); it is based on the eighteenth-century manuscript Berlin, Staatsbibliothek, Mus. ms. 2681.

**28.** Johann Sebastian Bach (1685–1750), Prelude and Fugue in G from *The Well-Tempered Clavier*, Part 1

## EDITION

This edition is based on Bach's autograph manuscript of 1722 containing the entire first part of the *Well-Tempered Clavier*.[33] The source is a so-called fair copy, meaning that Bach had copied it from an earlier manuscript (perhaps his original composing score) now lost. Indeed, a dozen or more manuscript copies by other eighteenth-century musicians may also have derived from the lost older autograph; one of these preserved an earlier version of the prelude that is four measures shorter.[34]

The unusual position of the key signature in the upper staff reflects that in Bach's manuscript (where this staff uses soprano clef). In the prelude, the apparent conflict between the time signatures of the two staves is merely a shorthand for the notation of triplets: each eighth note in common time is worth three sixteenths in $\frac{24}{16}$.

## PERFORMANCE ISSUES

Bach does not specify a keyboard instrument, and both prelude and fugue could be played on clavichord, harpsichord, piano, or even organ, although harpsichord was probably the composer's first choice. The two hands cross somewhat awkwardly in the prelude, in measures 2–3. But this does not necessarily indicate the use of two keyboards, such as were present on some harpsichords. Bach wrote the work primarily for study, and thus the prelude might often have been played separately from the fugue. Tempo and expressive character must be determined from the music; the lively style and brilliant figuration of both movements suggest a quick tempo and, on the harpsichord, a strong (loud) registration throughout. An ornament table in the Little Notebook for Wilhelm Friedemann Bach provides an introductory guide to the ornament signs in the fugue, although other contemporary music and treatises furnish valuable suggestions as well (see Selection 29).

## SOURCE

This edition is reproduced from *Joh. Seb. Bach's Clavierwerke*, vol. 3, *Das Wohltemperierte Clavier*, ed. Franz Kroll, *Johann Sebastian Bach's Werke* 14 (Leipzig: Bach-Gesellschaft, 1866), 52–56.

---

[33]Berlin, Staatsbibliothek, Mus. ms. Bach P 415.

[34]This earlier version lacks mm. 7b–8a and 14b–17a; it was found in the so-called Konwitschny manuscript, now lost but preserved on microfilm.

**29.** Jean-Henri D'Anglebert (1628–1691), François Couperin (1668–1733), and Jean-Philippe Rameau (1683–1764), Extracts from Ornament Tables

| ORNAMENT NAME | ORNAMENT SIGN AND REALIZATION | | |
|---|---|---|---|
| | D'Anglebert (1689) | Rameau (1724) | Couperin (1716) |

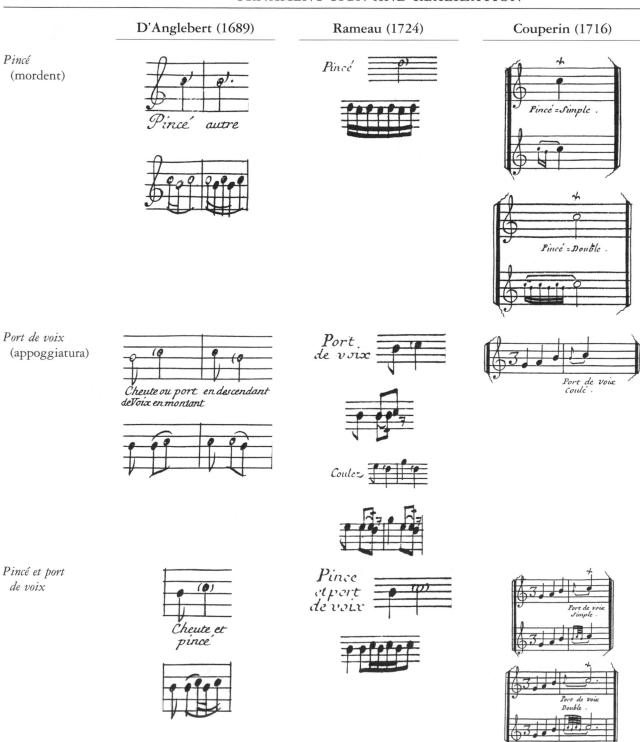

**ORNAMENT
NAME**

**ORNAMENT SIGN AND REALIZATION**

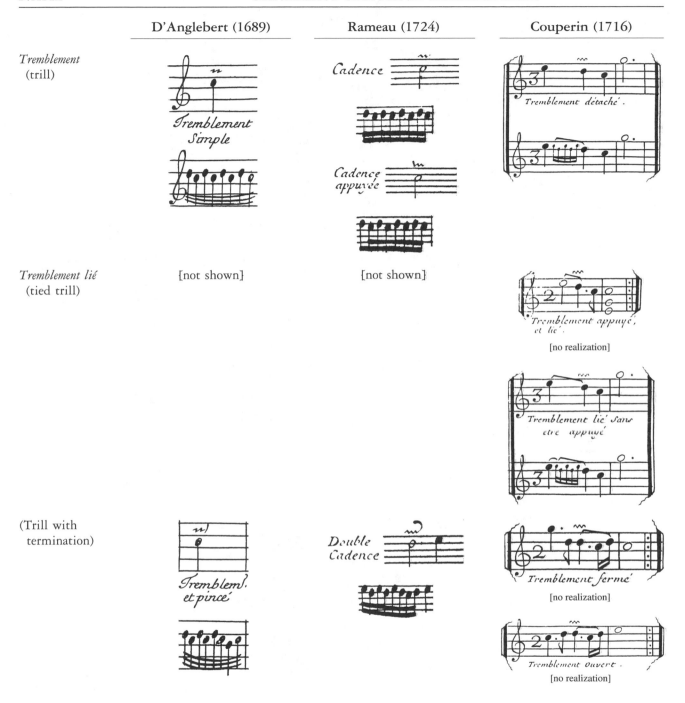

| | D'Anglebert (1689) | Rameau (1724) | Couperin (1716) |

*Tremblement*
(trill)

*Tremblement lié*
(tied trill)

(Trill with
termination)

## ORNAMENT NAME

### ORNAMENT SIGN AND REALIZATION

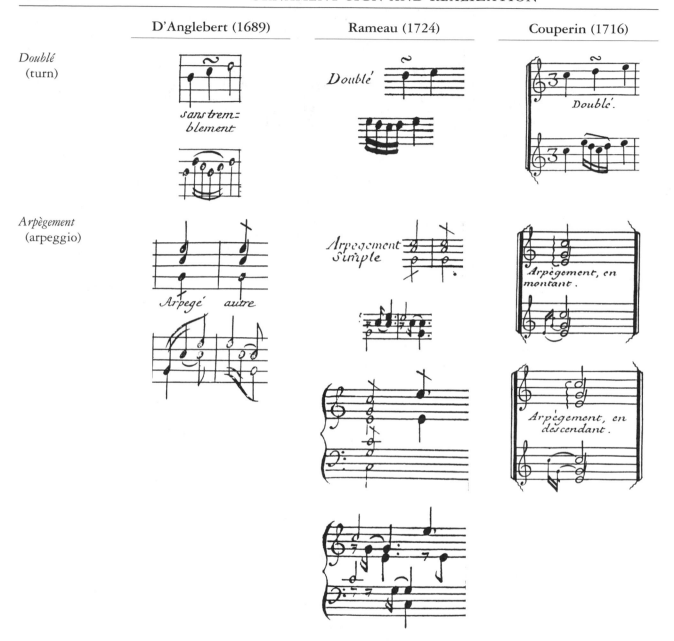

| | D'Anglebert (1689) | Rameau (1724) | Couperin (1716) |
|---|---|---|---|
| *Doublé* (turn) | | | |
| *Arpègement* (arpeggio) | | | |

| ORNAMENT NAME | ORNAMENT SIGN AND REALIZATION | | |
|---|---|---|---|
| | D'Anglebert (1689) | Rameau (1724) | Couperin (1716) |

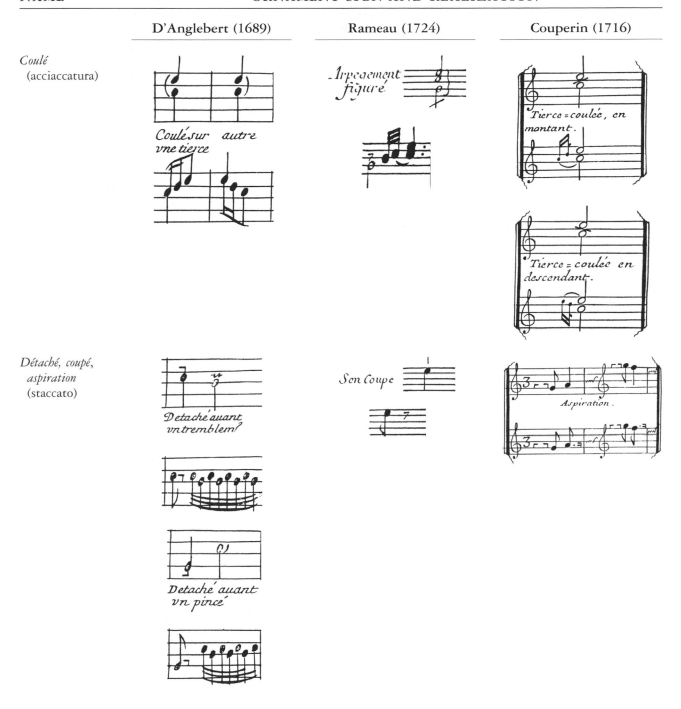

*Coulé*
(acciaccatura)

*Détaché, coupé,
aspiration*
(staccato)

## PERFORMANCE ISSUES

Detailed attention to ornaments was typical of Baroque performance in general, but it was especially cultivated in France. Keyboard music tended to be particularly precise in the notation of ornamentation through symbols, but the same ornaments were used by all musicians, including singers.

These extracts are from the ornament tables that were included in three published collections of French Baroque harpsichord pieces. Each shows both the ornament sign and its performance or realization. Probably none of the realizations should be taken literally. The somewhat different signs, names, and realizations for each ornament given by these three French composers suggest that what is shown in each case is only a suggestion of what a good musician might have actually played. Certain common principles are nevertheless apparent. For example, trills normally start on the upper note, not the main one, and most ornaments seem to start on the beat.

## SOURCES

The examples are reproduced from D'Anglebert's *Pièces de clavecin* (Paris, 1689), Rameau's *Pièces de clavessin* (Paris, 1724), and Couperin's *Pièces de clavecin . . . Premier livre* (Paris, 1713).[35] Rameau's work was published after Couperin's, but his ornament signs are illustrated in the middle column because of their closer similarity to those of D'Anglebert in column 1.

---

[35] All have been published in facsimile (New York: Broude).

**30.** François Couperin (1668–1733), *Vingt-unième ordre*
(selections)

a. *La reine des coeurs*

b. *La Couperin*

D'une vivacité moderée

## EDITION

Our score is based on the first edition. Modern clefs have been substituted, but otherwise the music retains much of the appearance of the original. Even the shapes of the ornament signs and slurs have been specially engraved to resemble the elegant but somewhat angular forms of Couperin's original publication.

## PERFORMANCE ISSUES

Unlike Bach's keyboard music, these pieces are unambiguously intended for the harpsichord—specifically the large, resonant French type of the early eighteenth century. A technique particularly idiomatic on such instruments is the so-called *overlegato*, whereby certain notes are held beyond their written lengths in order to blend together with the notes that follow. In some cases, Couperin indicates this through the use of extra stems on the noteheads (as in *La reine des cœurs*, left hand, mm. 3–7). Slurs can have the same meaning, even where the notes are adjacent (as in the *port de voix* in the right hand, m. 3).

Naturally, a performer must consider as well the many other conventions of the French style, including *notes inégales* and overdotting. Also notable here are Couperin's unusually precise tempo markings. It goes without saying that a player should also consult Couperin's ornament table (see Selection 29) as well as his treatise *L'art de toucher le clavecin* (The art of playing the harpsichord).[36]

## SOURCES AND ACKNOWLEDGMENTS

This edition is reproduced with the permission of the publisher from François Couperin, *Pièces de clavecin: Quatrième livre*, ed. Kenneth Gilbert (Paris: Heugel, 1970). The source for the edition was Couperin's *Quatrième livre de pièces de clavecin* (Paris, 1730).

---

[36]Paris, 1716; 2d ed., 1717; English trans. by Mevanwy Roberts as *The Art of Playing the Harpsichord* (Wiesbaden: Breitkopf und Härtel, 1961).

## 31. Jean-Philippe Rameau (1683–1764), Suite in G from *Nouvelles suites de clavecin* (selections)

a. *Les sauvages*

b. *L'Egiptienne*

# EDITION

Our score is a facsimile of the original edition. The notation is essentially identical to that of modern scores; it is necessary only to understand a few abbreviations and certain conventions regarding repeated material.

In the first piece, *Les sauvages*, the first section (mm. 1–16) should probably be repeated. One then plays the second section (mm. 17–32) and a repeat of the first section. The third section (mm. 33–48) follows, and one concludes by again repeating the first section, ending in measure 16 at the word *fin* (end). The word *reprise* in measure 17 is puzzling, since in French Baroque keyboard music it was more often applied to the second half of a binary form (as in *L'Egiptienne*). Possibly the expression *1$^{er}$ couplet* (first couplet) was intended here, with *2$^{e}$ couplet* (second couplet) meant to follow in measure 33.

*L'Egiptienne* is in binary form, meaning that the two halves are each repeated. The last two measures of the first half are joined by curved lines that look like slurs or ties. Actually, these are a common eighteenth-century way of indicating first and second endings at a repeat.

Also in this piece, one should observe the hand crossings, which are indicated by the abbreviations "g." (for *main gauche*, left hand) and "d." (*main droite*, right hand).

# PERFORMANCE ISSUES

The same considerations arise here as in Selection 30, despite the more virtuosic, perhaps more Italianate, style of the music.

# SOURCE

The music is reproduced from Rameau's *Nouvelles suites de pièces de clavecin* (Paris, ca. 1728).

## 32. Domenico Scarlatti (1685–1757), Two Sonatas in A, K. 181–82

### K. 181

# K. 182

## EDITION

The edition is a literal transcription of the principal manuscript source (see below). Hand crossings in K. 182 are indicated by letter abbreviations, as in Selection 31b; "D" and "G" stand for "right hand" and "left hand," respectively.

## PERFORMANCE ISSUES

There are no eighteenth-century Italian or Spanish writings on keyboard performance comparable to the French and German ones that inform our understanding of the music of Couperin, Bach, and their compatriots. Thus it is somewhat less clear how to interpret the ornament signs and other aspects of Scarlatti's scores. Even the instrumentation has been cast in doubt by arguments favoring the use of the fortepiano, although the one-manual Italian-style harpsichord used throughout the seventeenth and eighteenth centuries in southern Europe was probably the most common choice for these pieces. Such instruments encourage a generally lively and relatively detached (non-legato) manner of playing that seems in keeping with the spirit of the music.

## SOURCES AND ACKNOWLEDGMENTS

This edition is reproduced with the permission of the publisher from Domenico Scarlatti, *Sonates*, vol. 4, *K. 156–205*, ed. Kenneth Gilbert, Le pupitre 34 (Paris: Heugel, 1976). The edition is based on the eighteenth-century manuscript Parma, Biblioteca Palatina, Sezione Musicale, AG 31407 (known as Parma II), nos. 10–11.

## 33. Biagio Marini (ca. 1587–1663), Sonata for violin and continuo, *La variata*

## EDITION

Our score is based on the first edition, which included both a violin part and a score for the continuo player. Barlines, absent or irregularly placed in the original, have been regularized to modern usage, and the editor has also revised the notation of the triple-time sections at measures 38 and 59, substituting smaller note values. The changes of "key" signature at measures 16 and 87 are original, although they were probably understood as representing different transpositions of the Dorian or Aeolian mode rather than changes of tonality in the modern sense. The word *tardo* at measure 95 occurs in the original score and would seem to signify a ritard. But it might have been misplaced (intended for m. 101), or merely a warning not to execute the three eighth notes in measure 95 at the same speed as the preceding thirty-seconds.

## PERFORMANCE ISSUES

This sonata was published as part of a large collection of instrumental music, much of it (including this work) suitable for performance as part of a church service as well as in domestic (chamber) settings. Hence organ as well as harpsichord or lute is a possible choice for the continuo instrument. The violin employed here was the early Baroque version of the modern instrument; Marini's music reveals sophisticated use of bowings, double stops, and high notes up to e''' (probably played in third position, with extension).

The style resembles that of a keyboard toccata in its frequent changes of character. Tempo changes are largely written into the music, as in the use of large note values at the beginning and much shorter ones in measures 8–12. It is uncertain whether the time signatures imply precise tempo relationships between the sections; Marini might have expected considerable freedom in this regard. Thus the editorial equivalences marked at several points should be taken only as suggestions.

## SOURCE AND ACKNOWLEDGMENTS

Our edition is reproduced with kind permission of the publisher from Biagio Marini, *String Sonatas from Opus 1 and Opus 8*, ed. Thomas D. Dunn, Collegium Musicum: Yale University, 2d ser., vol. 10 (Madison, Wis.: A-R Editions, 1981). The edition is based on Marini's *Sonate symphoniae . . . Opera ottava* (Venice: Magni, 1626).

## 34. Hans Ignaz Franz Biber (1644–1704), "Mystery" Sonata no. 9 in A minor for *scordatura* violin and continuo

## EDITION

The score reproduces an early twentieth-century edition based on the sole surviving manuscript copy of the work. The latter is a score, but because of the *scordatura* or "mis"-tuning of the violin (indicated at the beginning of the first system), it shows not the pitches that one hears but rather the notes that the violinist fingers. In this work only the two lowest strings of the violin are affected—that is, notes written below a′. Because these are used relatively infrequently it is possible to read the violin part with less trouble than in some of the other pieces from this collection, which use more radical *scordatura*.

In the opening system, for example, only two notes are transposed; in measure 4 written f♯′–d′ sounds as g♯′–e′. Similarly, in measures 8–9 the actual pitches are a′ (tied), e′–f′–g′–f′–e′. In the double stops in the first line of the courante, the notes are f′/a′ (m. 2), d′/g′–f′ (m. 4), and c′/e′ (m. 5).

## PERFORMANCE ISSUES

*Scordatura* creates technical challenges for the violinist, since the irregular tuning results in abnormal physical tensions on the strings, making good intonation and even bowing somewhat more difficult than usual. Otherwise, the interpretive issues of the work are similar to those raised in other virtuoso seventeenth-century violin music.

It is uncertain what continuo instruments might have been used in this work. The sacred image in the surviving manuscript ("Christ on the Way to Calvary") implies church performance and thus use of the organ. But the presence of a dance movement suggests that the piece might not originally have been composed for sacred use. Even in church, accompaniment by harpsichord or lute, perhaps joined by bass viola da gamba, would not be out of the question. In any case, the editorial realization of the figured bass in this edition is probably more elaborate than Biber would have expected. This is especially true in the section marked *Finale*, which is composed largely over a dominant pedal point. Here an organist might have held the first chord for a couple of beats and then rested, sustaining only the bass note until three measures before the end, where the figures call for specific chords.[37]

Although the courante and its variations constitute a distinct movement, the entire work can be played without any significant breaks. The virtuoso figuration in the opening and closing sections implies considerable rhythmic freedom. The abbreviation *t* in the violin part stands for *tremolo*, which in seventeenth-century usage is the equivalent of our "trill," although unlike most eighteenth-century trills it often started on the main note, not on the upper neighbor.

## SOURCE

The edition is taken from Heinrich Franz Biber, *Sechzehn Violinsonaten*, ed. Erwin Luntz, Denkmäler der Tonkunst in Österreich 25 (Vienna, 1905), 38–43. The manuscript source is Munich, Bayerische Staatsbibliothek, Mus. ms. 4123.[38]

---

[37]Later composers indicated the omission of a realization through the words *tasto solo* at the beginning of a pedal point.

[38]Facsimile with commentary by Ernst Kubitschek, 2 vols. (Bad Reichenhall: Comes, 1990).

**35.** Arcangelo Corelli (1653–1713), Sonata in D for two violins and continuo, op. 2, no. 1

*Preludio.*

## Allemanda.

## EDITION

This is a nineteenth-century edition based on Corelli's original publication together with some of its numerous later reprints. It contains small deviations from the original, particularly in the figures for the continuo part, but is otherwise very close to what Corelli presumably wrote. The original publication consisted of a set of three partbooks, each containing all twelve sonatas of Opus 2.

The editorial tempo mark for the first movement is incorrect; the first edition specifies *Adagio*. In addition, our score omits the indication *Da Capo* at the end of the last movement, suggesting that the latter is to be repeated in its entirety.

## PERFORMANCE ISSUES

The word *violone* probably indicates a cello or related instrument, not the double bass instrument designated by that term today. In Corelli's Rome the *cembalo* would naturally have been an Italian-style harpsichord. The original edition actually called for violone *or* harpsichord (*violone o cimbalo*), suggesting that the figured bass realization is optional. It is uncertain how often such works would have been played as string trios without keyboard.

The *largo* marking of the second movement probably does not imply so slow a speed as it does in later music. In all four movements, Corelli no doubt expected the two violinists to embellish their parts, listening carefully to one another and imitating whatever trills, scales, and other figuration the other might introduce.

## SOURCE

The score is reproduced from *Les œuvres de Arcangelo Corelli*, ed. J. Joachim and F. Chrysander, 5 vols. (London: Augener, 1888–91), 1:75–77. The first edition was entitled *Sonate de camera* (Rome: Mutii, 1685).

## 36. Arcangelo Corelli (1653–1713), Sonata in C for violin and continuo, op. 5, no. 3

## EDITION

Our score is reproduced from the same nineteenth-century edition as Selection 35. The editor has combined the score published as the first edition with the embellished version of the violin part published by the Amsterdam printer Estienne Roger in 1710. The latter is shown on the staff labeled "Corelli's Graces," echoing Roger's claim that the embellishments were "composed by Corelli as he plays them."[39]

## PERFORMANCE ISSUES

Roger gave embellishments only for the two slow movements, but it is likely that players added ornaments elsewhere as well. Roger claimed in a catalogue of works for sale that he possessed letters from the composer proving that these were Corelli's own embellishments. These documents do not survive, but in any case it seems unlikely that Corelli would have always played the same improvisatory embellishments. Surely, most good players would have varied the embellishments from one performance to the next. Hence these "graces"—an old expression for "ornaments"—were probably intended to serve primarily as models for inexperienced players to imitate.

The fugue (second movement) contains difficult multiple stops for the violinist. Those involving just two notes are self-explanatory. Chords of three or four notes (as in mm. 17–18) were probably executed differently from similar chords in later violin music. The lowest note was probably placed on the beat, not before it, and the bow drawn over the strings smoothly, without holding out the lower notes in a momentary double stop (as in modern technique). Unfortunately, Roger did not indicate how the violinist is to play the passage at the close of the second movement, where Corelli marked *Arpeggio* (mm. 46–50). Some sort of rapidly broken chords was apparently intended, despite the notation with ties (which misleadingly suggests sustained notes).

## SOURCES

Our edition is reproduced from *Les œuvres de Arcangelo Corelli*, ed. J. Joachim and F. Chrysander, 5 vols. (London: Augener, 1888–91), 3:26–35. The original edition was entitled *Sonate a violino e violono o cimbalo* (Rome: Pietra Santa, 1700).[40]

---

[39]The title of Roger's edition reads: *Sonate a violino e violone o cimbalo . . . Troisieme edition ou l'on a joint les agremens des Adagio de cet ouvrage, composez par Mr. A. Corelli comme il les joue* (Amsterdam: Roger, 1710). For a facsimile, see Arcangelo Corelli, *Sonate a violino e violone o cimbalo*, ed. Marcello Castellani, Archivum musicum 21 (Florence: Studio per Edizione Scelte, 1979).

[40]A facsimile of the first edition is published alongside the facsimile of the embellished edition by Roger; see previous note.

**37.** Arcangelo Corelli (1653–1713), Concerto Grosso in G minor, op. 6, no. 8, "Christmas"

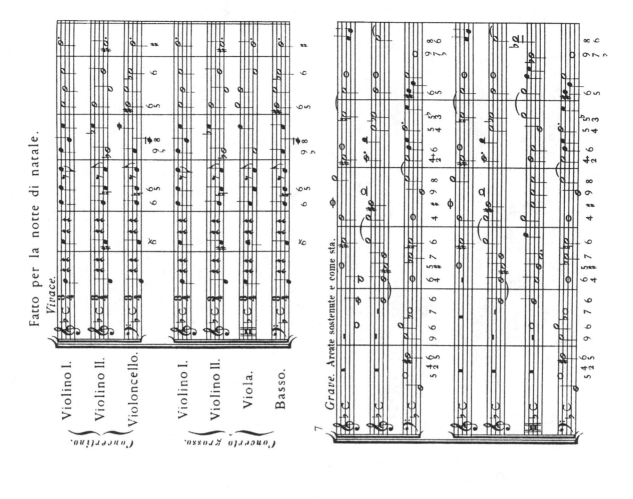

311

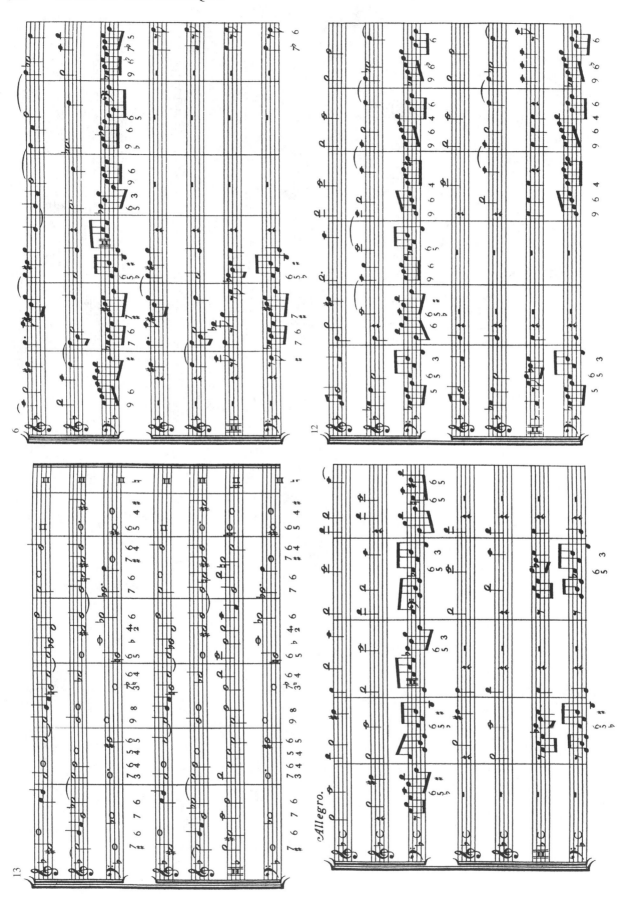

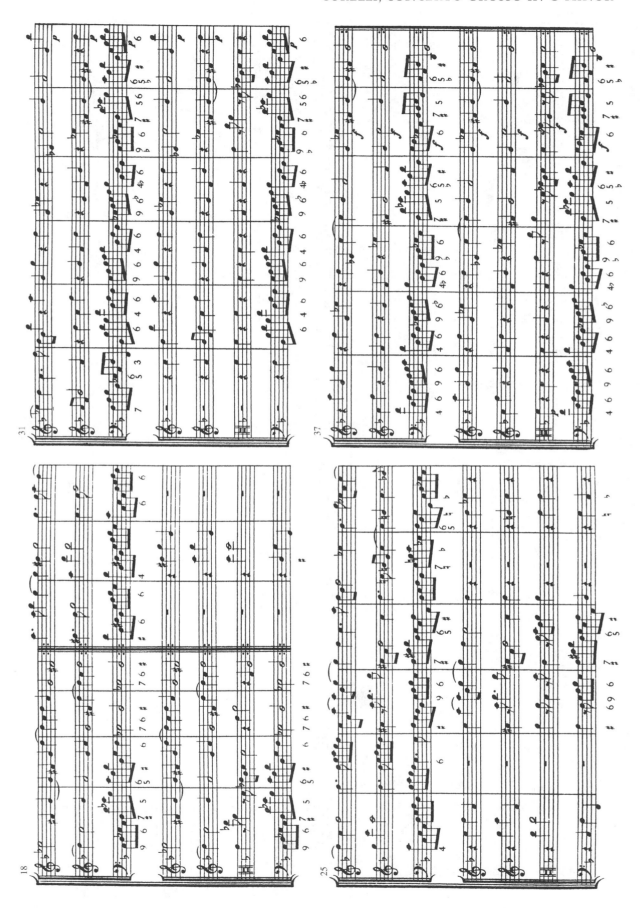

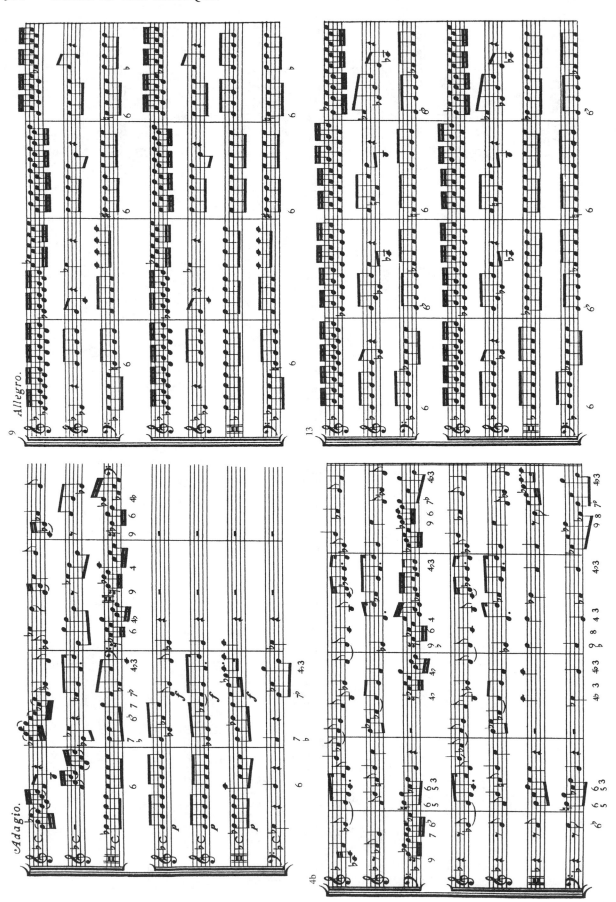

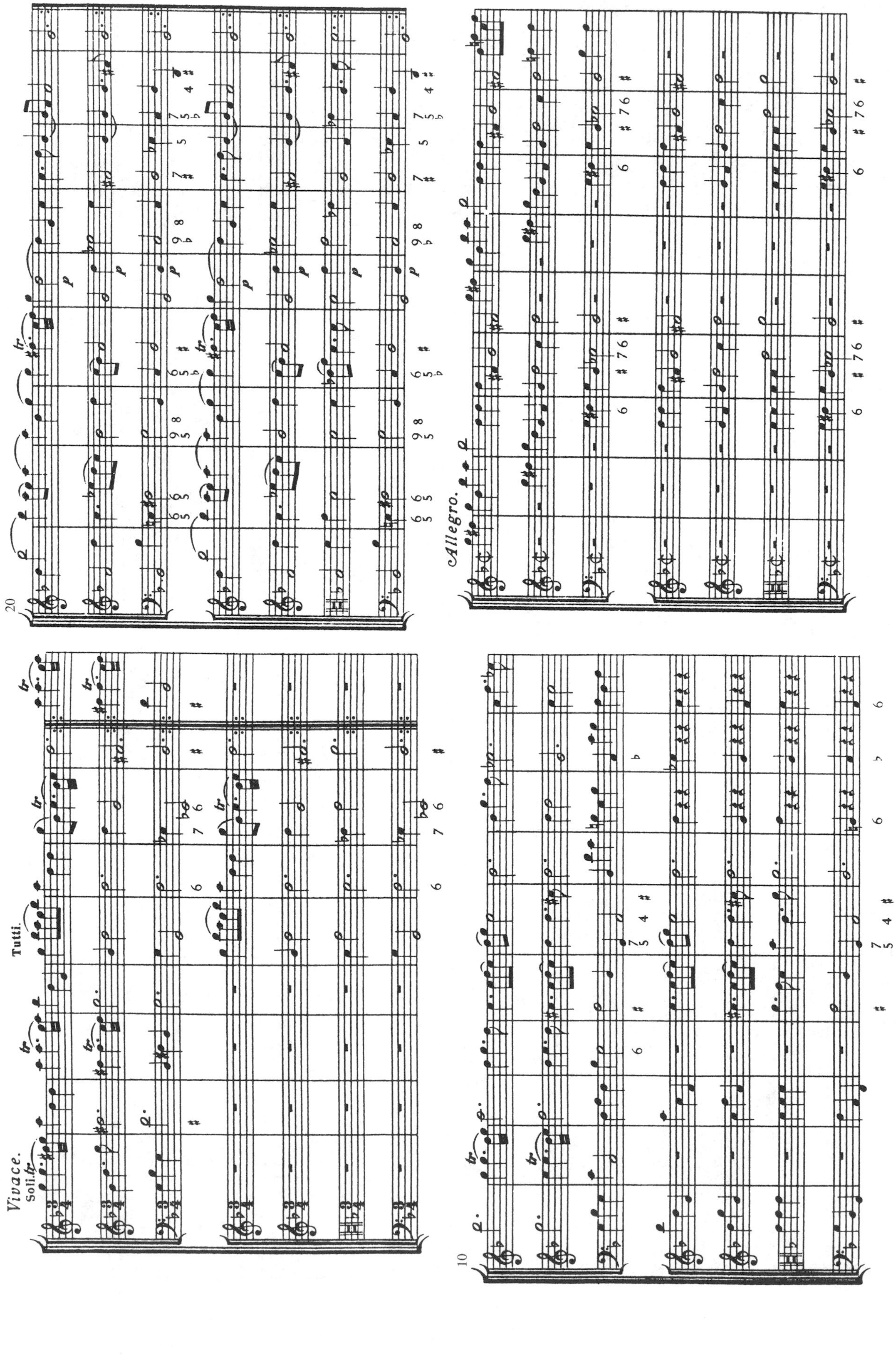
Vivace.
Soli.
Tutti.
Allegro.

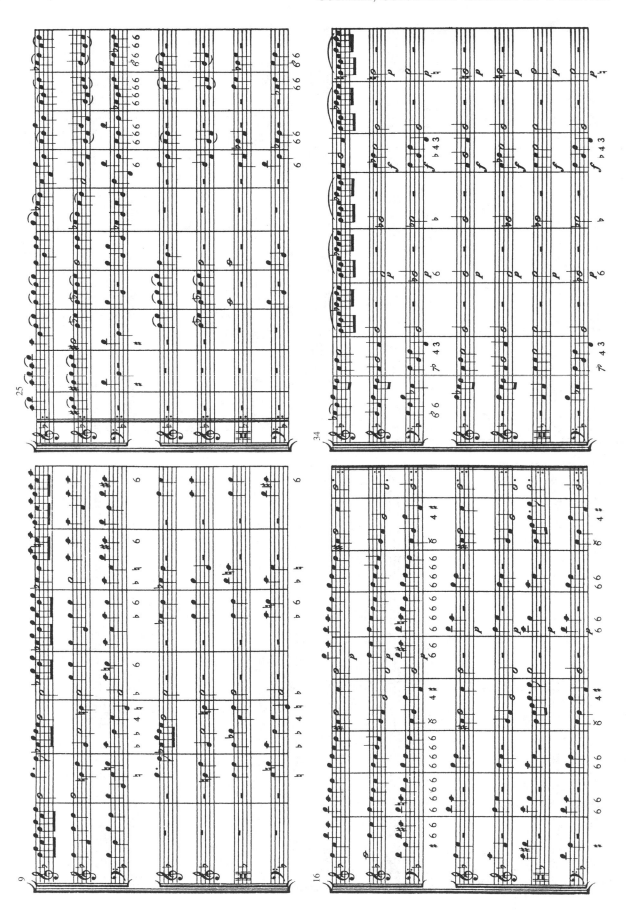

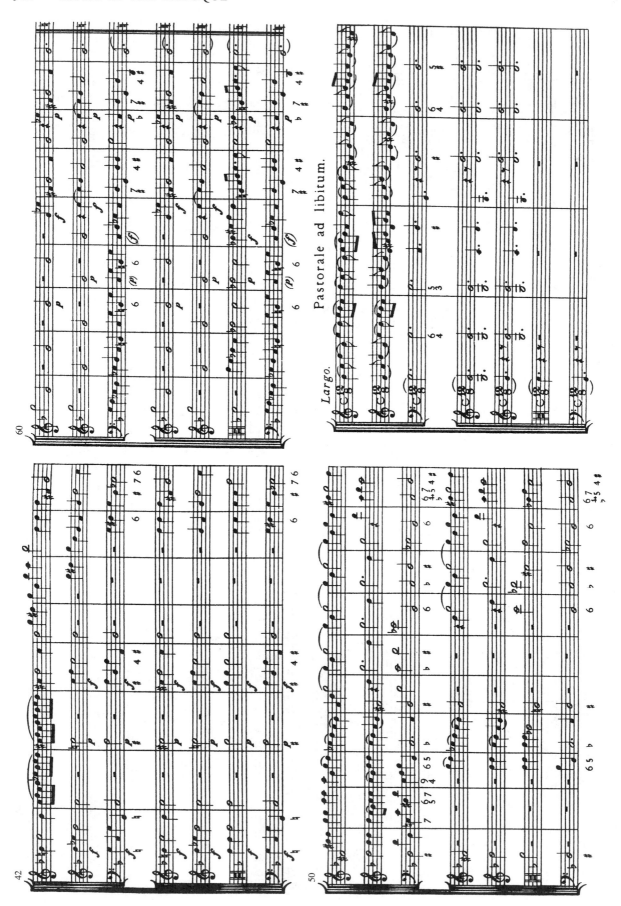

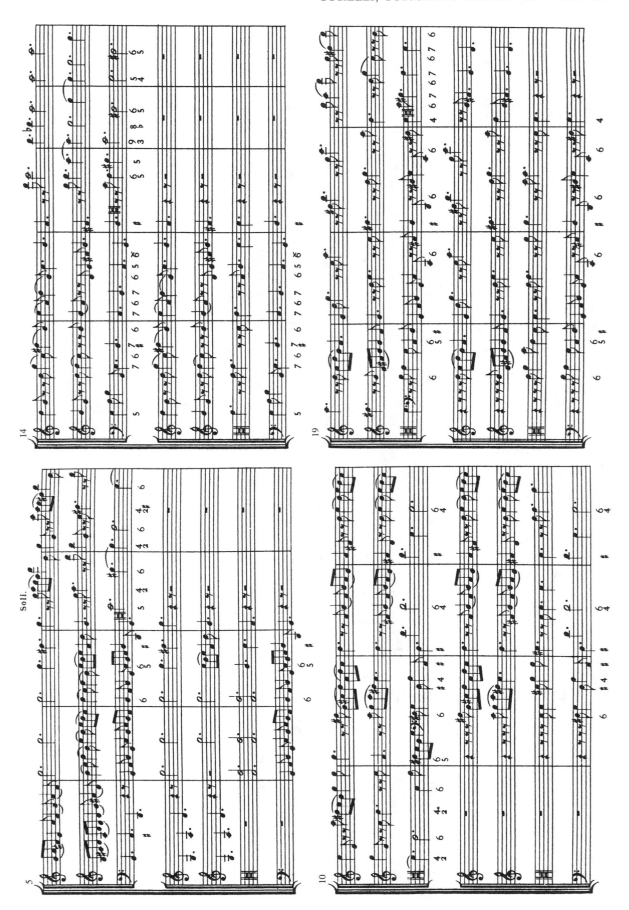

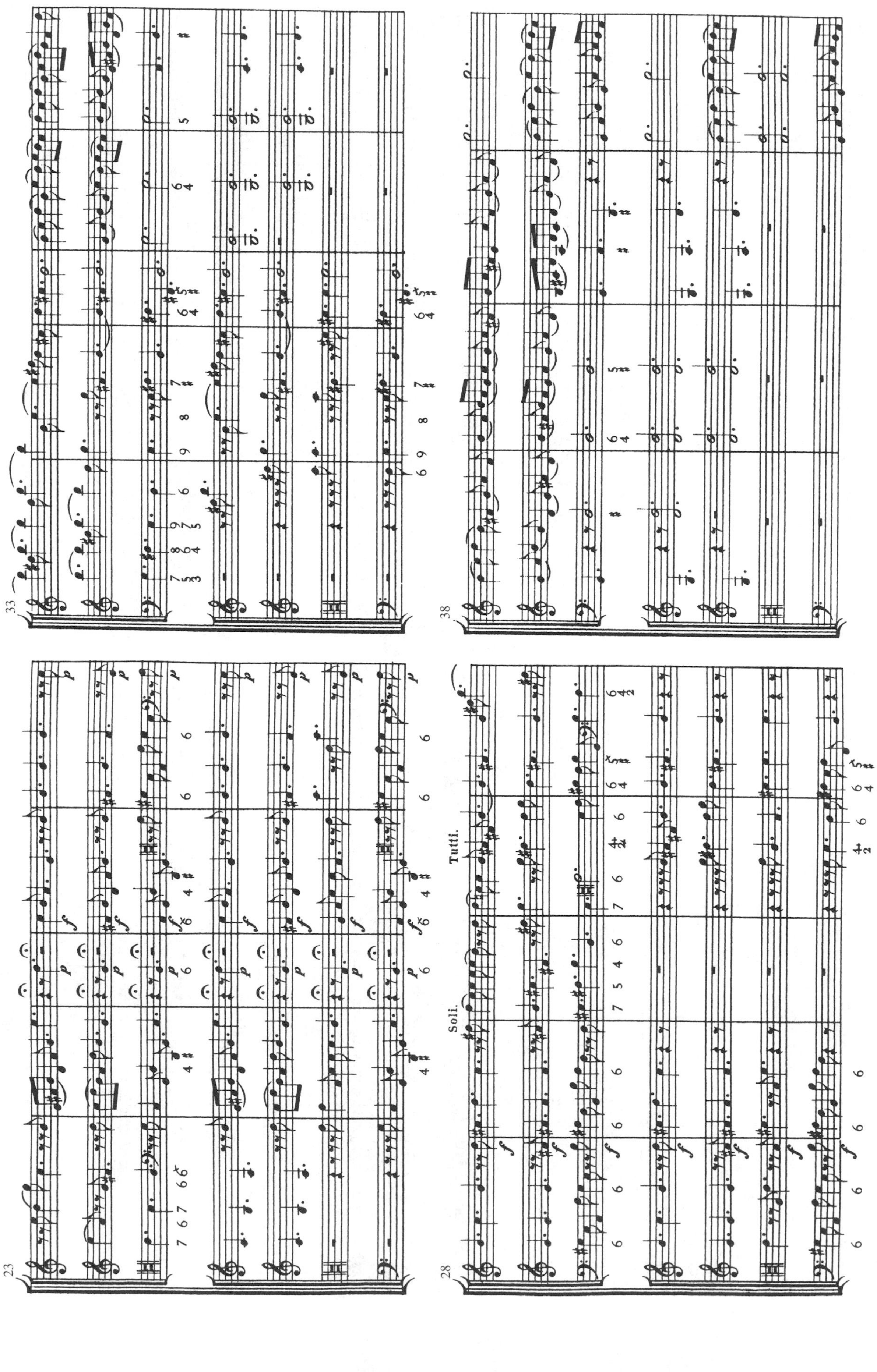
23
28
Soli.
Tutti.
33
38

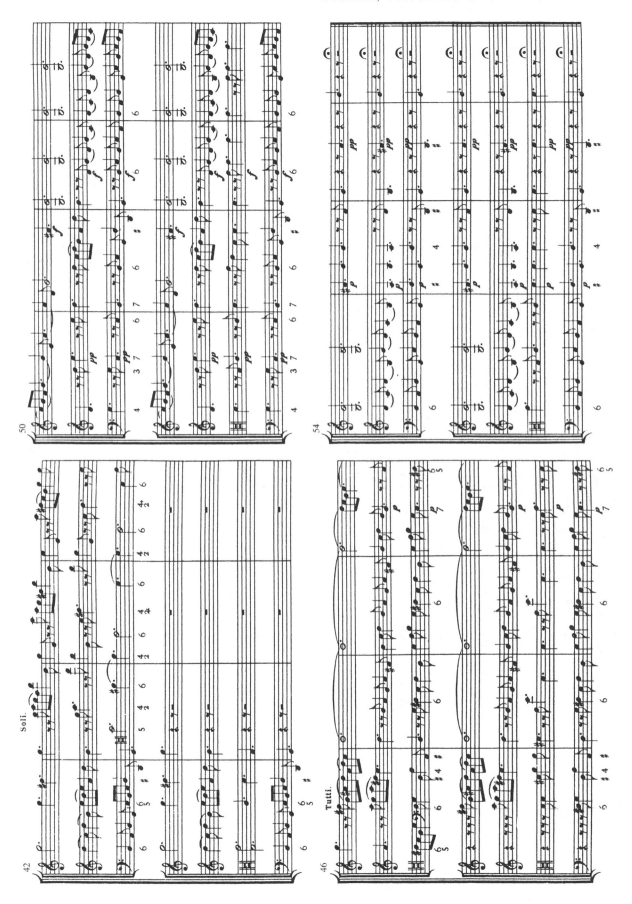

## EDITION

Again, our score is from the nineteenth-century edition of Corelli's works, based on eighteenth-century editions of his Opus 6 concertos. The work was originally published in a set of seven individual partbooks. The layout of our score, with the solo parts at the top, is editorial; in Corelli's manuscript, all four violin parts are at the top, with the viola, solo cello, and *basso* (continuo) parts beneath, in that order.[41]

The opening textual rubric, *Fatto per la notte di natale*, means "written for Christmas Eve." At measure 7, *arcate sostenute e come sta* means "with sustained bows, as it is"—that is, without improvised embellishment. The last movement is headed *Pastorale ad libitum*, meaning that this closing dance can be omitted if one likes.

## PERFORMANCE ISSUES

As a sort of modified trio sonata, this work raises similar performance issues as Selection 35. It can, in fact, be performed satisfactorily without the *ripieno* parts (labeled "concerto grosso" in our score). The figures in the part labeled "violoncello" imply a keyboard realization, but the part was unfigured in Corelli's score and may have been originally meant for cello alone. The preferred keyboard instrument for the ripieno basso continuo part was perhaps organ, in light of this piece's use as a church concerto for Christmas Eve.

The *ripieno* string parts might be performed by a string quartet—one player to a part. But at least one contemporary account reports the performance of this type of music by large ensembles, with multiple players for both the *concertino* and *ripieno*. Any such large-scale performance would include at least one double-bass instrument doubling the *ripieno* bass part.

## SOURCE

The score is reproduced from *Les œuvres de Arcangelo Corelli*, ed. J. Joachim and F. Chrysander (London: Augener, 1888–91), 5:150–70. The first edition was entitled *12 Concerti Grossi* (Amsterdam: Roger, 1714).

---

[41]Facsimile of the autograph score of the concluding *Pastorale* in Arcangelo Corelli, *Gesamtausgabe*, vol. 4, ed. Rudolf Bossard (Cologne: Arno Volk, 1978). Corelli's manuscript for the remaining movements does not survive.

**38.** Antonio Vivaldi (1678–1741), Concerto in E for violin, strings, and continuo, op. 3, no. 12 (R. 265)

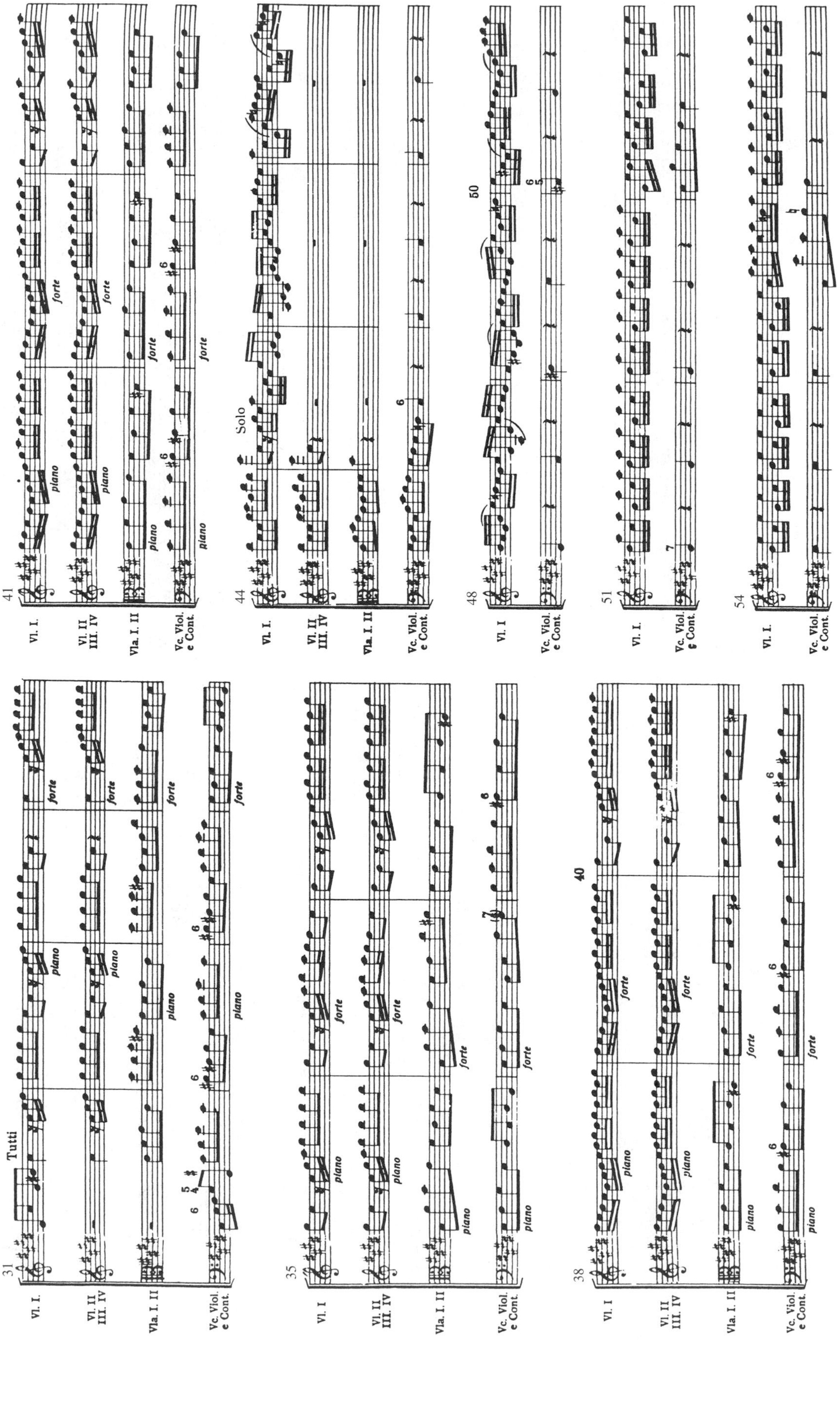
31
Tutti
Vl. I.
Vl. II
III. IV
Vla. I. II
Vc. Viol.
e Cont.
piano
forte
35
Vl. I
Vl. II
III. IV
Vla. I. II
Vc. Viol.
e Cont.
38
40
41
44
Solo
48
50
51
54

II
Largo
Tutti
Violino I
Violino II
Violino III. IV
Viola I. II
Violoncello
Violone e Cembalo
Solo
Cantabile e piano
piano
pianissimo
Vl. I
Vl. II
Vl. III. IV
Vla. I. II
Vc. Viol.
e Cemb.
forte
pianissimo
tr

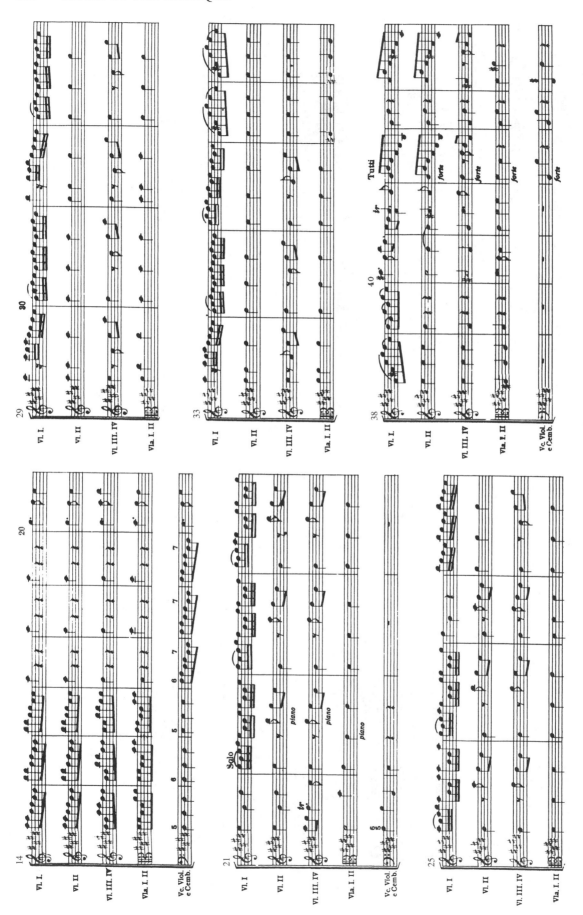

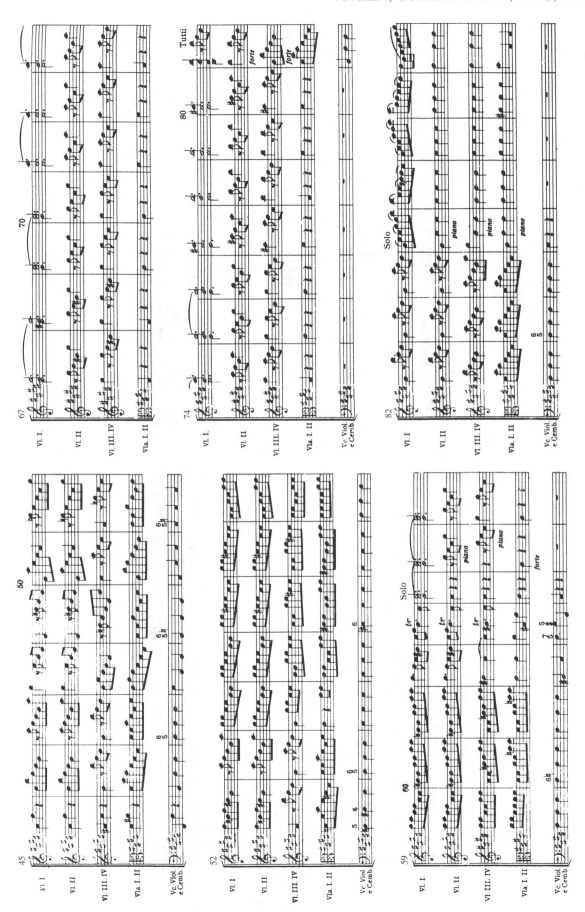

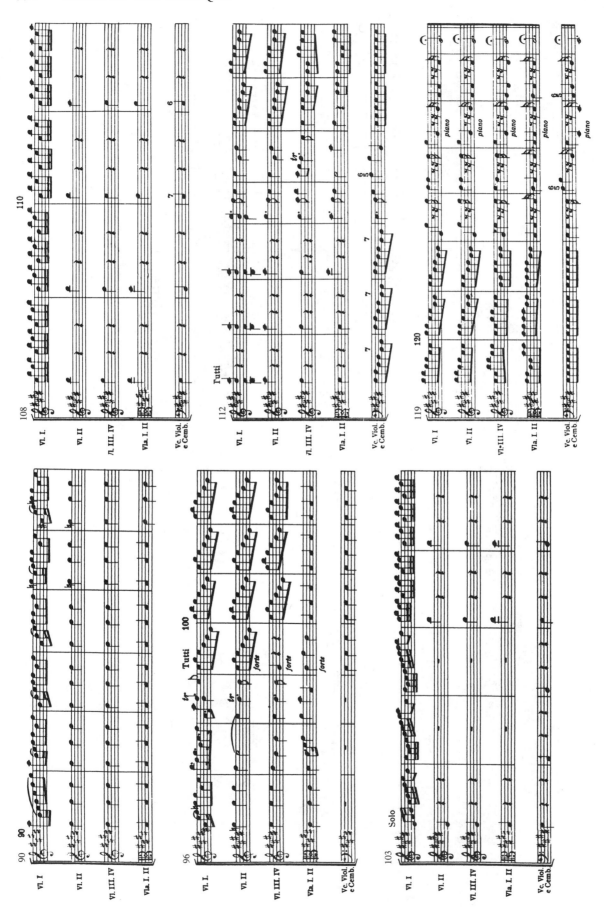

## EDITION

Our score is reproduced from a pre–World War II edition based on the eight partbooks that constituted the early editions of Vivaldi's Opus 3. The part labels reflect this, naming four violin parts and two viola parts. But the present work is, in effect, a concerto for one solo violin, two ripieno violins, viola, and continuo. The part designated as the second violin functions as the first ripieno violin, and the third and fourth violins (whose parts are identical) function as the second ripieno part. The two viola parts are also identical, as are the two bass parts.

## PERFORMANCE ISSUES

From the publication of Opus 3 in eight partbooks, it is doubtful whether Vivaldi intended any doubling of the parts (beyond that mentioned above) except for the violone and keyboard continuo. The words solo and tutti in various passages in the first violin part serve merely to alert the player to the presence or absence of the ripieno parts of these points.

As in any Italian Baroque concerto, the soloist might well add embellishment, especially in the second movement. The apparent double and triple stops in the first movement (mm. 58–65) were surely meant to be broken in sixteenth notes, following the pattern of the preceding measures. Similarly, in one passage in the third movement, the solo part is notated as sustained chords (mm. 64–80) but is presumably meant to be played as arpeggios (cf. Selection 36).

## SOURCE

This edition by Heinrich Husmann (Zürich: Eulenburg, 1939) is based on Vivaldi's L'estro armonico (Amsterdam: Roger, 1711; numerous reprints).

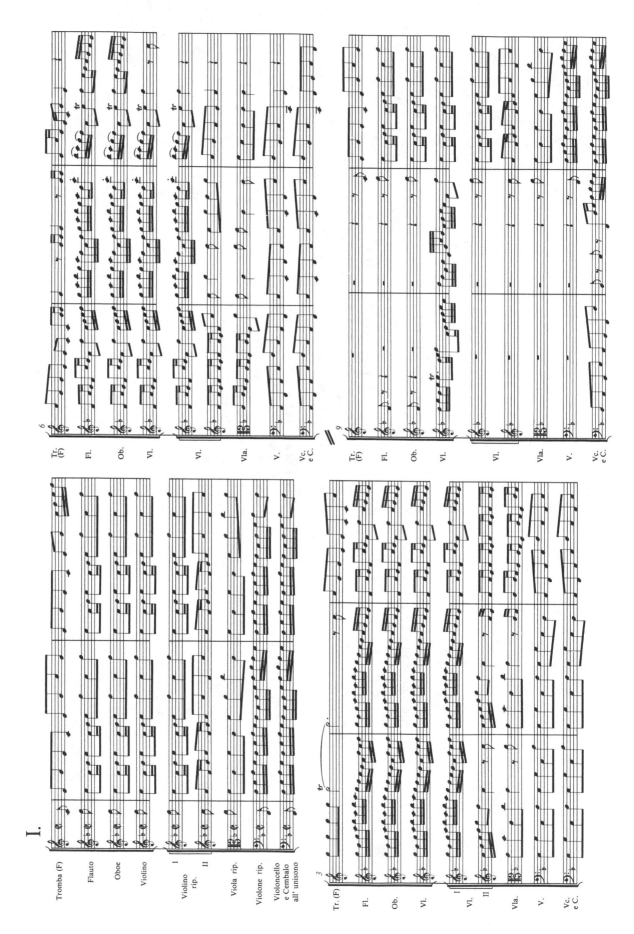

**39.** Johann Sebastian Bach (1685–1750), Brandenburg
Concerto no. 2 in F, BWV 1047

I.

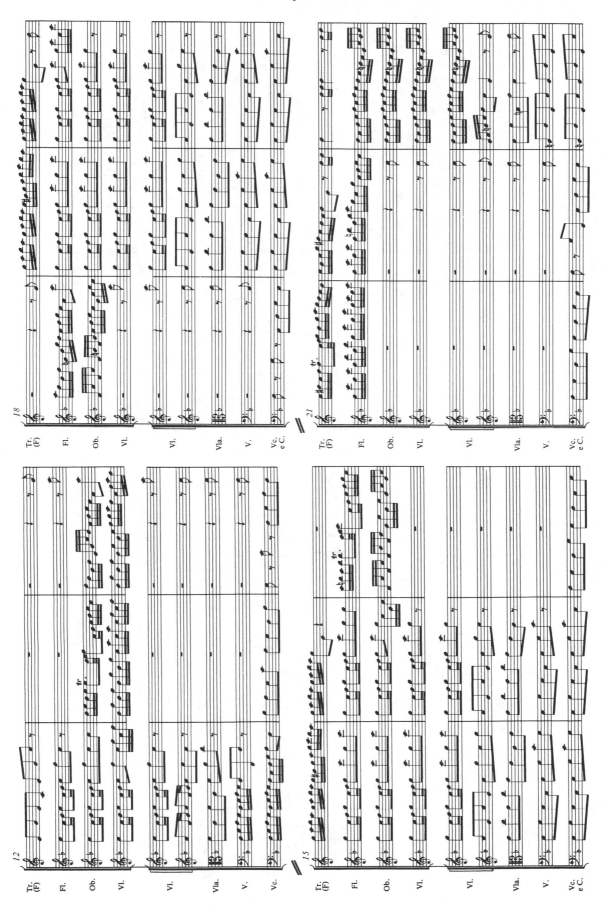

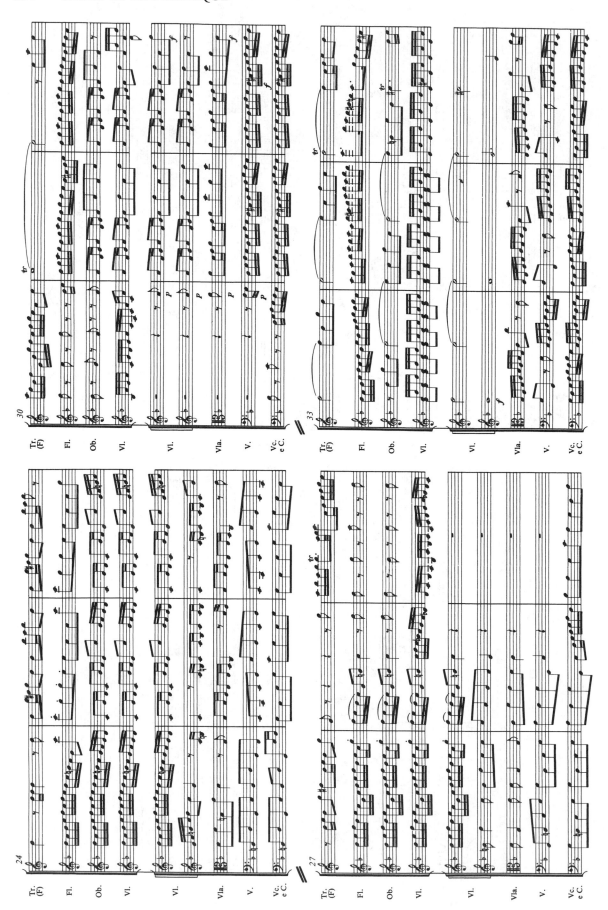

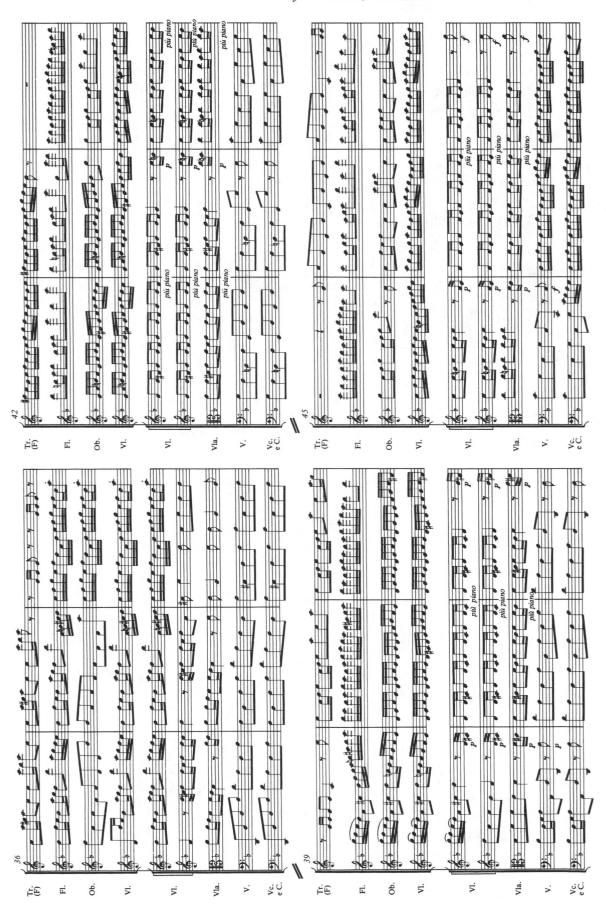

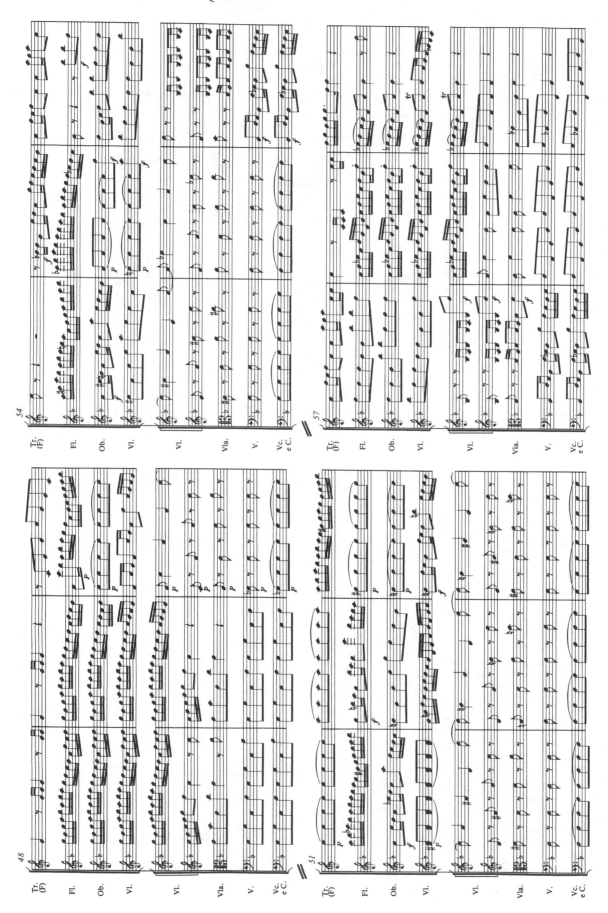

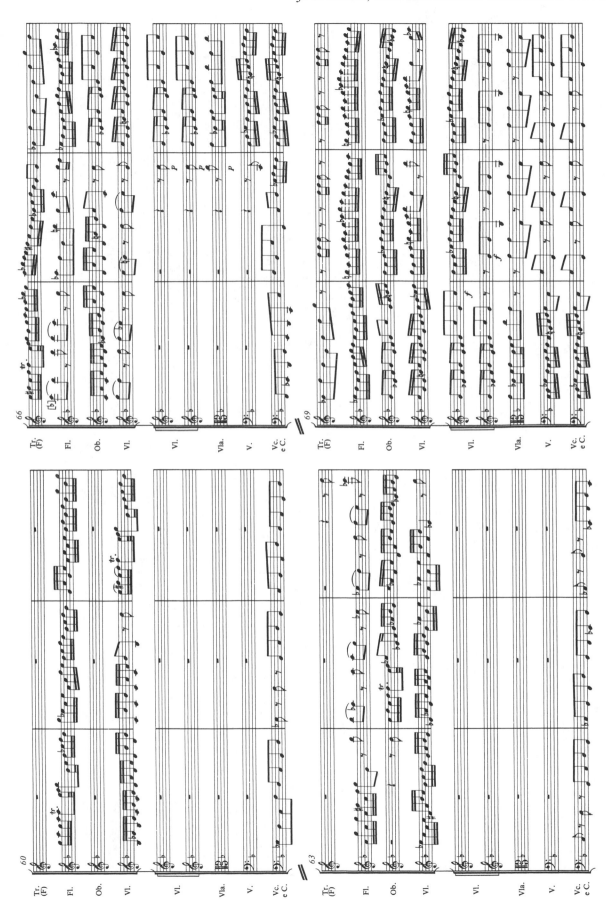

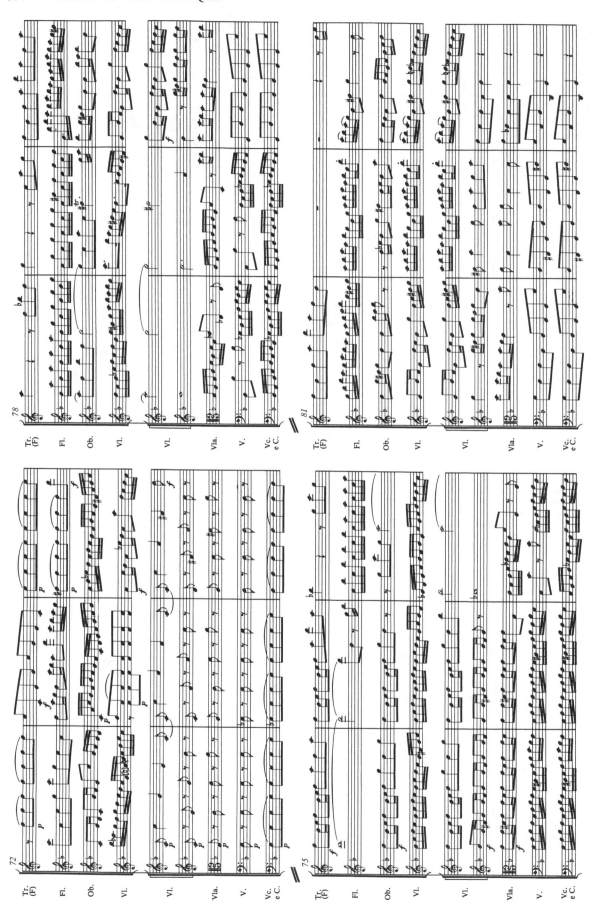

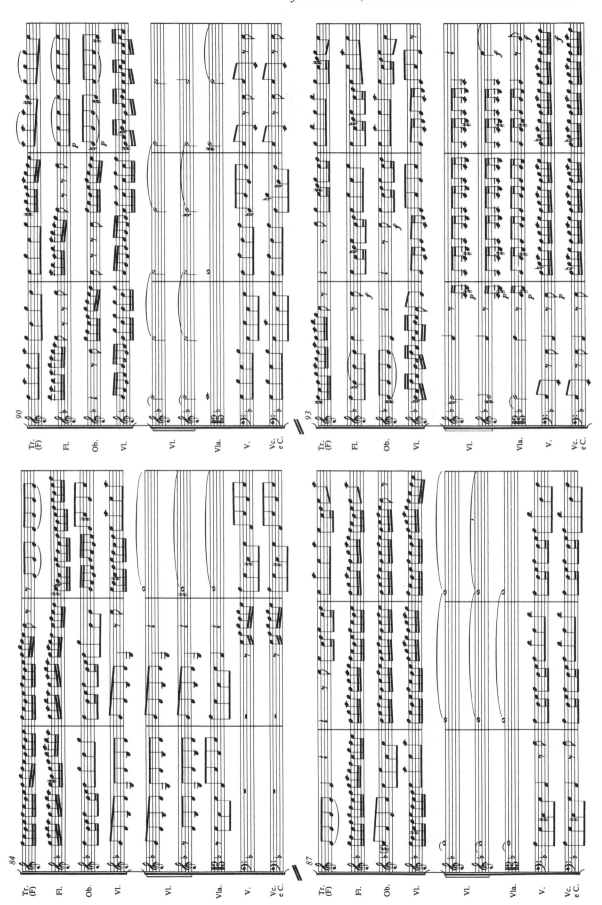

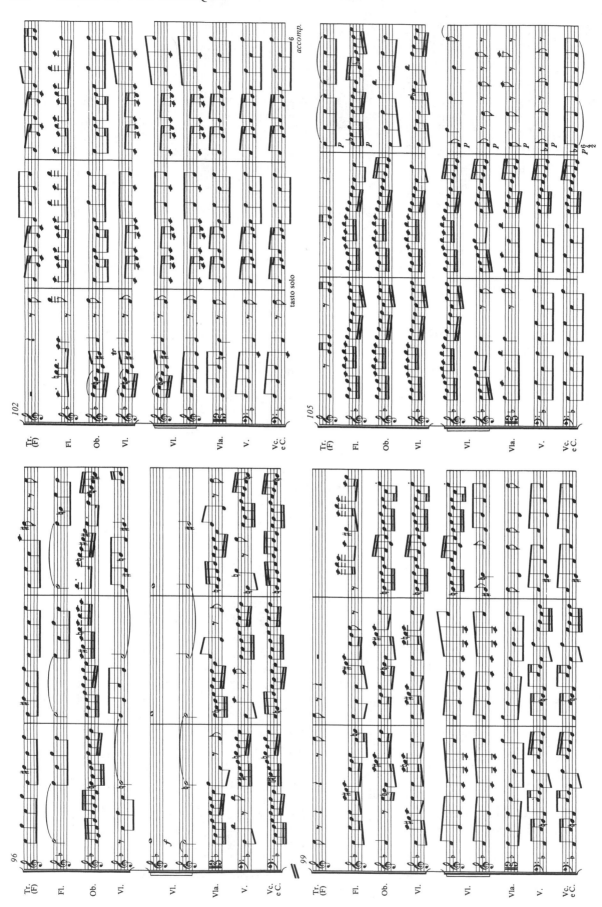

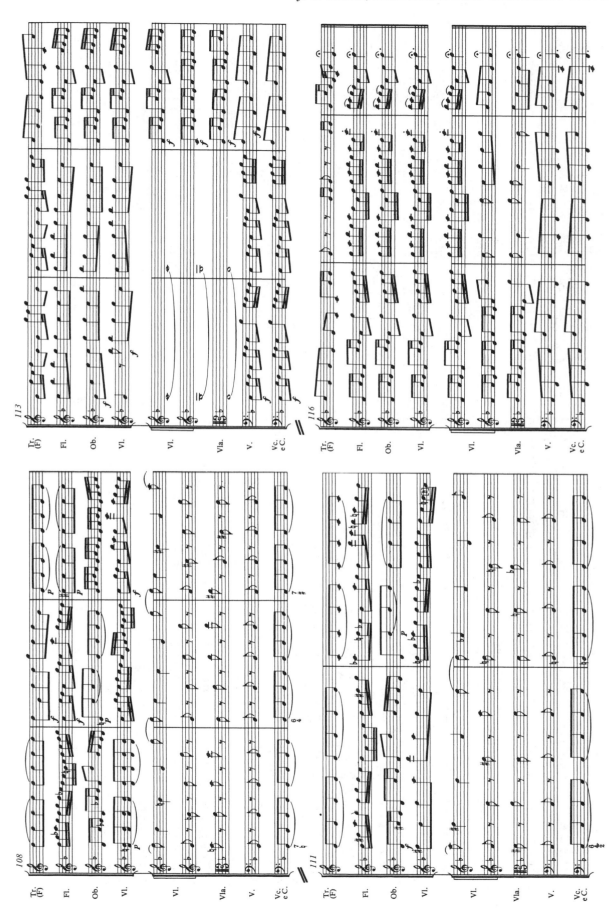

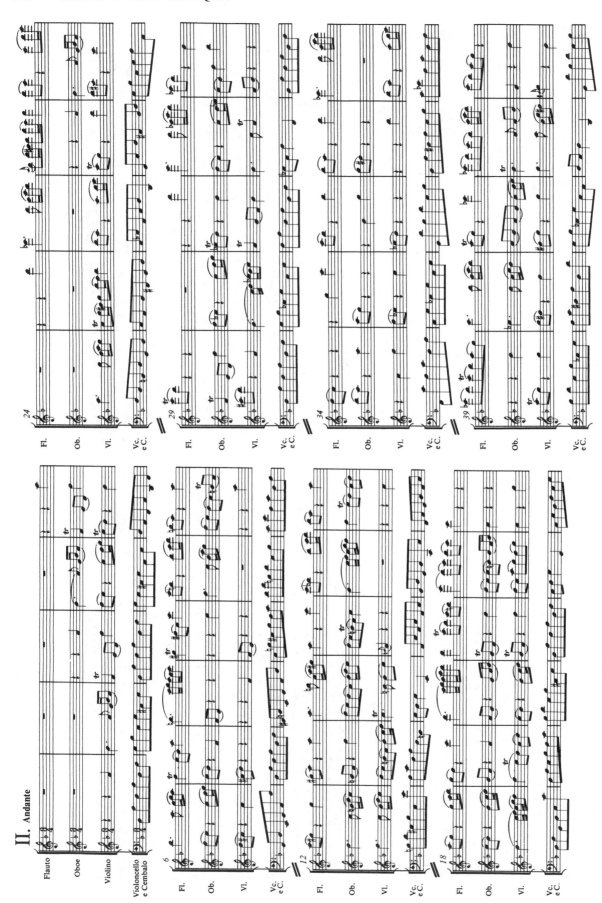

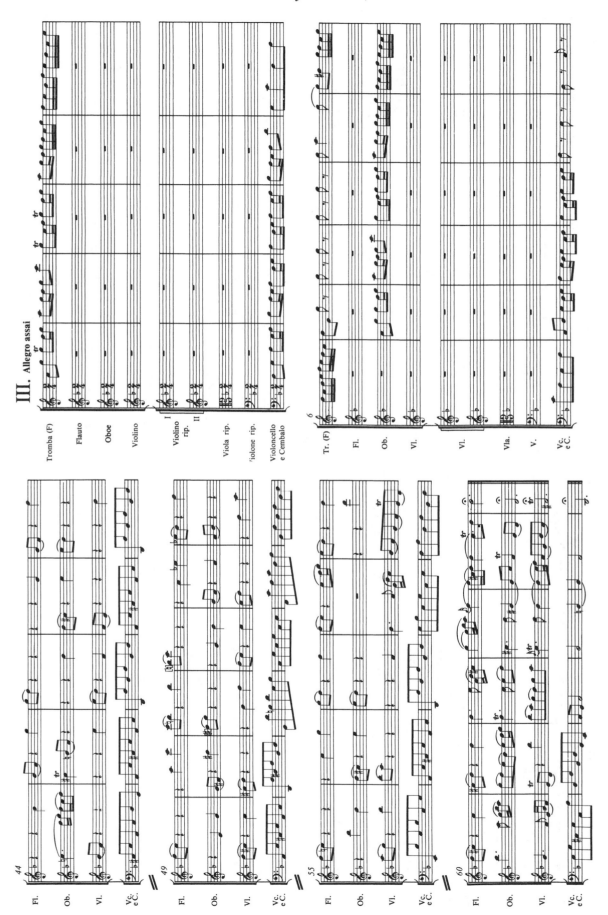

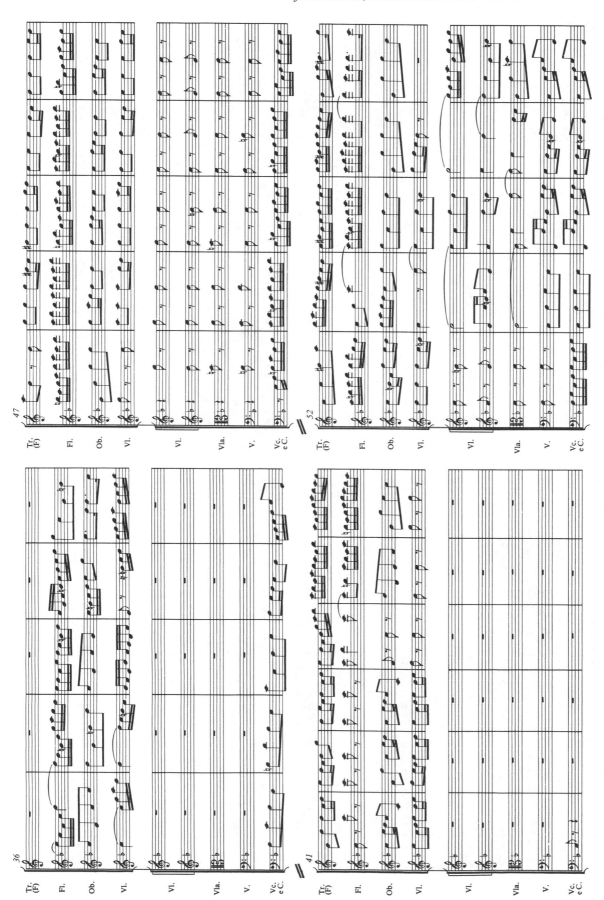

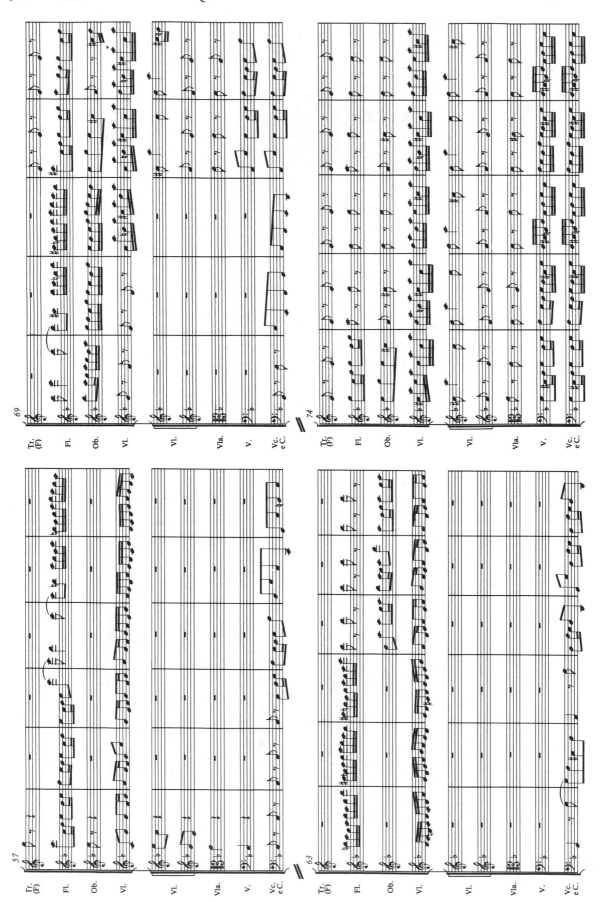

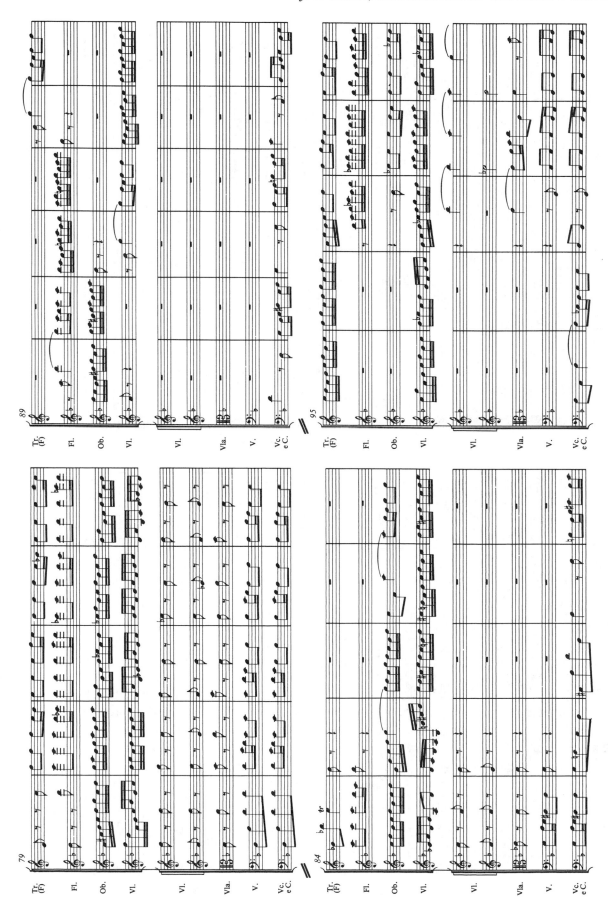

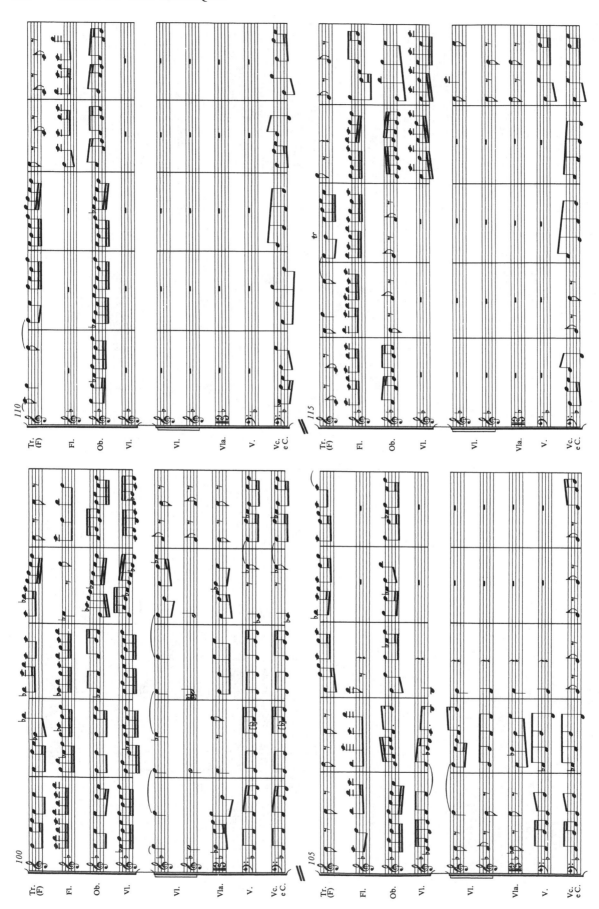

## EDITION

This is edition based closely on Bach's autograph manuscript score of the six concertos, which he presented in 1721 to the margrave of Brandenburg. Bach's manuscript is unusual in its careful listing of the instruments, including the specification of *ripieno* parts. Nevertheless it is incomplete for performance purposes, for the continuo lacks the figures that Bach often notated only in the individual part after it was copied from his score.

The part labels of our score, adapted from Bach's, can be translated as follows: trumpet; recorder; oboe; principal or solo violin; first and second *ripieno* violins; *ripieno* viola; *ripieno* viola; *ripieno* bass instrument—possibly a bass violin or a large viola da gamba sounding at written pitch; and cello and harpsichord, doubling one another at the unison.

## PERFORMANCE ISSUES

Like Selection 37, this work was very likely intended for performance with a single player on each part; moreover, it could be performed without the *ripieno* parts.[42] The trumpet has a transposing part, notated in C but sounding a fourth higher. Today, players of "modern" instruments often use the so-called Bach or "piccolo" trumpet, a small valved trumpet. But Bach's trumpet was a "natural" brass instrument lacking valves, and its somewhat mellower tone and smaller volume are less likely to overbalance the much quieter recorder.

## SOURCE

Our score is reproduced with permission from Johann Sebastian Bach, *Brandenburg Concerto no. 2, F Major, BMV 1047*, edited by Karin Stöckl (London: Eulenburg, 1984), which is based on Bach's autograph score in Berlin, Staatsbibliothek, Amalienbibliothek ms. 78.

---

[42]An edition has been published in this form, including as well a few alternative readings found in early manuscript copies: see Johann Sebastian Bach, *Concerto da camera F-dur*, ed. Klaus Hofmann (Kassel: Bärenreiter, 1998).

**40.** Georg Philipp Telemann (1681–1767), *Nouveau quatuor* no. 6 in E minor for flute, violin, viola da gamba (or cello) and continuo, TWV 43:e4 (first, second, fifth, and sixth movements)

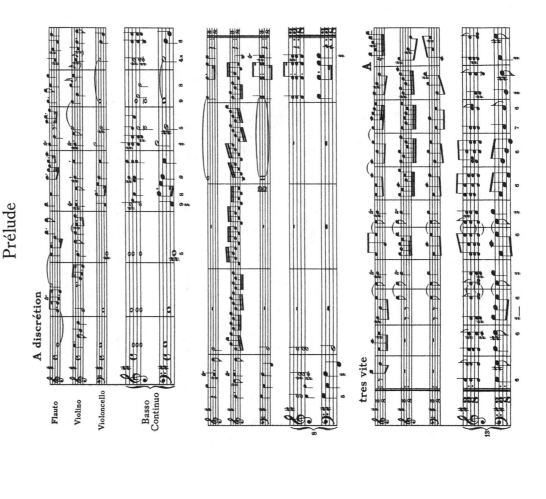

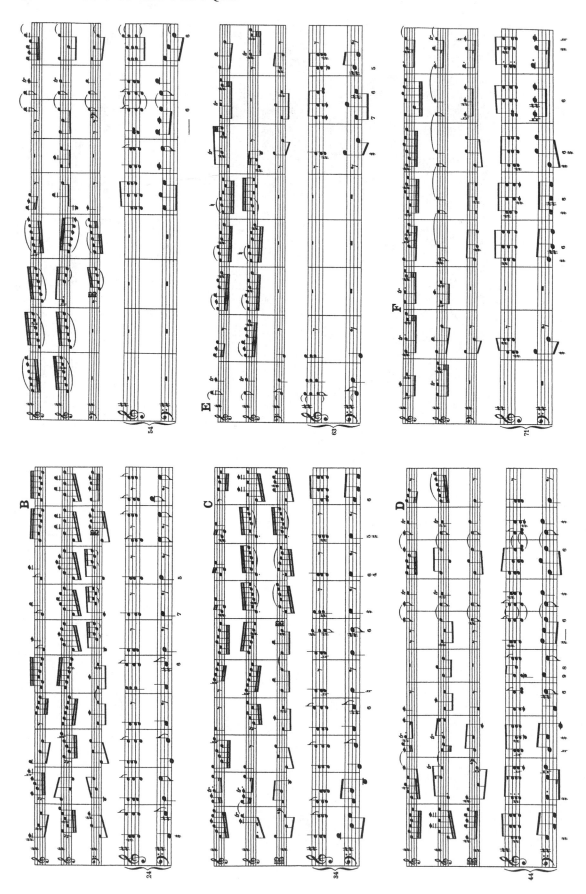

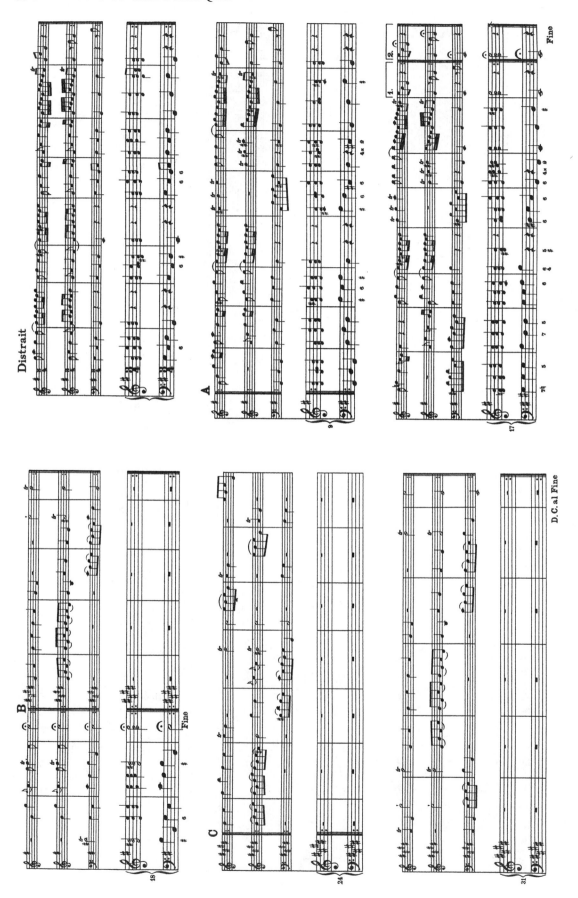

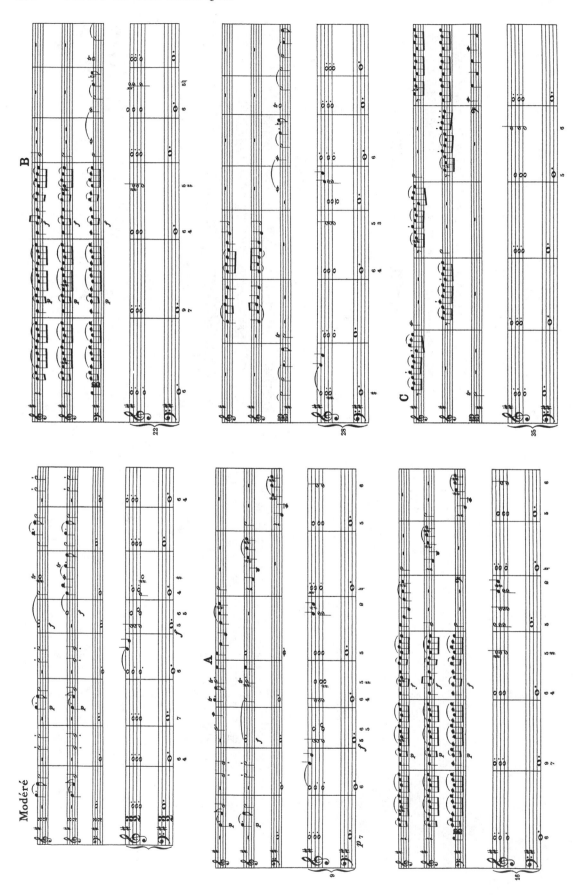

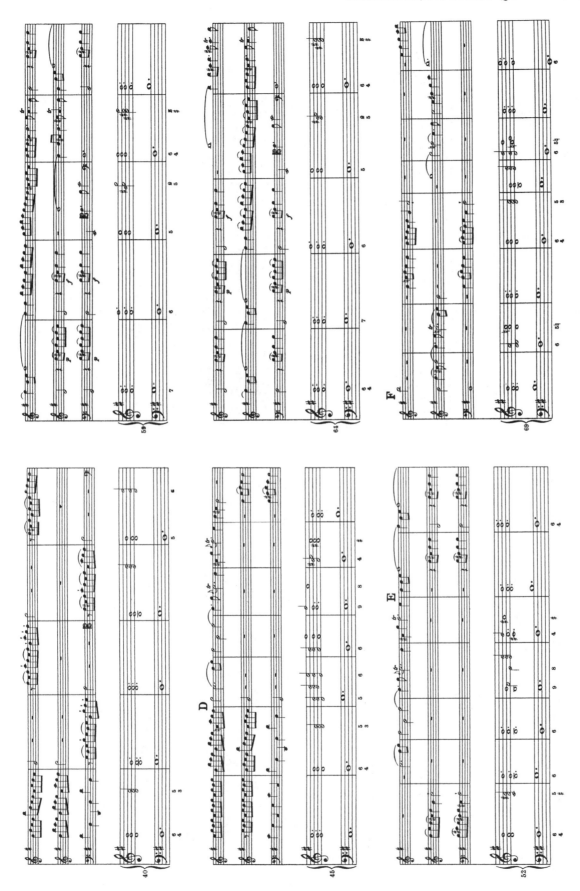

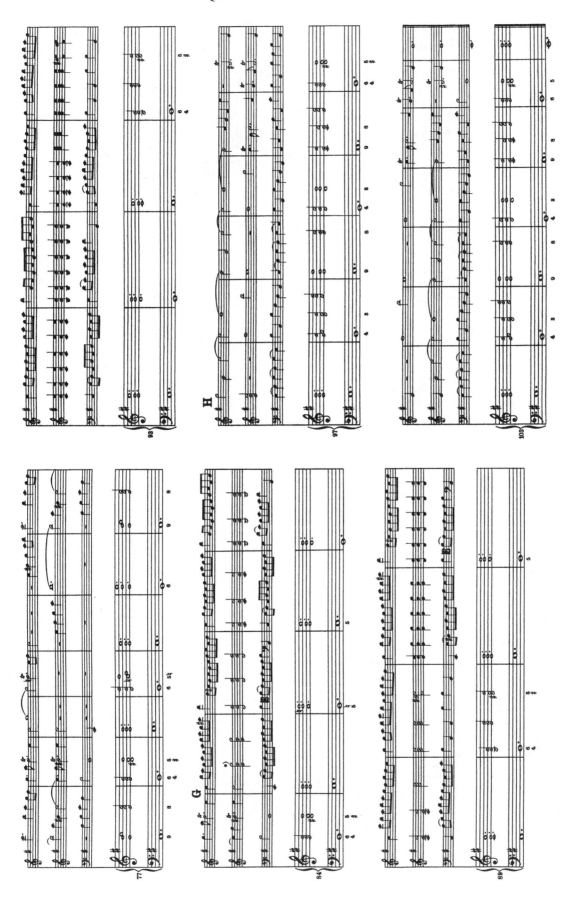

## EDITION

This pre–World War II score was intended to serve as a keyboard part. Thus it includes an editorial realization of the figured bass, and the three melody parts are printed in small notes. The rehearsal letters (the large "A," "B," and so forth) are also editorial. Otherwise, it is an accurate transcription of the original publication in separate parts, although it omits the part for viola da gamba (see below).

## PERFORMANCE ISSUES

The individual parts of Telemann's first edition included both the original viola da gamba part and the composer's adaptation of it for the cello; either could be used as the lowest of the three melody parts. Telemann and his contemporaries often gave players such options, thus making compositions available to performers who lacked one instrument or the other.[43]

The figured bass realization is appropriately simple in style. But like many from the era of this edition, it errs in rising too high, often crossing above the highest melody part or doubling it. Moreover, the steady three-part chords of the right hand would sound clunky and dull if played as written. A good player will improvise a lower and more flexible part, arpeggiating many of the chords and varying the number of voices.

## SOURCE

This score is based on the first edition, *Nouveaux quatuors en six suites* (Paris, 1738).[44]

---

[43]For the viola da gamba part, see the facsimile edition listed below or the edition in Georg Philipp Telemann, *Musikalische Werke*, vol. 19, *Zwölf Pariser Quartette Nr. 7–12*, ed. Walter Bergmann, BA 2944 (Kassel: Bärenreiter, 1965), 133–55.

[44]A facsimile (in separate partbooks) is published by Performers' Facsimiles (New York, 1998). The present score is reproduced from Georg Philipp Telemann, *Quartett in e-moll*, ed. Ellinor Dohrn, Nagels Musik-Archiv 10 (Hanover: Nagel, 1928).

**41.** Carl Philipp Emanuel Bach (1714–1788), Concerto in D minor for harpsichord and strings, W. 23 (H. 427) (first movement)

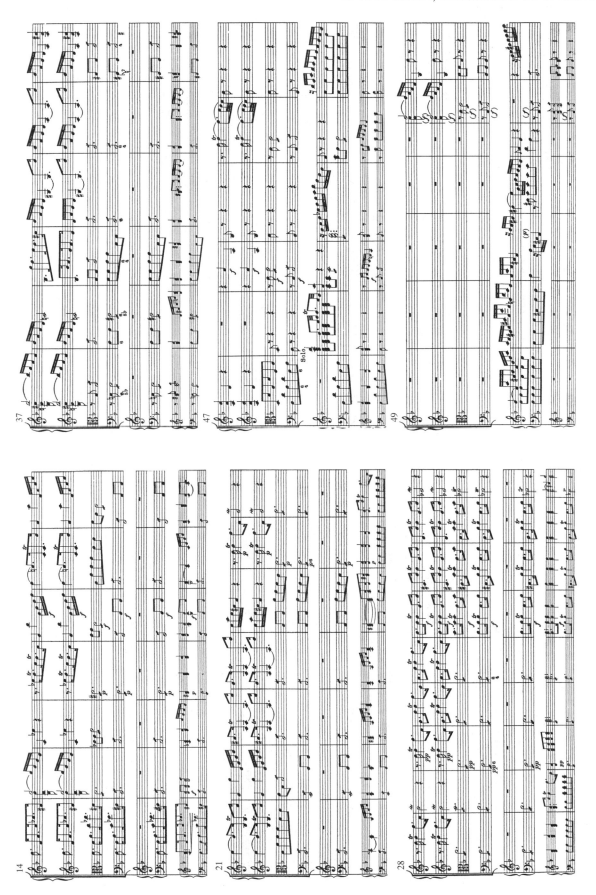

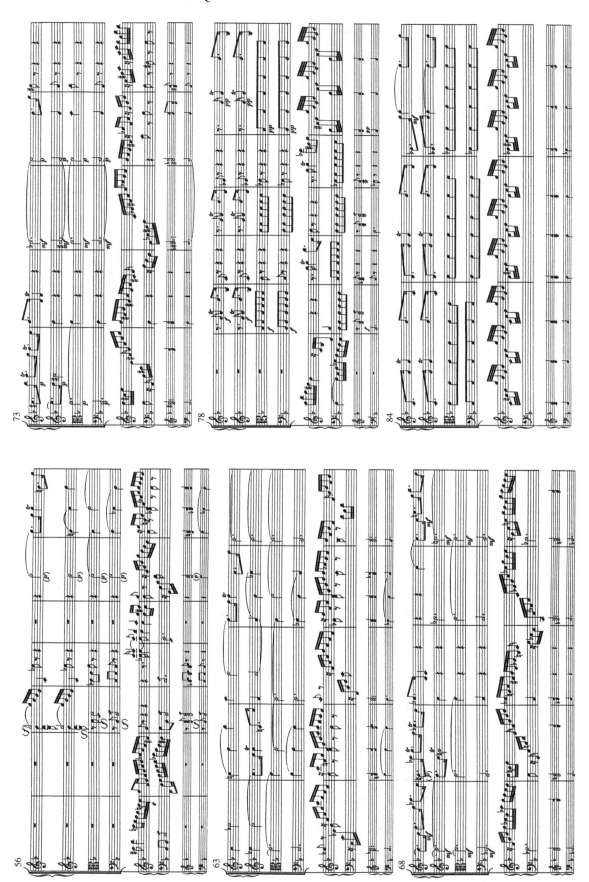

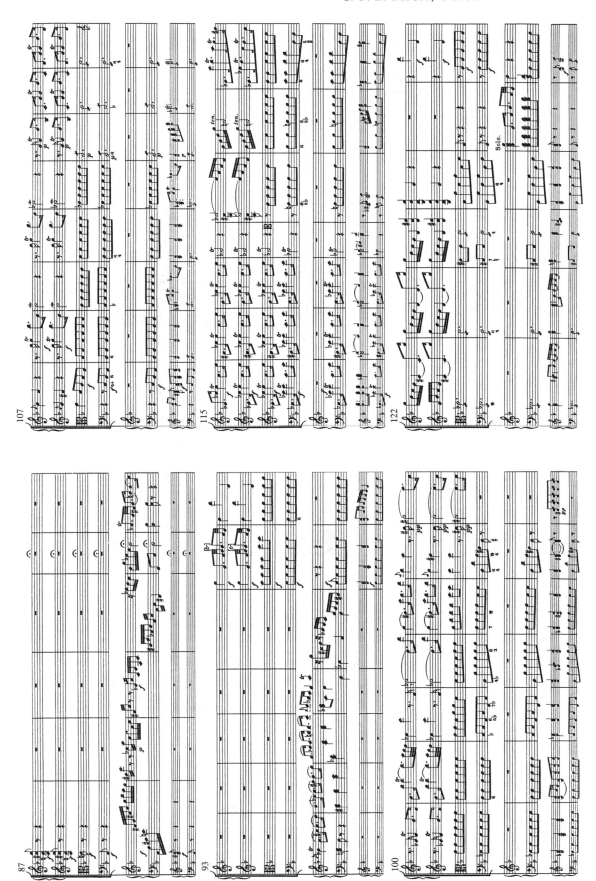

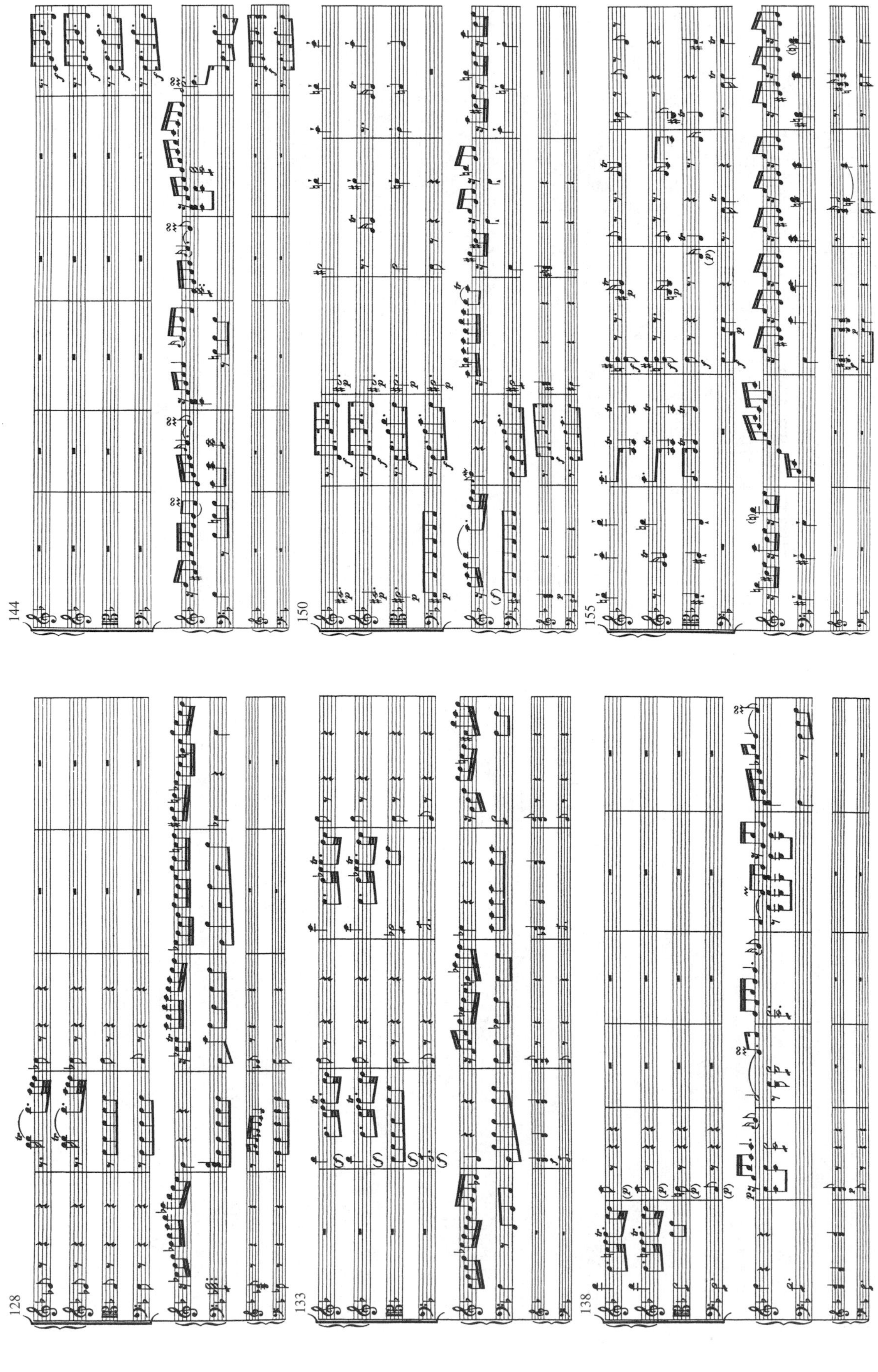

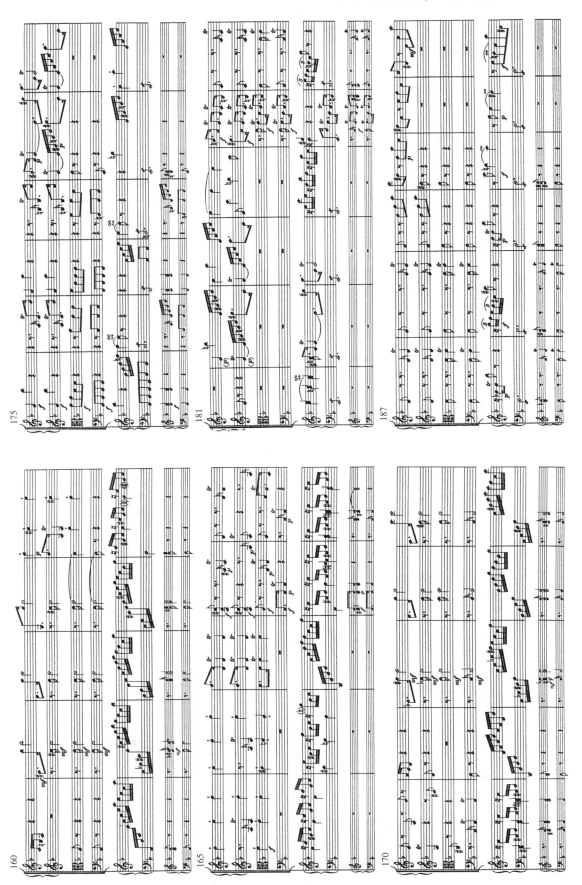

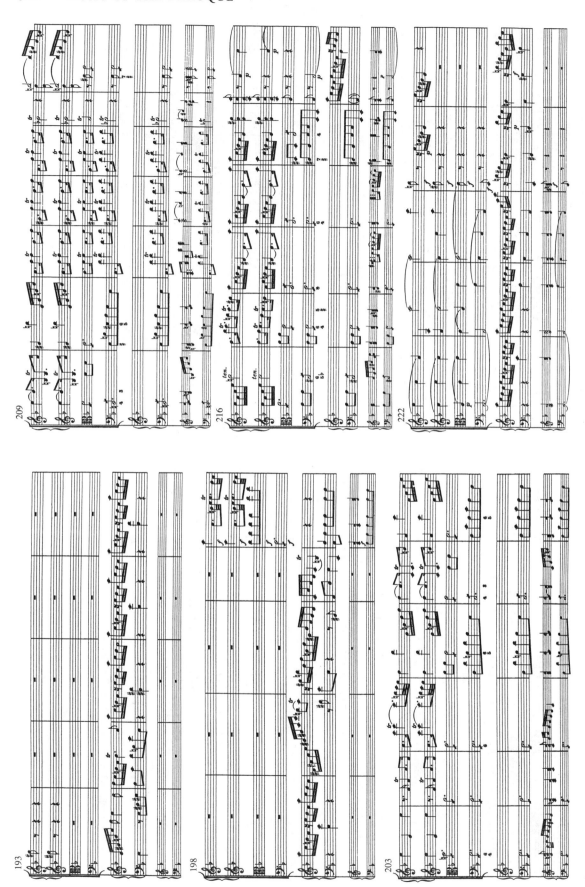

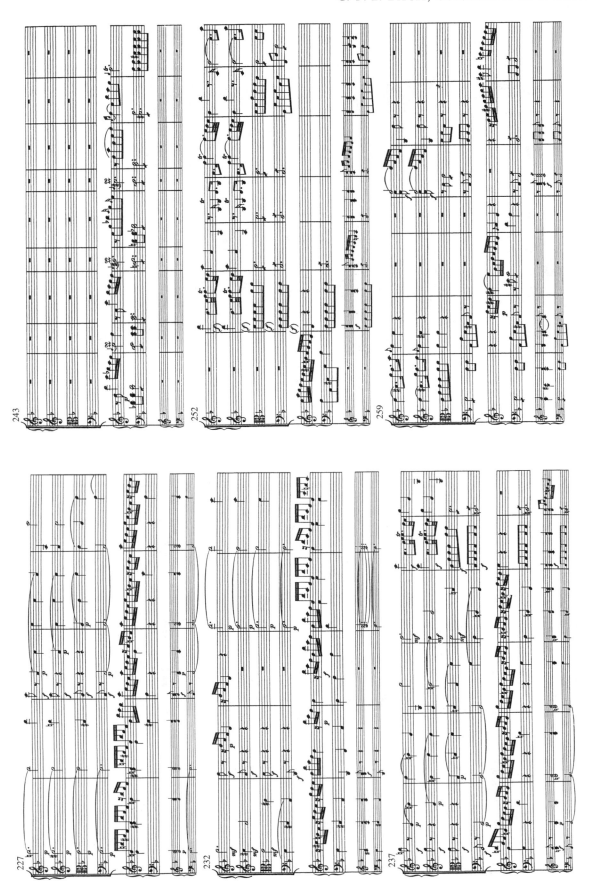

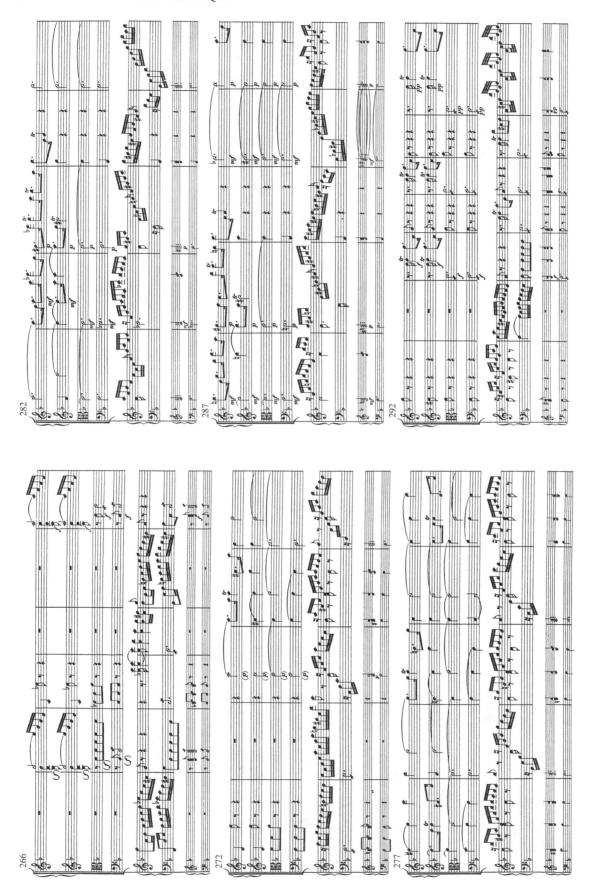

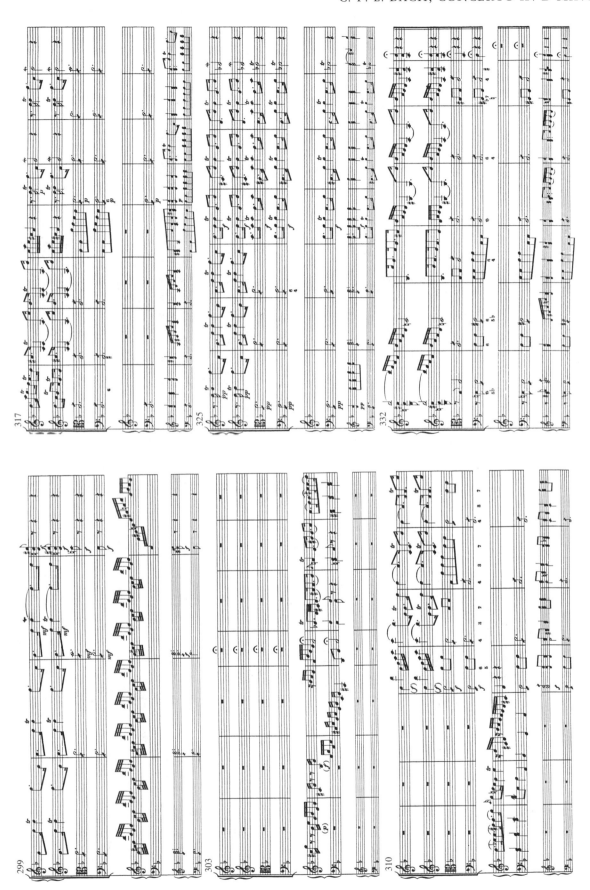

## EDITION

Our score is an early twentieth-century edition based on the composer's autograph composing manuscript. The editor has inserted a second keyboard part ("cembalo ripieno"), complete with editorial figured bass realization, at the bottom of each system.

## PERFORMANCE ISSUES

Eighteenth-century performances would not have included the second keyboard part. The soloist ("cembalo concertato") would have realized the figured bass in the ritornellos, and the solo passages would have been accompanied by the strings alone. The latter must often have been played by a string quartet, one instrument on a part, although performances by larger bodies of strings are possible. In the latter case a double-bass instrument might join the cello on the line marked *basso*.

In 1753, five years after the composition of this concerto, C. P. E. Bach published the first volume of his famous treatise on the performance of keyboard music.[45] The treatise has much to say about the performance of this type of music; much can also be learned from the nearly contemporary treatise on the flute by Bach's Berlin colleague Johann Joachim Quantz.[46] Quantz's treatise goes far beyond the flute, including detailed instructions on the performance of continuo parts and on the number of string players appropriate to a concerto such as this.

At least one basic question, however, is not settled by either treatise or by Bach's manuscript score: what instrument should play the solo part. Although harpsichord is the usual choice today, the early piano (called today the *fortepiano*) was being cultivated at Berlin at precisely the time this concerto was written. It is likely that the composer wrote this concerto for his own performances at semipublic gatherings in private homes in Berlin, where either a harpsichord or the small, rather quiet fortepianos of the period would have been appropriate.

## SOURCE

This edition, from *Denkmäler deutscher Tonkunst*, vols. 29–30, *Instrumentalkonzerte deutscher Musiker*, ed. Arnold Schering (Leipzig: Breitkopf und Härtel, 1907), is based on the autograph score Berlin, Staatsbibliothek, Mus. ms. Bach P 354.

---

[45]*Versuch über die wahre Art das Clavier zu spielen* (Berlin, 1753–62); English translation by William J. Mitchell as *The True Art of Playing Keyboard Instruments* (New York: Norton, 1949).

[46]*Versuch einer Anweisung das Flöte traversiere zu spielen* (Berlin, 1752); English translation by Edward R. Reilly as *Essay on Playing the Flute*, 2d ed. (New York: Schirmer Books, 1985).